A Journey of a Thousand Miles

Dearest Mavy,

Daughter of the Most High God.

There is a woman in you Get it out of her for God's glory.

22.09.2020

Sarah Moloi

Sarah Moloi

Copyright © 2020 by Sarah Moloi

All rights reserved. No part of this publication may be reproduced, stored in any form of retrieval system or transmitted in any form or by any means without prior permission in writing from the publishers except for the use of brief quotations in a book review.

Table of Contents

Preface iv
Dedication v
Chapter 1 9
Chapter 2. Early Years 19
Chapter 3. Matome Village 59
Chapter 4. Matladi High and Early Years in My Career 78
Chapter 5. Marriage 114
Chapter 6. New adventures in Christ 135
Chapter 7. Another tragedy 142
Chapter 8. Relocating to the UK 148
Chapter 9. Coming Out of the Upper Room 176
Chapter 10. Getting the Human Soul Saved 197
Chapter 11. God's Faithfulness 208
Chapter 12. Greater Works 235
Chapter 13. Total healing 255
Chapter 14. Abuse 264
Conclusion 299

Preface

I know that He who writes my story is in my story.

I can't change the past but I have grown to know the Power of Him who holds my future.

— **Jeremiah 29:11**

Dedication

To my children, Dineo and Moses

I would like to thank you both for being so strong and always being there with me through everything. You have stood with me throughout my life experiences, in recent times, even playing a rock for me at a time of unbelievable life events that negatively affected me in the long run. The support, advice and unconditional love you showed me is beyond words.

I can't imagine life without you two.

You grew up so quick, not only physically but mentally and spiritually.

You are precious to me.

Your Dad would have been very proud of you.

To my mother Florah Mahlo

You taught me to be strong, not only verbally but mostly by the way you lived your life. You were always the rock in our immediate family and beyond. The whole entire clan of relatives from your brother's side and your sister's side looked up to you. I grew up seeing this and vowed to be like you.

I saw your reliance on God, the heartfelt prayers, always knowing you had no one but God.

I saw how you always touched people with the Gospel; how your salvation was solid and secure.

I saw you starting your days in the early hours of the morning with prayer and ending them the same way.

I saw your dedication to serve the Lord even at a ripe old age, sharing the Gospel at every minute you got with everyone you met.

It stayed with me forever.

Your love never failed anyone.

You lived long enough to see your great-great-grandchildren.

God preserved you and took you at the right appointed time, peacefully, as He did with His servants.

To my siblings, my two older sisters, Maria and Anna.

Maria

You are, and have always been, a delight to be around. You would never harm a fly. Always composed, calm and peaceful. Never got moved much by anything. A helper, always available to lend a hand. What would I have done during the times I had to work and required help with my small children? I am who I am, and became who I have become mostly because of your unending support from birth to date.

Anna

My toughest role model and sometimes rival; dearest Anna.

You are the rock; tough and never giving up. I always admired you for these virtues. Always daring, always pushing to advance, going against the tide. The word 'difficult' does not exist in your life.

You remain a rock for the family, a pillar firm enough to provide security to the rest of the family and relatives at large.

I can close my eyes and still see you fighting your way out of a mob of girls surrounding you, trying to team up in beating you up, just because they were afraid of you; your toughness. They wouldn't dare challenge you individually but needed a mob to bring you down and you always fought them and conquered. You never ran away. I never saw you run away. You would be in the middle of that mob as they surrounded you, almost hidden from my view as I watched with tears silently rolling down my cheeks.

This reminds me of the day we fled from the Military police in Voortrekkerhoogte, Pretoria whilst visiting you. You and your friends were illegally selling alcohol to augment your low wages. Even though we nearly got caught and put in prison, that experience never daunted you; it never stopped you. After we managed to successfully hide and evade them, you went straight back, bought more alcohol, as they had destroyed the leftovers when we fled, and continued with your business. This never left me. The tenacity you have, the inner strength, the determination that nothing shall stop you. This particular incident scared me to death, but not you.

I always looked up to you.

I love you both,

Words cannot express.

May you live to see more of life than you have already seen.

May you continue to set this example to your children, grandchildren and great-grandchildren.

To my younger brothers,

Joseph, Simon and Sipho

I still remember playing with you in the fields whilst shepherding Grandmother's goats, chasing you through the thick grass in the afternoons.

How much fun that was!

I only pray and wish I could have been a good older sister to you all; that you could look up to me.

Your existence in my life made it possible for my children to have someone to call uncle.

May the Lord preserve you and make you strong. May you come to know Him more, not only personally but through developing a deep relationship with Him.

To my friends

Some of you have been more than a friend, almost like siblings.

You know yourselves.

Without you, I wouldn't have become who I have become.

It's been good knowing and meeting you in my path travelling along Life's Road.

May the Lord bless you and keep you.

May He make His face shine upon you,

And be gracious to you;

The Lord lift up His countenance upon you,

And give you peace. Numbers 6:24-26

To the Church of Jesus Christ my Saviour, Friend and Lord

I extend my sincere gratitude for the love, acceptance, understanding and patience which you showed me.

I wouldn't have come thus far without you.

You played a major and vital part in grooming me, pointing me in the right direction, presenting God to me as He ought to be, teaching me His ways, helped me discover who He says I am. You guided and helped me to reach out to others with His love and Salvation.

You have been built upon a rock and the gates of hell shall not prevail against you. Matthew 16:18

We will still journey together until the trumpet sounds.

To the reader:

I am not looking for sympathy or attention by telling this story of my life. I am past that stage.

I am looking to help those who are struggling with the effects of abuse and need encouragement to know, that it may take time; yes, healing and restoration do take time, and you will make some mistakes about how you rewire your mind but it is possible to recover.

Nothing is impossible or too difficult for God. Luke 1:37

Chapter 1.

I was born in the early 1960s. It was in the then Transvaal province, which became the Northern province and it is now called Limpopo province, in the Northern region of the country of South Africa, in a small farm called Marsfontein, just about three hours' drive from Johannesburg.

It was a few minutes after midnight on Sunday 17th October, which meant it was actually Monday.

My mother chose to name me after the day, hence my middle name is Sondaga, meaning Sunday. Sondag is Sunday in Afrikaans. The 'a' at the end is to make it sound more African.

Black languages in South Africa are greatly influenced by Afrikaans words which have been slightly changed or have vowels added to make them more African.

Being born on Sunday was an honourable thing. Even though people were not evangelised and most areas never had missionaries, they still somehow saw Sunday as a special 'Holy' day. Most babies born on Sunday were named after the day.

This name became a great part of me. I grew up being called by it till my mid-teens when I attended a traditional girl-to-woman ceremony whereby the name you grew up being called changes to the one that depicts you as a young woman and not a girl any more.

The little farm was owned by the European Settlers, the Dutch East India company that came into the country from the Netherlands in 1652 and settled first in the region of the Cape province, the Cape of Good Hope, but later spread themselves across the country.

I am a third-born. The middle child. My sister Maria is first-born, then followed my sister Anna and then myself, followed by my three brothers, Joseph, Simon and Sipho.

I was born at home. I was illegitimate. My mom never married. I never knew or met my biological father. My mom never breathed a word about him. By the time I was born, he had moved on.

The only hospital available was miles away. It was common and was the norm for babies to be delivered at home by their grandmothers or older family members like aunts or other relatives.

Birth registrations would be rarely carried out. My one was only made when I was 16 and was old enough to apply for a National ID book, which at the time was called a 'Pass'. The people used to call it Dom pass, meaning, a fool's pass.

This applied especially to people who lived in farms as they never got to go to town or any government offices but relied on their farmer bosses for everything. Some farmers were kind and would do this for their people but some wouldn't bother.

It was not until 1986, when the old Government was under great pressure to make changes, and one of those changes was to get rid of Dom passes and issue Blacks with the same National ID as Whites. I got my first one in July 1986 whilst training to be a nurse in Pretoria.

My sister, Maria, has three children; two daughters, Sarkie and Miriam and one son, Lucas. She is blessed with nine grandchildren and one great-grandchild.

My sister, Anna, had one daughter, Florah, who had a misfortune at age 24 whilst attending a Technikon in Pretoria in 1999. She went missing overnight from her rented room and has never been found. Rumour had it that her then boyfriend, who happened to be a professional thug and hitman, known by the locals there and unknown to her at the time, was heavily involved. We learnt later that he used to visit her and stay for some time in her room. Her best friend informed us later that Florah got to know about his involvement in gang-related murders and crime as well as hitman affiliations, and she wanted to end the relationship. That's when he reportedly eliminated her. It still remains to be proven. The then corrupt police Departments and courts made many cases disappear into thin air. Florah's case was the same.

These types of people are known to be working with corrupt policemen and tend to bribe the courts and get away with it. Unfortunately, that's exactly what happened. The case dissolved into thin air and original files went missing, police officers and magistrates resigned and it was left unresolved until recently.

In winter of 2019, (SA) police officials came over to my sister's house and announced to her that the man had been arrested for questioning regarding the case and that many more such cases that disappeared were being reopened. They were going round collecting information from witnesses. It is still ongoing at the time of writing this.

Florah had a son who unfortunately drowned in a nearby pond whilst playing with his friends at age 6.

My sister, Anna, by the grace of God, is still recovering from all this and is going strong.

Chapter 1

I was named after my grandmother. She got the name from the then local farmer she lived under. It was the norm for people to be given names which would be English and mostly Afrikaans by their farmer bosses as they couldn't pronounce African names. People were at least allowed to keep their surnames.

When the time came for me to change my name depicting my transition from girlhood to womanhood as per tradition, I then began to use Sarah as I was named after my grandmother.

The traditional girl-to-woman ceremony usually took three weeks during winter, whereby the girls would leave their homes to go and live in the village Chief's compound. They had an older sister or a relative or anyone organised for them for that purpose, to come and look after them.

The girls and their carers were not allowed to go home or leave the compound at any time during the period.

The purpose of this event was to mature girls who are nearing adulthood, mainly between the ages of 14-17, to train and teach them about their cultural values, beliefs and customs. I was 14.

They would be taught special cultural songs. These songs would talk about what they were to be taught.

The harsh winter months were preferred to get the girls tough and get accustomed to severe uncomfortable weather conditions with very little covering.

They would walk around with the upper part of their bodies bare day and night. Only the bottom part from the waist down would be covered with a very scruffy hard material. No shoes were allowed. Most parts of South Africa have quite cold winters. The girls' feet would crack and bleed. It was considered a necessary way to toughen them even more.

Food would be very scant; below basic. It was a way to get them used to times of famine and teach them to survive with very little or nothing.

Some activities involved getting girls accustomed to and strong enough to conquer fear. They would create late evening activities and games that were very scary. One of them was getting girls to take a lone walk through thick bushes on a very narrow footpath in pitch darkness. They would have organised people to hide at certain parts along the route within the bushes and would make certain scary noises or sounds when the girl came past near where they were hiding. The girls wouldn't have been warned about this beforehand, so it became unexpected and extremely scary and terrifying.

Those who completed the journey were separated from those still to go, to avoid running the risk of them warning the others.

This one freaked the heck out of me.

They would engage in special activities designed to train them in what was deemed adult and grown-up, preparing them for the times ahead in life. These activities were non-sexual as only women ran the whole thing and men or boys were never allowed anywhere near the compound. The good thing is, those days, virgins still existed, and most if not all girls of that age group were all still virgins. The grandmothers made sure to keep a close eye over them and protected them from boys. It always worked. This was to make sure your daughter would get married, as virginity was a prerequisite to marriage.

During the period of the ceremony, whilst girls had the top part of their bodies exposed and were bare-breasted, it was a good way for older women to watch their breasts to ascertain their virginity. A virgin's breasts were expected to be smooth, round, full and pointed, not shrunk and floppy. They wouldn't need a brassiere.

Most of the time, girls would be grouped according to their tribes, as part of the purpose was to teach and train them in things pertaining to their tribal beliefs and way of life.

Boys of similar ages had their own similar thing, at the same time of year, for the same length of time, but theirs were carried out on the mountains or forests as it involved circumcision and they didn't want women to see them walking in pain. What was happening in there was kept a secret, but older women knew as their husbands would tell them. The reason to choose cold months, in addition to training them to gain the ability to withstand severe, difficult and uncomfortable conditions, was so the wounds inflicted through circumcision would heal quicker and properly with no danger of becoming septic.

The boys would be regarded as grown up and ready to marry at any time after this, especially those in their late teens to early 20s.

Those days, any boy who was not circumcised was not considered to be a man, good and strong enough to have a wife and family.

As in the case of girls, where virginity was a prerequisite to marriage, with boys, circumcision served the same equal purpose.

A virgin deserved a circumcised man. Those were the days.

At the end of this period, for both girls and boys, but separately, there would be a great celebration in the village beginning in the Chief's compound and home. He would then meet the girls and pronounce some blessings over them,

Chapter 1

then release them formally back to their families where individual family celebrations would be held. These celebrations were usually done as per tribal groups. Each group would have their own joint celebration in one place, usually in a home of one of the girls, but each family would take part in the preparation and financial contributions towards it.

At our house In Lebowakgomo with my eldest sister Maria's daughter, Sarkie and her family. December 2017.

A Journey of a Thousand Miles

Last time my mom was taken out to visit family and close relatives. Christmas Day 2017, surrounded by people. She lived just over a year after this.

Chapter 1

My younger brother Joseph and I used to visit her at the hospital every weekend. This is one of those times. I was 14 and my brother was 9.

My mother when she was working in Groothoek Hospital - Nursing college.

Chapter 1

From left to right: Recent photo of my older sister Anna, myself and eldest sister Maria.

My grandmother holding my cousin

Chapter 2.
Early Years

My first seven years were spent living with my mom and grandmother and my siblings, except my brother Sipho, as he was born when I lived in another region with my aunt.

When I left, my brother Simon, born in the late 1960s, was just a baby.

We were very poor. My mother never had anyone helping her with the family. My grandmother was the one chipping in to help financially with her pension.

My sisters were compelled to leave school very early to go and find work to help out. My sister Maria literally didn't have any formal education. My mother taught her to read and write.

My mother was taught mainly by her white farmer bosses' wives and her friends. She's never been to school.

My sister Anna left school in Standard 2. This is the fourth year after starting school.

I was lucky because I lived for 5 years with my aunt and the last three years of the five, I was in school. Then, when I returned to my family, my mother was now working as a housekeeper in the local hospital as we moved from the farm to a village nearer the hospital.

I got a chance to continue with school.

My grandmother had plenty of chickens, some goats and a few pigs.

They were viewed as a fortune. The only 'wealth' we had.

In those days, most families were very poor like us, so things like these were viewed as luxuries.

We still wouldn't get to have any of them for a meal though. My grandmother was very strict when it came to that.

Once or twice a year, mostly Christmas and Good Friday, we would have either a pig or goat slaughtered for the family to feast on, and chickens were mostly used any time we had visitors.

There were no baking facilities. We didn't have stoves then. The only time we would bake was making 'vetkoek' at Christmas and Good Friday. These were a kind of donuts made to a very traditional Afrikaans recipe.

During special events in the community, the women would make a makeshift oven by digging a shallow rectangular hole a few feet long and use corrugated iron sheets. They would then place hot piles of wood on top of them and put the iron sheet on top of the makeshift oven, whilst the scones would be baking on a large pan inside.

They were very delicious. These women were very creative. It worked very well.

My sister Maria is the light-hearted one among us all. Always likeable, calm and peaceful.

She helped me a lot when I lived in Vereeniging, Sebokeng, with my small children. She was always handy.

My sister Anna is the tough one. She has guts.

She used to get into fights out on the streets; not because she was troublesome, no, mostly because she was tough to tackle by one person and the other children in the village knew that and envied her for her toughness. They would set out to bring her down by inviting her to join a team for basketball, which she loved playing.

They then would trap her and bring her in a circle, taking turns trying to beat her. She always beat them all up and won the fights. They would then team up to beat her but still she managed to beat the whole team up. I used to watch these fights but was helpless to lift a finger to help her. I remember one time when they teamed up against her and brought another tough girl to challenge Anna. The fight was really tough that day. I was crying outside the circle and at one point, I just couldn't take it any longer; I jumped in to help her but Anna gently pushed me back to stay out of it, saying she could handle it.

She didn't want to see me hurt. One of the girls tried to hurl me inside so they could beat both of us up. Anna punched her on the face and sternly told her to "leave my sister out of it, you hear me?"

She is also very good at business. She can do anything to make money, no matter the obstacles.

I remember one time when I visited her at her workplace in Voortrekkerhoogte, Pretoria, a national military training base. She worked there as a waitress.

The wages were very low so the women would buy alcohol from bottle stores at affordable prices to sell them out in parks or anywhere outdoors at a much more expensive price to make commission. It worked. My sister was good at this. Bottle stores were closed from Saturday at 1 pm till Monday at 8 am. So, drinkers were at their mercy during these hours.

It was very risky and one could be imprisoned by the military police if found doing that.

One particular time, whilst I visited her over the weekend, she took me along with her. I was still at school, doing Standard 9, which is equivalent to the last year of secondary school education.

As usual, we carried the boxes of beers to a secluded area at the far end of the park. It was always done in secret and hidden from the military police. The military knew about these endeavours and were always patrolling and looking out to catch the women as well as the customers.

That day, they managed to find the group. We ran for our dear lives. As we scattered, Anna grabbed my hand and tried to drag me along. I was so scared and terrified, my knees were knocking and I couldn't run fast. Anna ran ahead.

I fell over a barbed wire fence trying to get through to the other side.

The wire hooks caught the flesh on the side of my right knee and pulled it out, tearing my dress as I tried to pull away. There was a searing pain and blood gushed out. The military police were catching up with me from behind by this time. There was no time to look at the wound or even scream or cry. The thought of going to prison was way too scary.

Luckily, I did manage to jump through, ran as fast as I could, found a shrubby bush and hid behind it. The military policeman who followed me came very close to the bush where I was hiding, looked around, gave up and I saw him walk away in resignation. By this time, I was not even breathing, in case he heard my breath.

Gosh!! Was I afraid? You bet!

I waited until they had all got into their van and driven off.

I was surprised to see that Anna was not too far away from where I was. She had also taken cover behind a bush.

She came over to where I was. By this time, I was crying and in shock.

We nursed the wound on my leg and managed to stop the bleeding.

I thought we were now going to go back to her place. No, we headed straight back to where the boxes were left. All the other women and the customers emerged from all directions and came back. I thought, "Are these people alright in their heads?"

The boxes got kicked around by the police, bottles of beer were shattered; it was a mess. Everything we left was destroyed. The military police took what they needed and destroyed the rest. All the military police were made up of

Whites, although there were few Blacks among the Army but not in the military police.

They were vicious. We called them MPs, short for Military Police.

If they caught you, they would beat you to near-death before they took you to court or questioned you.

No one wanted to be in their hands.

Some of the women left and went back to their places. Anna and a few went back to their places, not to stay there, but to fetch whatever leftover beer they had, then they returned to sell again.

The show must continue. Nothing was going to stop them, vicious military police or not.

That was the attitude of Anna and her friends.

I admired her for this grit but that day, I hated her for putting me in that situation, making me go back to it after a narrow escape.

Anna also had a very funny way of finding and giving people nicknames according to something they did, said or wore or how they looked or talked.

For example, if someone had a bald head, she would call them Ellis Park, which was the name of the big famous football stadium in Johannesburg. She had a name for everyone and people just responded to those nicknames. It was so funny.

When he was a small boy, she used to call my brother Simon, hare. This was only because, when he was small, he looked chubby and very active.

My brother Joseph was 5 years younger than me. He was very bright at school and liked playing football. He was good at it. He was always among the first 5 in all the primary school classes.

His performance dropped gradually when he started secondary school. I discovered much later, when we were adults, that he was subjected to severe bullying which affected him psychologically.

This was not at school but mainly during playtimes in the village. There was one older boy, much older than him, by the name of Reuben, who apparently targeted Joseph so much so that it was well-known among the village football club and all the boys. He was not part of the club. He was a school-leaver, a good-for-nothing loafer. His only joy was to make my brother's life hell out there, making himself look strong.

Unfortunately, due to not having an older brother to help him out, and having kept this to himself and not shared it with any of us who could have intervened on his behalf, he continued to endure it by himself, but it ultimately affected him very badly.

His performance in secondary school was greatly affected. He did manage to get a pass in his matric results. This is a high school certificate.

He got a medium grade.

My second brother, Simon, was born a breech presentation. Breech is when the baby's bottom shows first during birth. It can be a very difficult and dangerous birth, especially when delivery is carried out at home. Unfortunately, those days, the hospital was very far from the farm, as he was born when we still lived on the farm. My grandmother had always helped deliver all of my mother's children at home.

With Simon, he happened to be breech and his birth was very difficult, resulting in some degree of brain damage. Most babies with breech presentations born at home didn't survive. He survived but ended up with mild learning disabilities.

He only managed to get to Standard 2.

With no facilities for children with learning disabilities in those days for Blacks, he couldn't further his education.

He began to work, but just odd jobs here and there.

He is married but they have not had any children yet.

Sipho was the last to be born in the early 1970s. He was a bit wayward from an early age. He got involved with the wrong group. He dropped out of school at age 15 and unfortunately never went back. He began getting involved in petty crimes, ending up in jail for a few months and few years at a time. His first imprisonment started at age 15.

Joseph, Simon and I would take care of my grandmother's herd of goats every day after school. This was the time we got a chance to play together in the fields, running around and playing hide and seek, sometimes riding on the bigger goats, climbing trees and all.

It was the village norm for children to take their herds of goats, sheep or even cattle to graze in the fields after school.

I loved these times.

My mother was a very good storyteller, just like my grandmother. They used to take turns at it. Every fairy tale they told us felt so real. I loved those moments a lot.

Later on, I went to live with my aunt and these times were the ones I missed most.

That time, when I lived in Zebediela Estates with my aunt, I began to retell all those stories to other children I played with.

I would have a whole bunch of them, every evening, gathered in a home after supper before a huge fire made out of wood in one of the huts or outside. Those days, food was either cooked outside the huts or inside. The weather was always warm unless it was raining.

My mother had another side to her. She was very strict and overly protective of us. She wouldn't allow us to go out to play with other children often. It was the norm that on Sunday afternoons, children, especially teenagers or those just about to become teenagers, would get a chance to go out and mix and play with other children. There were a whole lot of games to play, from skipping ropes to basketball.

My mother wouldn't let us go. She would come up with a whole-day chore on Sundays and get us all busy with it. I used to resent this but Anna resented it the most. I was not that very outgoing by nature and would have very few close friends. Anna had great social ability and liked to be among other groups of children. For her, it was quite a loss. My sister Maria was more like me. She didn't have many friends either. Most teenage girls those days got pregnant quite a lot.

My mother didn't want her children to experience what she had, becoming a young unmarried mother, so she used to hammer this into our hearts.

I guess part of what she was doing by refusing us permission to go and play with other children was due to seeing a prevalence in teenage pregnancy amongst those teenage girls whose parents allowed the freedom to go out.

She had my sister Maria in her late teens as a result of poverty that compelled her to leave home early to go and find work somewhere. The father disappeared as soon as she discovered she was pregnant.

This made my mother very over-protective and cautious about having her daughters impregnated out of wedlock at an early age.

She was a bit intolerant of what she deemed bad behaviour. She would deal very harshly with it. I will relate two incidences here involving both of my sisters individually.

The year could have been around 1965/66. My sisters Maria and Anna were bored and silly and decided to go and break into the farm foreman's house whilst he was out working in the field.

Apparently, all they did was to eat the food they found in there and didn't take anything. Someone saw them and went and told the foreman who came and caught them red-handed.

A complaint was made to my mother and she went berserk. She concentrated on my sister Maria as she was older.

She took them home and got her in one of the huts, locked it and beat the heck out of her. She beat her so much that when the stick broke, she used her fists and anything she could grab. By the time she was done, my sister was just left with a mere moan, unable to even open her mouth fully when crying. She lay there for some time unable to get up.

When she finally managed to get up, she ran away and fled into the forest. It was the middle of winter.

Maria disappeared and did not return home for three days. My grandmother, on the morning of day four, set out to find her. She feared that Maria may have died somewhere. My grandmother liked Maria a lot.

She challenged my mother about her oblivious attitude towards the disappearance of Maria.

My mother thought that Maria would return by herself when she was done crying, but it was now past three days.

My grandmother went out early in the morning in the freezing cold. It was a very cold winter.

My grandmother later brought my sister back. She had to literally carry her on her back as she was so frozen from frostbite and freezing temperatures that she was unable to walk.

Grandmother quickly made a fire, laid her beside it, removed the cold frozen clothes and put fresh warm ones on her, applied hot compresses on her body, cooked porridge and fed her. She gradually recovered. It was a near miss. One more day and she would have died out there.

Don't get me wrong, I guess my mother meant well. She wanted to teach her a lesson and set an example for us all so we would never do anything like that, ever, but unfortunately, it went way too far.

The second time was in the mid-1970s. My sister Anna was in a relationship with a young man next door to us. They were our distant relatives. We were not blood-related but just shared tribal origin, beliefs, culture and language.

The old members of that family were well-known to my grandmother. They came from the same region, in the far North of the Transvaal.

It was considered taboo and forbidden for relatives to engage in a sexual relationship.

Even though, in this case, these people were not really our blood relatives as far as my mother was concerned, it was still taboo and she was concerned about it being seen as a shameful thing by everyone.

She spoke several times about it to Anna, urging her to stop it. One time, she got a beating for it. Anna, as stubborn and tough as she is, refused to listen.

My mother gave her an ultimatum, either to stop it or leave home.

I believe that my mother never thought Anna would leave as she was only 16 and didn't have anywhere to go. She probably thought this time she had got her.

Anna told her boyfriend who, at the time, was working in the city of Pretoria. He lived there and only came home on special occasions like Christmas, Good Friday or family events.

When Anna told him about what my mother said, they set out to flee together.

He took her to Pretoria without permission. This was the time when my mother worked in the hospital. She was based in the Nurses' training college which was a stone's throw from the main road which linked our village to the hospital. Between the road and the college was a large football ground for hospital staff. If you were outside the college building, you could see anything out on that road clearly.

Anna knew this, so she set out to have my mother see her with her boyfriend, to show her she had gone with him and there was nothing my mother could do.

Anna and her boyfriend loitered around waiting for the time when my mother came out. Indeed, she did come out to hang laundry on the washing line.

They deliberately made themselves very visible to her and when they caught her attention, they waved at her and got into the taxi to town to catch the train. There was only one daily train from Potgiersrus, a town 45km away from the hospital. It operated at night to arrive in the early hours of the morning, between 5 and 6 am.

Off they went in plain helpless sight of my mother. If she didn't have a heart attack that day, she wouldn't have any.

My mom had a very good side. She was warm-hearted and known for this. She seemed to be a bit harder with her own children; I guess that was her way of making sure we grew up with good manners, but at times, she could be too hard and punitive. People looked up to her a lot. All her siblings relied on her. She had the brains even though she didn't really get to attend school, as there were no schools where they lived when she was a child. She taught herself to read and write. She always put others first. We learnt, very early in life, that people come first. If there was food, the best would be given to others and then we got what was left. When we had visitors, she would give them her bed, putting fresh, clean or new linen out for them. She was known by everyone as the kindest person ever.

We grew up having all sorts of people constantly coming to our house just to chill. I am talking about the rejects of society, people with mental health issues who were shunned and no one would have them come near them. The outcasts, the poorest of the poor. They frequented our house. When they were there, you wouldn't even think they were odd. Only their appearance would give you a hint into their mental state. They would be so happy and felt accepted and welcomed and that would make them behave well. They would then come again and again. When people in the village feared them, we found them very safe. They never harmed us or threatened us. They could become violent, but it was provoked by how people treated them.

Drunks also frequented our home. They felt accepted and loved. I grew up with this and always talked to this kind of people on the streets when other people stayed away from them.

My mother was an encourager. She always made sure she praised her child when they had done well. She always saw potential in us. She would tell you that you could do something that you felt inadequate to do. She made you feel so capable. That's the one thing that made me persevere with school, even when I started late because of ill-health.

She worked hard to make sure we were fed. I remember when she would get up at 2 am to prepare food for my brothers for their lunch break before she went to work to start at 7 am. She had to walk a distance of about 20km or more, twice a day, to and from work for a long time as public transport was very unreliable; many times, the bus wouldn't be seen for months on end.

She always refused to follow the traditions. She rebelled against them. This helped her to find God. Where we lived, in the farms, there were no churches. There would be one church very far away, about 10-15 miles, with no transport to get there.

She took me along once when I was about 5 and we walked that distance there and back. It was a small European-style building that was long-established by the Dutch missionaries who, together with the British missionaries, built churches, schools and hospitals at the most. Most of these were in villages and big cities. The farms were deprived of these privileges. Most of these missionary churches were Dutch Reformed and Wesleyan. (Methodist)

The Dutch Reform in our part was more prevalent. It was popular, even though apartheid laws made the congregation divide even seating inside the church, utensils used for communion, baptism and everything. We didn't know any differently at the time, so this didn't really bother us.

She was a great influence on me in the things of God.

I loved her very much.

We always have been very close and shared a lot in common. My sisters used to complain and say she favoured me over them. When my husband passed away and after a few years I decided to come to work in the UK, she helped look after my children. This made my children love her. They had a very strong bond with her. They were with her for three years before I brought them over to join me. She had moved into my house. She lived in my sister Anna's house before, when I lived in Sebokeng, (Vaal Triangle) Gauteng province, with my husband. After my husband's passing, I went back to Limpopo province in preparation to come to the UK. I sold the house in Sebokeng and built a bigger one in Lebowakgomo, a newly established suburb near Pietersburg/Polokwane.

She passed away recently, August 2019, after two consecutive strokes within a week. I miss her.

My grandmother loved us very much, me and my sister Maria. But perhaps me slightly more as I was named after her. She taught me how to recite my name according to the tradition of our tribe.

She would spend time telling me stories and things about my grandfather whom I never met as he died before I was born. She told me how jealous and possessive he was. My grandmother was very pretty even in her old age with sharp nose. She was much younger than my grandfather. My grandfather was a well-known traditional healer. He was regarded as one of the most powerful ones in his time.

Chiefs and Kings regarded him highly and employed him in their homes and villages. He was always gone from home doing work in some village. He met her when he helped my grandmother's parents one time and he asked for her hand in marriage as payment. He had another wife who had children of her own. It was common and expected of men those days to have more than one wife. Men were respected and valued by their ability to marry several wives and have many children.

Chapter 2. Early Years

My grandmother was given to him. He took her to another village and built her own home there, but further away from everyone else. They started a family. They had 8 children, including two twin girls who passed away. My mother was number 6.

She told me stories of how possessive he was of her, always paranoid that the younger men would snatch her away from him. One day, my grandmother said he asked her to accompany him to an event in the neighbourhood which was some distance away from their house, as he put her far from others for fear of losing her to other men.

My grandmother said these were rare occasions when he would ever take her along or allow her to go anywhere.

She prepared herself and put on her best traditional gear. How pretty she looked, she said.

Travel was by foot. Halfway through, he decided they would sit under a huge tree. He would proceed to the village to buy alcohol and return to her, then they would have their own little private party away from everyone else and celebrate there.

He did and indeed returned. My grandmother never got to get to the event; after all the effort and hard work to get prepared, choosing the perfect dress, looking her best once in a while and happy that at least she got a chance to be with other people, she never got there. Her voice sounded still disappointed even when she told me this. He was just a typical jealous, insecure, possessive and controlling man.

My grandmother used to go to the field to get organic vegetables and medicinal herbs. Her father was an amateur traditional healer and taught her a few healing tips.

He showed her some natural herbs effective to heal some ailments.

Occasionally, she used to take me with her to fetch them. I got to know some of them. Some were just green leaves from shrubs, some were roots and some were their fruits.

I used to love those times.

She also trusted me and chose me to be the one, if not my sister Maria, to accompany her to get her pension from the Chief's offices.

Those days, pensions were delivered to the village Chiefs and old people would collect them there.

Our village was listed under Potgietersrus, whilst my grandmother came from Pietersburg region. This is when we lived on the farms. She obtained her pass booklet whilst she was there.

She didn't want to change it so she had to travel to another village which was under Pietersburg to get her pension.

We would get up early and set out on foot to the village. I loved these trips as she would buy me anything I wanted whilst there with her.

She didn't get on well with Anna and didn't really like the boys.

She used to accuse Anna of stealing her pension money. She didn't really steal it. It was just because she didn't like her. These accusations used to cause Anna a lot of pain.

With the boys, she always disapproved of their poor work when herding the goats, accusing them of mucking about.

She didn't sleep on a bed. She used to sleep on a cane mat, handmade by herself. I would be the one preparing her sleeping area. I knew which blanket came first and so on.

She loved it.

Grandmother was a great storyteller, just like my mother. They took turns in doing this, mostly in the evenings after supper, whilst sitting around the fire.

Moving from Marsfontein to Watervaal

I was around five and a half when we moved to Watervaal from my place of birth, Marsfontein. Both of these places were farms owned by Dutch Farmers.

Life in Watervaal was great for me. I was still a small child, not attending school, but had no friends as the neighbours were scattered. My friends were my sisters mostly, as my brother Joseph was still a baby.

I used to have an imaginary friend; a doll made of pieces of clothing by my mother. I adored the doll. I called it Moleketlana, meaning floppy, as it was very floppy and had long floppy legs. This was my best friend.

I talked to the doll like talking to a living being. I would hold conversations, playing its part and my part in the conversation.

My sisters told me it was fun to watch me.

It was so real that they used to sit quietly and watch me.

When I was with the doll, I wouldn't need anybody or anything.

It was a real friend.

Chapter 2. Early Years

There were times when I would give it instructions to do something or say something and of course that wouldn't happen as it was not alive. I would get upset with it and either throw it around or smack it.

Then the scene would move from there to an imaginary point where Moleketlana would be upset and cry because I spanked her.

Then I would apologise and ask for forgiveness and reconciliation. Moleketlana would comply and I would give her a hug and a cuddle, tell her I loved her and then we were friends again.

I suffered a lot from recurrent tonsillitis, hay fever, and eczema.

My mother said eczema and hay fever were worse when I was little. She said my whole head was covered with weeping sores and dry scales.

She informed me that I had difficulty suckling on the breast as I often breathed through my mouth.

She related to me one particular incident that frightened her. She said I got a bout of measles at the time when I also had tonsillitis. My mother said it was so severe that I almost died. My immune system was already weak from the ongoing tonsillitis.

We were living on the farm in Watervaal at the time. I had to be taken to hospital and the hospital was very far.

My mother was working as a housekeeper in the farmer's house. She had a very good relationship with them. Transport was a big problem. The bus operated only once a week.

The farmer, Mr Boshoff, offered to take me to the hospital in his van.

My mother said I was laid down on the floor of the van and she covered me up. I was running a temperature.

I was at the back of the van with her so she could keep an eye on me.

My mother said, at some point, she was convinced that I was not breathing any more. The breathing was so shallow that my tiny chest couldn't be seen moving up and down; my mouth was open but I looked like I was dead. She didn't want to disturb the farmer whilst he was driving so she let the journey proceed. She was convinced I was dead.

I had recurrent upper respiratory infections from birth. My tonsils tended to be inflamed quite often throughout the year. As a result, I started school late. I had numerous hospital admissions as the doctors of the time were not confident or competent enough to operate on a child below the age of 7.

I had to be treated with intravenous antibiotics whenever the infection attacked. This would be 5-7 times a year. I also had severe eczema. My mother told me that it was far worse when I was a baby. She said my whole head was covered with weeping sores and dry scales. She said my whole head would be covered with bandages.

I had severe hay fever which graduated into sinusitis. This caused problems with breathing through the nose. I would use my mouth to breath as my sinuses would be inflamed, swollen and blocked.

Suckling became difficult.

That particular day, in the van going to hospital, was worse than all the other times.

Convinced I was gone, she silently wept, alone in the back of the van.

We arrived in the then emergency department, which looked like a small flat with three or four rooms for examination.

I was observed to be still alive but critical. They quickly transferred me to what was the intensive unit at the time. I stayed there for a few days whilst they pushed oxygen, fluids and intravenous antibiotics. I had to be in isolation due to the measles.

When the worst part had cleared, I was moved to an open children's ward.

My mother was very traumatised and frightened by this experience and decided to have me live near the hospital. The only way to do this was to move me to my aunt's house as she lived closer to the hospital. It still wasn't that close, but people from there could walk to the hospital, even though it may be a couple of hour's walk.

They talked and I was moved there. My brother Simon was a baby at the time.

I continued to get bouts of attacks of tonsillitis and sinusitis several times a year and my aunt would take me to hospital as soon as it occurred, as instructed by my mother.

It happened so many times that my aunt began to complain to me about it.

Being in hospital in those days was not a nice experience.

I developed separation anxiety when my mother left me with my aunt. I was only six and a half then.

This, coupled with poor health, multiple hospitalisations and an aunt who was now at the end of her tether with me, took its toll on me. I started to wet the bed, especially whilst in hospital.

The nurses then had power over patients and could get away with anything. It was the norm in that particular children's ward that whoever wet their bed would be taught a lesson in the morning, whereby all the other children would come to their bed, then the nurse would remove their sheet to expose their bottoms so the children could scratch and prick them with their nails. Some children's nails were long and sharp and I would bleed. The nurse would allow them to carry on despite my screams and cries, begging them to stop.

They would sing a mocking song that said, "The granny with a beard wet the bed". This meant that you were big enough like a grandmother, but were still bed-wetting. They would sing this chorus as they pricked and clawed at my bottom over and over till I couldn't cry or scream any longer. When they finished, the nurse would order me to carry those wet sheets and take them to the laundry bag. I was so humiliated and hurt that I began to feel worthless and useless, worse than all the children in there. The matrons wouldn't be around when it happened but they just weren't doing their job properly to check regularly.

This was so physically and emotionally traumatising, that it drove me into despair.

I began to isolate and was fearful of other children. I started to have terrible nightmares, dreading the nights in case I wet the bed again and got mocked and punished again in the morning.

The nurses' idea about this was that the punishment was necessary to stop the child from bed-wetting.

In that hospital, all the doctors at that time were white. There was a huge language barrier. Patients relied on nurses for translation. There was no way a patient could report anything to a doctor. The matrons were not bothered. They were mostly unapproachable. Patients couldn't report to them either, let alone children.

Some days I wouldn't be the only one, but there would be one or two more to take the punishment in turn with me.

My mom would only come to visit once when I was in hospital. As I mentioned, there were no transport means; the bus was only once weekly and my mom worked as housekeeper for the Farmer, and they needed her every day.

One day, she visited and she found me sitting outside the ward. As soon as I laid my eyes on her, I cried, bitterly. She didn't understand. Nor did everyone else, including the nurses. She expected me to run to her, hug her, smile and shout for joy. In my heart, I was grieved knowing that as usual, she had come but for a very short time, then she would be leaving me, not only in this terrible hospital but with my aunt.

This was what made me cry, but since I wouldn't communicate it to her or anybody, they didn't know why I was upset. The dread of being left abandoned again was way too much to bear and outweighed the joy of seeing her.

I never told her, nor my aunt, what was happening to me when I wet the bed. In my little mind, I thought that was such a bad thing that if I told her, she would be very upset with me.

The journey from my aunt's to the hospital was a bit far on foot. With no means of transport whatsoever, the only way was to walk. Frail, sick and weak, I still had to make those journeys several times a year.

One day, my aunt was so fed up with my recurrent need to go to hospital that she asked a young man, a total stranger, to take me. He was to put me on his bike as the last journey with my aunt had been way too heavy for me, requiring several stops on the way to let me rest.

I had never ridden on a bicycle. I was terrified of the thing. The young man forced me onto the back of the bike and requested me to hold fast on his waist. I tried, but got so scared when he started to move that I screamed and let go, risking a fall. He got so angry with me and all throughout the journey, he would try again, change positions and get me in the front or put only me on it whilst he pushed it. It didn't work. I freaked out and he ended up giving up and just pushed the bike and the two of us just walked, me behind him, as he was so angry with me.

He was afraid that I would not be able to make the journey on foot due to the condition I was in, and also my aunt had told him to make sure he got me on the bike and didn't let me walk all the way for fear of getting my condition worse, risking collapses and inability to reach the hospital.

By the grace of God, I managed to reach the hospital. The man was so angry. Luckily, I was admitted so he rode back on his bike.

My aunt lived in Zebediela Estates in one of the sections called Tangwaneng, named after the many dams, pools and rivers that surrounded it.

Zebediela was a large region, about 60km from the town of Pietersburg where the Dutch Settlers established large orange plantations. Each section had its own numerous plantation fields full of rich orange trees. They were supplying the whole world with those oranges. It was huge. Outspan oranges. Maybe some of you may remember them. The region had about 14 Sections.

Chapter 2. Early Years

Above: The then Groothoek Hospital and the hospital tuck shop.

A Journey of a Thousand Miles

Dutch Reformed Church that served the hospital. It was founded by the Dutch missionaries. Many hospitals and some schools were built by them.

Chapter 2. Early Years

Above: Hostels for single migrants from Malawi and a few from Zimbabwe.

These were all men and young men who had been carefully selected, but as time went on, people began to learn about this opportunity and would just come by themselves. Sometimes, there would be grown men among the groups who managed to survive the long difficult cross-country journey on foot.

My aunt married one of the Malawian immigrants, Mr Thinifala Chintali. He was renamed John by the farmers to make it simple. Everyone was given either an English or Afrikaans name in those days.

My aunt's estate was slightly on the outside, but nearer to Groothoek hospital.

There was only one primary school which provided tuition from Sub A to Standard 6. After standard 6, students would either take further education, such as nursing or teaching, or proceed to secondary school.

The nurses and teachers with only a Standard 6 certificate would only be allowed to enrol for nursing assistant training and qualify as assistant nurses, whilst those who took teacher's training would be assistant teachers too, or lower primary teachers.

The education for blacks in those days was a bit limited. To get to secondary school was a luxury. Very few people managed to do so.

The year I started school, at age 10, Standard six was found to be needing review. They were looking at taking it out and reducing the tuition years to Standard 5 and make secondary school a bit more necessary if not compulsory.

Students would no longer be considered for either nursing or teaching after the last year of primary school.

I am talking about only nursing and teaching for a reason. In that time, those two professions were what was easily available and accessible to black people. Very rarely did people become anything else.

My aunt had two children from her previous marriage. She was a widow. My cousin Johannes worked in Germiston, a big town in the East Rand, in a factory.

He would come home only on special occasions.

My cousin Johanna was the last-born and she only did odd jobs. She was very spoiled by my aunt and wouldn't lift a finger.

Both my aunt's children loved me. They were way older than me and older than my sister Maria too.

I began to regard them as my own blood siblings and looked up to them.

My 'sister' Johanna was very wild. She was a bit promiscuous and had a child very early. She led a very reckless lifestyle of smoking and drinking. In those days, these things were taboo, especially for women.

She hung around with the wrong crowds.

She moved from one relationship to another. Her first child passed away as a baby because she left the baby soon after birth and went off with another man. My aunt tried to bring the baby up but unfortunately the baby died as there were no feeding formulas available then. At least, they were not known among black uneducated people.

The same thing happened again with her second baby. This time, my aunt and my uncle would often leave the baby with me at age 8, for two days over the weekend, as they used to visit their friends in another estate from Saturday and would return Sunday late evening, intoxicated with alcohol.

My aunt was tired of taking care of Johanna's babies when she wouldn't take responsibility for them.

The baby would cry with hunger till it slept, only to wake up again and cry some more. I cried along with it. I was helpless, hungry myself with no meal left and no one to get help from.

This went on for several months till the baby passed away.

Johanna was very irresponsible but it was my aunt's fault; she pampered her a lot. She was unable to look for a job, let alone keep one. She liked partying.

The doctors were happy to carry out the operation to remove my tonsils when I was age 9. It was initially said I would have the operation at age 7, but I was too frail and weak so they didn't want to take chances. Medicine was not that advanced then.

After I had them removed, I slowly began to thrive. I got stronger, had fewer illnesses and even my allergies reduced.

I didn't have to go to hospital quite so often.

I finally was well enough to start school at the beginning of the following year. I would be turning 10 that year.

The first two years of school were Sub A and Sub B. There were no pre-schools or nursery schools then, at least in my part of the world. We used slates and pens specially designed to write on the slate.

A slate is a hard but fragile flat plate made of a fine greyish-black metamorphic rock.

They were so fragile, once dropped, it would easily break and shatter depending on the impact, it may split in two parts or many pieces.

It used to drive parents crazy as they would be having to replace them countless times.

The pen was a hard almost metal pointed stick that would be used to literally scratch on the hard slate to write.

The policy was that pupils would then graduate from slates in the third year of starting school which in our case was Standard 1.

We used pencils and normal excise books. Then in Standard 2, we were introduced to pen and ink. This carried on till higher education. I was lucky in that the education system was progressively developed and by Standard 3, inks and ink pens were out of use. Normal pens were now in use.

The ink pens used to break or dismantle and ink would leak and spill onto your book as you write making such a mess of everything.

The ink bottles also used to tip over on desks and spill on your books, the desk and even your school uniform. Our white or khaki shirts, as they were part of our uniform, used to have blue marks on pockets in particular as we would put the ink bottles and pens in our pockets.

It was so good, when we did away with ink bottles and moved on to normal ball point pens.

Slate and Pen

Chapter 2. Early Years

Ink bottle and fountain pen

Classroom in the 1970's & 1980's. Most classrooms had two seater desks.

I was very bright and the teachers liked me a lot. My first teacher was Mrs Mphahlele. I used to look at her and think she looks so much like my mom. I missed my mom so much and this resemblance was making me think of her every day. By seeing her, I would get a little satisfaction.

The name of the school was Lehlasedi. It was situated in section 6, very far from our section, Tangwaneng. By this time, I was stronger and two years older than the average school starting age.

Winters were very cold with morning frost and ice. Most of the time, we would find water, left in cups or containers, had turned into ice overnight.

The grass and roads would be white with frost and ice.

I had no shoes to wear and during the winter months it was tough; my feet would crack and bleed.

My sister Johanna was working in Groothoek Hospital as a housekeeper this time. I had just started school and I was in the junior school choir. Once a year, the schools would set up choirs of all kinds; junior mixed, junior boys, junior girls, intermediate mixed, boys and girls and senior mixed, boys' and girls' choirs.

We were one of the best schools in the region.

The time for competitions arrived and each child had to have a clean or new black gym dress, a white shirt, black socks and a pair of black shoes. My aunt had enough of a burden with my ill-health already, let alone having to spend money on school clothes. She freaked out.

I had a friend in class whose mother worked in the hospital with my sister Johanna. She was also in the choir and needed the uniform. It was now very close to the choir competitions and the teacher sent home every child who didn't yet have the full uniform to get their parents to buy it.

I thought of my sister Johanna. I wasn't going anywhere near my aunt. She had told me already she was not buying them.

My friend and I discussed and agreed to go straight to the hospital. We got there on time and it went well. Her mom gave her the money and my sister gave me the money. Off we ran home. When I got home, I happily showed the money to my aunt and told her that my sister asked me to ask her to go with me to the local shop to buy the uniform.

My joy turned into mourning.

She retorted back at me and asked me why on earth I had even thought of going all the way to the hospital to disturb her daughter about this.

She had no choice, though, but do as my sister requested.

We set out to the shop and she gave it to me all the way, both ways.

I had to accompany her for two reasons:
- to select and show her the exact clothes
- to have the clothes tried on as she wouldn't have known my size.

The only thing I held on to, that made me happy despite everything, was that I finally got the uniform, and would be going to the competitions. This enabled me to ignore all of my aunt's tantrums and nagging.

The competitions were held in the Zebediela regional village, Moletlane. This is where the Chief lived, Chief Kekana who overlooked all the villages in Zebediela region. Every village had its own Induna, who was accountable to and reported to Chief Kekana.

All the schools in Zebediela competed there for sports, debate, music and other major events.

Going there was like Christmas. The village was better developed compared to all others, with better shops, better schools, and other facilities.

It was like a farm girl going to town.

I was thrilled.

Then, two years later, my sister relocated to Venda, a region in the far North of Transvaal, with her boyfriend who was a plumber in Groothoek Hospital. They had a baby and he got transferred to another hospital in Venda, Tshilidzini Hospital, to help with plumbing duties. This baby was her third, with the first two having died due to negligence.

My sister gave up her job and moved with him. She returned home after a year and luckily got her job back. The problem was she needed a baby-minder as she worked shifts.

I was now in Standard 1 under Mrs Tladi. Standard 1 was year 3 in school. She was a very good teacher and she liked me. I was lucky to be liked by most teachers, if not all, because I was too grown-up for my age; a tough life had made me a bit wiser ahead of my age group and I acted too responsibly. They also loved the fact that I was bright. They used to give me certain responsibilities that they wouldn't give to other students.

My sister decided to pull me out of school and get me over to the hospital to look after her baby. I informed Mrs Tladi and she was heart-broken. It was two months before the final yearly exams.

Groothoek Hospital was a missionary hospital, having been built and founded by the Dutch Reformed church missionaries. There was a church building in the hospital compound and all employees were to be trained in the Dutch Reformed Faith movement for a year, learning the basics of Christianity and the Bible by memorising certain verses. They were to study a strategically designed booklet. This booklet would take a whole year to learn, with students demonstrating to class leaders, mainly on Sundays after the service, that they know the contents of the book by heart, chapter by chapter.

At the end of the year, there would be a huge celebration where students would then be confirmed and baptised by having water sprinkled on their forehead. A baptismal certificate would then be issued to them to take to employment and educational institutions.

My sister Johanna could not read or write as she never went to school. She then gave up the job as she couldn't fulfil this one requirement of reading and learning the booklet to qualify for the hospital job.

This helped me a lot as I could now go back to school in time to sit the end of year exams.

Life with my aunt continued. My sister later left her baby, who was now a toddler, with my aunt and went back to join her plumber boyfriend in Venda.

This time, even though it was still difficult, the toddler survived and lived. That child is a grown woman of 49 now and has 5 of her own children. She happened to have been affected by the early childhood abandonment and must have been psychologically traumatised by it as my aunt was not caring at all. She developed some mild learning disability and slowness of thought in life.

This has affected how she raised her children. She left the first three to be raised by relatives whilst running around.

Her first son struggled so much that he fell behind many years through being kicked out of school for not having books and uniform.

Despite this, he worked hard, persevered and today he is in a Soshanguve Technikon in Pretoria, studying IT. He is 29 and persevering in spite of everything. He won a bursary after achieving excellent grades in high school.

He was several years older than everyone in his classes due to numerous drop-outs throughout his early years.

My aunt had a very hot temper. Everyone knew about it. She subjected me and sometimes her husband to constant shouting and nagging.

She seemed irritable and easily angered and would take it out on me. She would call me names and keep complaining about how my mother dumped me there burdening her with the responsibility and so on.

She was a bit cruel too. Those days, to have bread in the house was luxury. Shops were too far away and money was scarce.

Chapter 2. Early Years

Now and then, my uncle would buy bread and some cocoa as well as milo for hot drinks. I loved them but my aunt would hide them in their hut, high above things, so I couldn't reach them.

Then, every evening, when my uncle returned from work, it was routine to fill two big mugs each with those beverages, very rarely with bread too. My aunt would have me go outside as they consumed their delicious drinks. I used to go out and sit behind the hut and cry. It was during these times that I would really miss home and wondered why my mom left me here; why can't she come to take me back?

These were questions going through my head all the time.

The reader must not misunderstand my mom's intentions. She had four other children to single-handedly take care of, work full-time to provide for and take care of my grandmother.

I also never told her about all this at the time, so she had no idea things were bad.

I mentioned earlier that my aunt and her husband used to leave me by myself and go and spend the weekend with their friends in the nearby section, B3.

It was not that near but the distance was halfway to school.

They would leave me with no food. I used to hop from house to house visiting other children and sometimes they would let me eat with them and allow me to spend the night with them. Sometimes I would be asked to leave.

These were times when I would have to go home in the dark and cry myself to sleep.

Children used to come out in the evenings to play. I would join them. There was an older girl, could have been 3 or 4 years older than me, very strong and evil, who started to target me. Everyone in the neighbourhood knew that on weekends I was by myself.

Nana took advantage of this. She would get all the other children to form a circle and have me fight her inside the circle. I was no match for her. Nana used to be battered by her mom who had a very deep voice and looked like a man. She always subjected Nana to beatings. This hardened her heart and made her angry. She needed someone to take it out on and I became that person.

She would invite me to slap her or punch her and I wouldn't. She would then begin to punch me severely everywhere she could. As she did that, she would get the other children to cheer and this made her feel great and powerful. She loved it and made sure it happened every weekend.

It wouldn't have happened during the week as my aunt would be home.

I now began to isolate and avoid coming out to play.

At first, she would come and beg me for forgiveness and tell me she was sorry, she wouldn't do that again, that everyone missed me and wanted me to come out to play with them.

I would believe her and get out of my house and go with her to join others. Already, she would have prepared them to form a circle as soon as we arrived and lock us inside it so she could beat and punch me to her satisfaction.

She managed to trick me for a few weekends, but I started to refuse to come out with her. She then devised some plans to send a child she knows I liked to come and convince me to come out, that everything was alright. As soon as I got there, she would have everyone ready to encircle us so she could beat me up again.

I started not to trust any of the children any longer. This drove me to isolation. The only time I got to play was during the day, as she wouldn't touch me when adults were about.

How I longed for my mom to come and get me. How I missed her. I cried a lot. Small things would trigger my emotions. I was always on edge and frightened. I never felt safe at all.

My aunt was not someone you could open up to. There was no way I was going to tell her about Nana.

We had a shop which was in another part of the area where we lived, quite a distance away. The only route to get there was through a thick bushy footpath.

My aunt used to send me to the shop to buy her stuff. At one point along the route, there was a dried-up valley, not too deep, but deep enough to only see the head if someone stood in there and you were passing by the footpath.

I began to have some awkward and scary experiences. At the point where the valley was, as I passed, I would look in the direction of the valley and see a pale-looking face with what seemed to be hollow eyes and a bald head. The distance between where I was walking on the footpath and the valley was just a stone's throw. One could see clearly.

I felt chills go up my spine. I was scared. I looked again to make sure I was not making it up; it was there. I walked past as fast as I could, bought the stuff and came back and tried not to look this time.

One time, again my aunt sent me to the shop, and the same thing happened. This time, I told her and she shouted at me as I was asking her to find another child to accompany me as I was scared. She pushed me to go and I did. The same thing happened. I wouldn't see the rest of the 'body' of this thing that looked like a human being with a pale, very fair complexion. It was just the 'head' which had no hair and eyes that appeared like two dark hollows. It scared me.

I began to ask some of the children to find out if they knew about this thing, as they also got sent to the shop by their parents and used the same path. None of them had seen it.

One of them said she wanted to come with me next time so she could see it. I took her with me the next time. The thing was not there. I didn't see it either. But each time I was on my own, it would appear. She laughed at me and said I lied. My heart was painful as I knew I wasn't lying. I saw this many times.

One time, I went by myself and there it was, standing in the middle of the valley, facing in the direction of the footpath, hollow eyes and bald head. I ran back and asked that child to come with me. She did, and this time she saw it. We both ran and went back home. My aunt nearly killed me that day, not physically but the shouting and the screaming at me was too much to take.

Over the next few times, she went to the shop herself as I refused to go.

By this time, my sister Johanna had returned. I told her about this thing and she believed me. She never questioned it at all. I loved my sister Johanna. Despite the fact that she was the way she was, deep down she had a warm heart.

She offered to come with me so she could also see this thing.

She came with me but unfortunately, I saw it but she couldn't. It was there when we got to the spot and as soon as I pointed her to it, it disappeared like it sat down in the valley. I was sure I saw it. My sister Johanna said, "Let's go check inside the valley and see if it's there". I refused. I was too scared; no way was I going to see this thing at close range.

She still believed me though. I guess she saw the terror on my face and that was enough.

I know it sounds like I made this up as a frightened little child but I know I saw this thing; it would just stand there and 'glare' at me with those 'hollow-looking eyes and follow me with its stare as I proceeded forward along the footpath.

I grew up with a heightened sense of 'knowing'. If there was anything sinister or evil, I would sense it very quickly.

Before this incident, I had an experience when I was around age 3. I was the baby at the time as my brothers were not born yet. My mother had a friend visiting, her very best friend. We used to visit the friend sometimes. This time around, she wore a black dress with white small dots all over it. It was not the dots or the colour per se but something was odd around her. I felt a very disturbing and frightening uneasiness each time I looked at her. This was mostly not coming from her face but the dress.

I began to grab my mom by her skirt and clutched with both hands at her as I cried pointing at the woman. My mom realised what was happening and she was really embarrassed and so was her friend but the more I looked at the dress the more I had that foreboding weird feeling as if something from her was coming to grab me. Trying to hide behind my mom, nothing was helping.

The woman decided to leave. She was not upset or angry, just ashamed and embarrassed.

She apologised to my mom and left. My mom tried to question me after she left as to what it was I saw but I was too small to explain. This time it was not something I saw but something I felt and sensed. A presence.

My uncle was from Malawi, as I mentioned earlier. Malawian immigrants used to hold festivals every quarter or so, whereby they would gather in the middle of nearby bushes and perform some ritualistic dances and wear very scary costumes and masks on their faces, singing their traditional songs in their language.

These festivals were always carried out in the middle of a thick bushy area. They would cut a few trees to make room or create a dance area but made sure there were enough trees and bushes to shield the happenings of the festival. As I said, all of them were men.

During these festivals, only women were allowed to come and watch as they performed. No men were allowed.

It was very strange.

My uncle played a very big part of these festivals. He took part in the performances.

My aunt would take me with her at a certain time to go and watch as my uncle would have left earlier to prepare with his group.

They used to get the women to guess who was who behind those scary costumes and masks. Everyone seemed to be alright and enjoying it except me.

I was so terrified, clutching at my aunt's clothes, begging her to take me home. The masks were the worst. The masquerades would come out one by one from behind bushes further away from where they allowed the women to stand. They then would come a bit closer to the women as they sang, beat drums and danced.

Everything was scary; the drum beats, the dances, the costumes and masks.

If they saw a man or a boy peeping through the trees or bushes, they would run to chase them away.

I learnt later, as an adult, that those performances were actually some kind of ancestral worship mingled with a degree of some devil-worshipping.

They held them a few times a year.

They were not known in South Africa.

Each time my aunt got me to go and watch these things with her, I suffered terrible nightmares for months afterwards.

I literally saw the 'creatures' and masquerades coming to grab me in those dreams. I began to be fearful of spending the night in my room. I would wake up in the middle of the night in terror and run to knock at my aunt's door, begging her to let me in.

The first few times, she would let me in and I would sleep in a corner in their hut. Then my uncle started to complain about it, that I was disturbing their privacy.

My aunt had to have me return to my hut and the nightmares continued.

I literally re-lived those events, everything I saw and heard, the songs, the drums, masks and costumes.

I began to beg my aunt to leave me with other children when she went to attend those festivals. Luckily, she agreed.

One of the things that made me later think that my aunt wasn't really a caring person, was when she sent me to the shop one day, and a young man, much older than me, emerged from the thick bushes and asked me to show him the money I had. I did and he pulled out a bag full of strange coins and said I must give him my money as it would not be accepted at the shop, that real money was what he had.

I believed him and took all those coins in exchange for my aunt's money. The shopkeeper told me that the money was not in circulation anymore; it was old British coins, pennies, half-crowns, farthings, crowns, pounds and so on. By this time, the currency was the Rand. These British coins were used during the time when the country was still colonised by the British.

That night, I got it from my aunt. She gave it to me, all she could from her heart. She was so angry, boiling with fury. She called me every name under the sun. Crying for me was a daily thing.

All she cared about was her money, not my life and safety. That man could have killed, raped or even abducted me.

Life was not all doom and gloom in Tangwaneng. I had plenty of happy moments and times. As I said, the section was surrounded by dams, pools, ponds and rivers, as well as lakes. It was water everywhere and the weather in summer and spring was quite warm. We used to swim a lot. This is where I learnt to swim. Every child learnt how to swim.

I also learnt how to fish. My sister Johanna taught me how to fish. She used to take me along when she lived at home.

The picture above is the Nkumpi river, one of the rivers that surrounded us.

The Zebediela dam pouring into the famous Nkumpi (formerly known as Gompies) river, which supplied water to the gigantic orange plantations and the whole of Zebediela region.

My sister Johanna died a tragic death in 1988 in her mid-forties. She had been working on a farm where she lived with her now elderly parents in the late 80s. We were informed that she experienced severe stomach pains and vomiting after eating her packed lunch. Apparently, farmworkers would leave their packed lunches in a particular area whilst working. It was believed someone put some poison into her food. She was vomiting greenish stuff. They put in tubes to try to drain it in the hospital but it was never-ending. It destroyed her insides and she died leaving all 4 of her children plus a 2-year-old daughter who was literally brought up by my elderly aunt.

The two-year-old suffered psychological issues as a result, and some learning disability. She struggled in primary school and I was informed years later that the teachers had been writing to my aunt, making her aware of this, but in vain, as I believe the letters were never read and the teacher never personally went to talk to her when there was no response to the letters.

I took her in when I was in the UK and had moved to my home town. I got her a disability grant and put her in a school for special needs.

We also played family games which I loved very much. We would make houses with stones and appoint fathers and mothers as well as children for each family. We would then each go to our house to take some foodstuff to come and prepare a meal, and when meals were ready, all families would come together to eat and share. This is how it was in real life there. Families used to do this. It was really fun.

Sometimes, we would get a hiding from our parents for stealing foodstuffs from the house to play with. This never stopped us.

Above: Picture of my favourite childhood playtime. Simulation of a house with rooms and the family in it, complete with furniture and household necessities.

Chapter 2. Early Years

Below and above: The Citrus plantations which produced Outspan Oranges. They are planting Mandarins today.

A Journey of a Thousand Miles

Above: what remains of Lehlasedi primary school in section 6.

Above: This is what remains of the clinic that catered for the whole of the Zebediela Estates. I frequented here due to recurrent tonsillitis.

We also used to go through the forests to pick fruits. There were so many there. Every season had its own. Summer was the best as there were quite a few different fruits.

We celebrated Christmas too but not in a Christian manner. Very few people were Christians in Tangwaneng. It was really still so unevangelised. Even those few were not knowledgeable about God, or their Faith, and no one read or studied the Bible. No one actually had a Bible. The most prominent denomination was the Dutch Reformed Church. The main church was based in Section 6 where the clinic and the primary school were.

As it was far, Mr Ndlovu was elected an elder to hold mid-week meetings in his house and then believers were expected to attend the main church service on Sundays in Section 6. It was just him and his family that used to attend. A few of the people attended the mid-week meetings in his house. I never got to attend the Sunday services in the main church in Section 6 but became a regular attendee in the weekly house meetings.

Christmas meant a new dress and new shoes if you were lucky. Food, mainly things that you wouldn't normally get during the course of the year, played a big part of the event.

In Tangwaneng, we would then put on our new clothes, and head to the farmer's house with the adults singing and dancing all the way. When we got there, we would gather by their front garden or driveway and sing and dance some more for the farmer and his family. They would be so happy and then would give us goodies, sweets, cookies, cold drinks, and alcohol for the adults. Then we headed back home to continue the celebration. That was about all.

It was not traditional to get presents for Christmas.

Back to the weekly meetings in Mr Ndlovu's house. I was a regular at those meetings. Very few of the people where we lived attended. Few children did, and I was one of them.

Then when I was about 8 1/2 - 9 years old, before I began school, Mr Ndlovu started targeting me. I guess it's because I didn't go to school at the time due to ill-health. I was just loitering around when children my age were in school. He worked in an office as a security guard for the dams and fountains as well as machinery and tools. His wife used to ask me to take lunch to him in his office.

Those days, if you are a child, any adult had the right to ask you to do things for them. So, when his wife asked me to take the lunch, I didn't hesitate, as it was the norm.

This was now a daily thing. After a few times, Mr Ndlovu started to expose himself to me. I would step into his office and found him having his manhood out and he would beckon me to come and touch him.

This frightened me so much as I had never seen this before. I trusted him as a leader of the believers in our area, preaching to us and singing very nice Christian songs. They were hymns, those days, translated from English to Sesotho. I used to love them. They were partly the main reason I attended.

And now this. I thought maybe he would stop as I indicated to him by running away that I don't like this.

No, it continued, day after day; Mr Ndlovu would be waiting for me, exposed and beckoning me to come and touch him.

Children were never listened to and things like this were never heard of or talked about. There was no way I could even say anything to his wife or my aunt, or even my friends, as I could get severely punished for 'lying'.

So, it became my little scary secret.

We used to fetch water from some of the fountains a short distance from the neighbourhood as they were considered cleaner than other sources.

It was the girls' tasks to fetch water. As I mentioned earlier, the place was surrounded by fountains, dams and rivers, so, on the way to this particular well that was believed to be cleaner than the others and suitable for drinking water, I would find Mr Ndlovu, 'bathing' himself in one of the small rivers along the route to the well. The river was very close to the footpath. One could see everything from the footpath. He would be just standing there as he splashed himself with water, stark naked and not trying to grab his clothes to cover himself when I emerged.

He would continue to indicate to me that I should come to him and touch him. This was so frightening and made me sick.

I started avoiding that route and took the longest route to the well.

One day, I gathered strength and told my sister Johanna when she came home as I had a good relationship with her. She believed me but was unable to do anything herself. I guess she was afraid that the people would think I was a little liar and it would cause her a lot of trouble with the neighbours.

This behaviour went on for a year or so as I then started school.

I was never the same. I got so frightened and distrustful of older men. I believe it somehow affected my trust in God then, as this man was a representative of God, leading us in singing these nice songs (hymns) and preaching the Bible. I believed everything he said, and not only loved the meetings but looked forward to them.

In my childish mind, I asked myself, "is God like this? Does He do these things to girls?"

I later discovered through my sister Johanna that it was known in the neighbourhood that he was sexually abusing his daughter Shadi, who was a couple of years older than me. My sister Johanna managed to speak to a few of her friends who happened to know about Mr Ndlovu's sick behaviour and told her that it had been discovered that he was actually abusing his own daughter.

Even though people knew, no one dared say anything. That was the culture then. You would be regarded as a bad person and a liar, especially if you were a woman.

I also was informed by my sister that his wife knew about the sexual abuse of her daughter in the house. I guess she opened up to some of her friends but everyone was powerless to do anything.

I believe this man did not just abuse me and his daughter but must have done the same things to a whole lot more girls there.

He carried on with his role as a church elder as no one reported him. I stopped attending the meetings.

Another traumatic thing happened as well during that time. This was at the time when Nana was bullying me, when my aunt and uncle went away for the weekend and left me alone at home. I hadn't started school yet.

My brother Johannes, my sister Johanna's older brother, was working in Germiston in the East Rand near Johannesburg then. He would come home during major public holidays like Easter, Christmas and New Year. When he came, he would throw parties at home. He bought a big music system and people would come from all the neighbouring sections and farms to have a good time.

There was this regular guy, who was more or less my brother Johannes's age. I knew him from the times he came to our house for these parties.

He somehow discovered that I got left alone on weekends. One night, he sneaked into the house and knowing that I was by myself, he knocked on the door of the hut I slept in. I inquired as to who it was and he said some name I didn't know and claimed that my aunt had sent him to come and give me some food.

I refused to open the door but he managed to break the door handle and came in. I started to scream and he put his hands around my mouth to silence me and threatened to harm me if I continued.

When he opened the door, I had a good view of his face from the moonlight that swept into the room from the outside. That's how I knew who he was. He was trying to loosen his trousers and let go of my mouth. I somehow managed to scream and mentioned his name and he got frightened and ran away. That saved me. He thought I wouldn't recognise him as it was night time, but I saw his face in the moonlight. The thought that I knew who he was freaked him out so much that he fled. He never set foot in our house again and I heard he even left the job in the farm. My sister Johanna told me as she set out to find him and get him arrested.

The psychological scars were left.

Chapter 3.
Matome Village

I lived with my aunt until December 1972. My uncle was transferred to another job in another Section, Section 8, and we had to move. It was mid-December 1972 when we moved.

By this time, my mother and the rest of the family were now living in Matome Village, one of the villages under Chief Kekana. Our elder (induna) was Mr Mojapelo.

My mother had given birth to the last-born in the family, Sipho, Emmanuel, in December 1971.

He was now a year old. I never met him as I never travelled or visited the family, and my mother stopped visiting when she got pregnant.

It was around Christmas time 1972 when my mother requested that my aunt bring me back as they now had a proper home. The village was near the hospital, the schools were nearer, and besides, I had fully recovered from recurrent tonsillitis and the frequent hospitalisations had ceased.

My aunt took me back that Christmas and in January 1973, I began a new class, Standard 2, in a new school. This was Phalalong school. I couldn't get a place in the primary school under Elder Mojapelo, as my aunt registered me in her husband's name, which was Malawian, and Elder Mojapelo didn't allow foreigners to live in his village.

The village was divided into two sections. There were the Northern Sotho speakers under Elder Mojapelo, with Matome primary school catering for them, and the other section which consisted mainly of the Tsonga/ Shanghaan-speaking people under Elder Maluleka. Elder Maluleka was alright with anyone from any background who sought residence in his area.

However, during the course of the year, my mother changed my name to hers so I could be moved to our section of the village's school.

My mother had not been working since she gave birth to Sipho. Her last job was in the Orange plantations in Section B3. When they moved from the farm in Watervaal, they moved to this Section and the only job available at the time was hard labour in the plantation. She was used to housekeeping jobs.

It was during that year that my mother got a job in the hospital as a housekeeper in the Nursing college.

She started her new job in August 1973. Sipho was just over a year and a half. My mother had to stay at the hospital as her job required early starts, 4/5 am to prepare breakfasts for Student Nurses and she would finish late due to having to prepare dinner for them.

The only solution was to take Sipho with her, as babies then were only breastfed. There were formulas but most people couldn't afford them.

Then, misfortune fell on my brother Joseph who was about 7 ½ years old. As school-going age was 8, he was due to start the next January but didn't as he was now looking after Sipho during the day whilst my mother worked.

This delayed him by a year.

It was in 1973, when I was in Phalalong school, that I got saved.

We were not Christians as I mentioned. The only time I tasted 'church' was when I lived in Tangwaneng and attended Mr Ndlovu's weekly meetings and years back when I was 5 years old when my mother took me with her to the church in another farm.

Our only teacher was Miss Tladi who was a sister to Miss Tladi who taught me in Lehlasedi school.

She was her older sister.

One of her subjects was Religious Education which was compulsory then because of the Missionaries that built the first schools in the country and incorporated Christianity in hospitals and Schools.

When my mother got a job in the hospital in 1973, the next year she had to do a whole-year Christian Foundation course which was compulsory for every hospital employee as the hospital was a Missionary hospital like many others in the country. Just like my sister Johanna.

On this particular day, Miss Tladi taught about the Cross, the death and resurrection of Jesus Christ. She didn't dwell so much on the resurrection, but on the death; the reasons He died, the sin of humanity, and mostly on how He died, the beatings, mockery, insults, degradation and went in details about the whole punishment He had had to endure before He died. I only knew years later, when I understood properly what Salvation is, that I actually got saved that day.

As she retold the story and explained in detail what took place there, what Jesus went through, I felt tears fill my eyes. I was sitting in the second row if not third. She went on to say that this was all because of us, people, with our sins, that He needed to die, suffer, so we can return to God. The woman was not a preacher, she was a teacher, only following the syllabus. But the presence of God came into that classroom and the truth of the true Gospel touched my little heart. I began to weep. I couldn't control it.

She was somehow oblivious to what was happening to me and just went on and on. I could feel her heart, her pain. I could sense her spirit, the hurt in it, the compassion for Jesus, the sorrow, and my spirit caught it. A wave of the Holy Spirit just came upon me, and tears began to run down my cheeks uncontrollably. I was afraid she would punish me for being stupid, so I quickly pretended I felt dizzy and asked to go outside.

She asked one of the girls to help me as I was really shaken. She told the girl to have me lie down on the school porch in the open air to get some fresh air. That helped. The presence of God was still so much over me that I continued to weep, now shaking and in my little heart seeing Jesus suffering, alone and forsaken. It touched me.

There was no big-time Theology in what she was teaching but the Holy Spirit took over that day and revealed the truth of the Cross, the suffering of the Messiah for mankind to a 12-year-old girl.

From then onwards, my heart started to search for more. As I told you earlier, I was somehow drawn to the mid-week meetings Mr Ndlovu held in his house. I was around 7 ½ - 8 then.

I believe my heart was searching and hungry. In the whole of my family, no one was really into church even though, of course, in those days and in the areas where we lived, there were really no churches around.

God was on the move. Slowly but surely. My mother was then requested to enrol for the Christian Foundation Course to keep her job in the hospital. This involved learning a special booklet and memorising some verses at least once a week and explaining what you had learnt from the verse to the course leader. This was the same thing my sister Johanna had to do.

As well as this, students were to attend services every Sunday. At the end of that year, if a student demonstrated good knowledge and understanding of those verses, they were baptised.

The thing was, with the Dutch Reformed Church, baptism was water sprinkling on one's forehead and not immersion. Only the preacher carried and read the Bible in church. Only the preacher prayed. The congregation just listened. There was no teaching about learning the Word for yourself, praying for yourself and others, talking to God on a one-to-one basis, no relationship, no worship in truth and Spirit. That was back then, but I'm not sure how things are today. Hope they've improved.

It was when my mother began the course and regular church attendances that I went with her. I also asked if I could enrol in the course as it was for those wanting to become church members and be baptised.

I was just about 13 ½ then. Only 16-year-olds and above were allowed as it was believed they were mature enough to understand their commitment.

The group facilitator and the Priest, for some reason, agreed I could join. I was the youngest.

I swallowed that booklet in half the time. Everyone was amazed.

At the end of the course year, there would be a huge celebration where students would then be confirmed and baptised. A baptismal certificate would then be issued to them to take to employers and educational institutions. They would then be considered full members of the church and be allowed to participate in taking communion.

The ceremony was held in the Chief's village of Moletlane, just like school competitions. All the Dutch Reformed churches around Zebediela would gather for a weekend from Friday afternoon till Sunday afternoon. A fee was required for board and lodging. Friday was the welcome and explanation of what was going to happen during the time there. Saturday, all day, was oral examinations based on the booklet we learnt during the year. The panel was made up of various congregational Pastors. Reverend Tladi, who was related to the teachers I mentioned, was our church leader. He was one of the panel members. He was well-liked by all. Full of jokes and fun, he was.

It was rumoured much later that he had alcohol issues and was drinking in secret during the services. People close to him revealed this. Who knows? He has gone to be with the Lord now.

Many years later, he was stepped down from preaching for unclear reasons, but some people said it's because he was selling alcohol in his shop.

I quite liked him. He was very gentle, very caring and loved everyone. The whole village knew him.

It was during the Saturday time of examinations and registrations that one of the panel members, who was dealing with registrations in particular for the certificate purposes, found out how old I was. He got concerned as the agreed age was 16 and above and I had just turned 14.

He asked me who my pastor was and went to have a chat with Rev Tladi about this. Rev Tladi told him he consented to my baptism, that I worked hard throughout the year, I was very mature for my age and that I deserved this. That's why I liked him so.

I went through but got stuck with another panel member who now wanted to fill in a form that would be used to produce my certificate. These Reverends were very strict, some of them.

The issue here was that I had left blank the space where the father's details are required. I did this because I never had a father, and my mother never told me the name of the man who fathered me. I never asked as, in those days, you just didn't ask.

It was an issue; the Rev told me I couldn't be baptised as I didn't know the name of my father. It was like torture to me. As a 14-year-old who never had a father or whoever fathered them had never been mentioned, how could this now stop me from becoming fully Christian? Was it my fault? These questions were now running in my head.

I began to cry and he sent me to my pastor to ask who my father is. I went to Rev Tladi again and tearfully told him what was happening. He quickly went up to that Reverend and told him that he knew me very well, he knew my mother very well, he knew my family and that the fact that my mother was unmarried should not be an issue or stop me from being baptised. He told him that he would take responsibility for whatever questions or consequences might follow.

This made my day. My baptism form was forwarded and I got baptised, got a certificate and became a full member at 14 instead of 16 and above.

God had begun.

By 1974, I had been moved to Matome primary school as my name had now been changed from a Malawian surname that my aunt's husband gave me when I lived with them, to my mother's one. Mahlo. This was accepted by the village Elder.

I was now in Standard 3. I mentioned earlier that I was one of the brightest children in all the classes. This was the same. There were three top pupils in this class but I was actually number one. Very shy, riddled with fear and insecurity from all the earlier life experiences, ill-health, the sexual abuse and attempted rape, my aunt's uncaring nature, the feeling of being abandoned by my mother, separation anxiety, Nana's bullying and all, my confidence was out of the door.

The good thing was, when working in silence by myself, I excelled. Times like exams, homework, tests, etc., I topped the class. It was the speaking in public part that really freaked me out.

The teachers noticed this and, luckily, they understood me so well. They never forced me to do anything that I didn't want to do. They worked with me very well. After all, I was their best student.

In those days, a class would be allocated a class teacher who would be responsible for all the lessons on a day to day basis.

There were times when a teacher would be absent for one reason or another and another teacher would be asked by the principal to step in and take care of two classes for the day.

All teachers were aware of my maturity and regarded me as quite clever and capable of leadership. So, what happened was that, during the times a teacher was absent, I would be asked to step in for the day and occupy the class as long as it was a junior class to my one.

I would be given work to write on the board and get the class to write as notes on a particular subject.

At times, some teachers, knowing that I was capable, would just say, "Do what you want to do, Sarah". I would then get them to recite poems, compete and give them little prizes such as marks like you got 10 out 10, you got 5 and so on. Or read a book, each one reading a paragraph, or get them to tell stories. It was fun.

The children really liked me.

We would sing at times.

This went on to where teachers began asking me to step in for them in the very class I was in.

In this particular year, in Standard 3, there came a time When the school inspectors came. They always did this a few times a year. This entailed sitting in class when the teacher taught and marking them, and also asking questions related to a particular subject they are studying.

This was one such time. The inspectors came and began asking random questions around the curriculum for our class. I must say I knew all the answers and my teacher knew this. I froze on that desk and didn't move a muscle. My hand couldn't go up. I just looked down. The other two students answered some of the questions and I just sat there with the answers in me, terrified to open my mouth.

After the inspectors left, my class teacher turned to me and said, "Sarah, I know you knew the answers to all those questions; why didn't you answer?" I couldn't say anything, I just looked at him. He was very loving and understanding. He didn't tell me off but I guess he realised that I was one troubled child, very shy and easily frightened by unfamiliar faces. He was just so disappointed.

I was good at recitations, like prose and poems and we would hold competitions in our school hall with other classes. I always won. I knew my lines like the back of my hand.

Literature teachers liked me for this. I remember learning the poem, 'All things bright and beautiful, all creatures great and small, all things wise and wonderful, the Lord made them all'.

The other prose I loved was Julius Caesar's speech by William Shakespeare.

I loved reading a lot. I exhausted all prescribed books within a short space of time.

Another one of my favourite poems was " Love at first sight".

I recited from my heart. I had the ability to heartily own up the words, make them real, and place emotion in them, so much so that listeners would be captivated and feel the words. I was so good at this. It's natural for me to do this. My emotions are easily accessible.

The teachers loved it. I made the classes a delight. I became the person in the poem. Over and over again, people have found me to be very empathetic. I guess I am able to feel what the other person feels, without judging them.

I started visiting our small dilapidated, impoverished school library and would get old Northern Sotho prescribed books. One of my favourite authors was H. Z Motuku. I devoured his books. He was the Shakespeare of the black Northern Sotho-speaking people.

Two of the books I loved were:
- Morweshi (name of a girl)
- Leratorato. (true love)

These two were his best-sellers.

They were used for decades in schools and libraries.

I would stay at home reading these books as a primary school student whilst other children my age were playing. I always seemed to be a bit different in a way.

I graduated from Standard 5 and was required to transfer to secondary school.

Primary schools were reviewed and Standard 6 was abolished and became Standard 5.

Secondary schools were very scarce at the time. In my region, the nearest was in Moletlane, Matladi High School, where there were secondary and high schools combined. It was one of the best schools that have ever existed for decades and produced great people. It still is.

If you studied there, you were considered educated. Parents in big cities brought their children there. It had boarding facilities for both boys and girls.

Matladi High was one of the popular boarding schools in the Transvaal Province. It indeed was very good. It produced professionals. You could do Secondary education or proceed to high school in the same school. Secondary education was from Form 1 to Form 3. Those days, if you obtained your Form 3 certificate, which I believe is an equivalent of the UK GCSEs, you were considered educated enough to become either a teacher, clerk, administrator, nurse or anything.

Those who aspired for more, and had finances to do so, would proceed to do the next two years of high school after Form 3. Qualification after these two years was called Matric. Now, if you had this certificate, you could access university, depending on your grades of course. Only those who passed with Exemption would be allowed into universities.

Fees were expensive. There was no free education and no loans. Bursaries were only awarded to those students who excelled exceptionally, especially in Science and Mathematics. It was very rare to get a bursary. Those two subjects were not my best.

My best were history and languages. I excelled in them.

January 1977: I began my first year of secondary schooling. I quickly settled. I loved the uniform, and the crowd, as there were so many students there. Each Form would have 3-4 classes. For example, we had Form 1A, Form 1B etc. The A classes were always for those regarded as 'intelligent'. But the intelligence was determined by the type of subjects. As I said, Science and Mathematics were regarded as the best subjects. Those who were good in them would be in the A-classes.

I sailed through and because I was so good in other subjects and participated in school debates, I was regarded as bright. The determination of who went into an A-class would be made in Form 2. From Form 3, all who were considered bright would be placed in A-classes through to Matric.

When I reached the end of Form 2, one of the teachers decided to put me in Form 3A, which was majoring in Mathematics, English and Science.

I struggled with Mathematics in particular. I was good at the Chemistry part of Science, but not Physics. Physics was still not too bad for me as compared to Mathematics. English was never an issue. In the end, I passed in Science and

English but failed Mathematics. This caused a problem for me. Even if I passed in good grades for the two, my overall grade was dragged down by my performance in Mathematics.

I achieved the grade to proceed to Form 4, though. The only problem was the subjects you majored in. You had to carry them through to Form 5. Forms 4 and 5 were seen as twins. Matric curriculum started in Form 4 and was completed in Form 5. Change of subjects was not possible once you started Form 4.

I knew I had to change but pressure from the teachers to remain with the intelligent was too great. So, I continued with Mathematics, but unfortunately, failed it through to Form 5 and I couldn't get my Matric certificate.

I approached the teachers and explained my situation and they looked at my grades and saw it. I had excellent grades in English and Chemistry. Mathematics was causing a blockage.

I asked to be moved to the history class in my repeat year of Form 5. This could never usually be done or allowed but they somehow understood my situation and allowed me to move classes. I enrolled in History, English and Geography this time round and passed my Matric with Exemption, a university-entry grade.

My mother couldn't afford university fees. I had to face the facts that university was not my pathway. So, I took Nursing as I needed to earn some money straight away to help my family. In nursing, whilst studying, you earned a small amount of money as you worked in between college times. Nursing education required this as you had to study theory behind the desk and go and apply what you had learnt under supervision in the hospital. It was those hospital-based hours that you would be paid for.

It was not much, but those days, things were affordable.

Whilst in Matladi High, I could not commute from Matome village. Transport was not good; besides, I wouldn't have been able to afford it.

Reverend Moloko was appointed to lead the Dutch Reformed Church based in Groothoek Hospital. As I mentioned, the hospital was a missionary hospital like many others those days. There had to be a church in the hospital vicinity to cater to the spiritual needs of workers as well as patients. They would appoint a leader whose job was not only to preach on Sundays but to provide Pastoral Care to staff, patients and their relatives on a daily basis.

Rev Moloko was given a house in the vicinity of the hospital. Those days, housing was not an issue. Doctors, nurses, administrators and other disciplines were provided with houses around the hospital grounds.

My mother thought it best to negotiate with the Moloko family to have me stay with them from Monday to Friday so I would be able to commute to Matladi High. As a member of the church, this was not too hard to do.

Groothoek Hospital had good transport links to the school.

My mother reached an agreement with the Reverend's family and I moved in with them in January 1977.

I was not charged anything but it was agreed that my mother would contribute towards food.

Lucy was the Reverend's youngest daughter. She was also attending school in Matladi. Lucy was two years older than me. Lucy was not too bright and she kept repeating classes. She was still in Form 2 when I began. She had started 4 years earlier.

We literally 'fell in love', so to speak. It was an automatic connection. I liked her and she liked me the same way. We became very good friends.

Living with the Moloko's was not easy. The Reverend was very strict, very controlling and harsh. Lucy didn't really like him. The mother was very nice, but every member of the family walked on eggs around the Reverend. He wouldn't say much but his look would say it all and you would know what to do or what not to do.

Lucy told me he had served in the SA Army Force before becoming a Reverend. That soldier toughness was still very much in operation. The way he dressed was immaculate. Everything put rightly in its place, his clothes had to be ironed and washed only by his wife, packed and folded in a certain way. He never smiled, let alone laughed. His look was very stern and frightening.

I always avoided him. The only thing that kept me there was my friendship with Lucy. Lucy loved me. We were inseparable. The whole hospital knew that. If you see Lucy, Sarah is round the corner. To be honest, I'd never had a friend like her. She was the first friend who managed to break through my defences and grabbed hold of my heart. I felt so comfortable with her, completely free.

We laughed, we cried, we fell out, we reconciled and life was just not complete for Lucy without me and neither was mine without her. We were the best of friends.

During that time, the hospital was sent a Dutch Reformed missionary from their Seminary school. Her name was Catherine. She was slightly older than Lucy and me. She was a black South African young woman on fire for God. Catherine was very evangelistic. She went to all the wards, singing and playing her accordion all by herself. It was part of her responsibilities as a hospital missionary, though, but she had the extra passion for it. She played and sang everywhere around the hospital compound; bus stops, taxi ranks and shops, everywhere. She shared the Gospel but she never led people to accept Jesus as personal Saviour and get them to pray the sinner's prayer. We quickly noticed her.

We started to be naughty and challenged the Reverend's rules. She worked jointly with Rev. Moloko, Lucy's father. We noticed her very quickly and befriended her. I loved her singing and the accordion she played. We began to go everywhere with her and sing along. We would listen as she stopped singing and shared the Gospel with the people who gathered to hear her sing. She was a saint. She had a very warm nature. We loved her company. We would visit her in her one-roomed house anytime and ask her to sing. She would gladly grab her accordion and began to play and sing, getting us to sing along. One of the songs she used to like singing was in Zulu: Si ya hamba thina, si ye ezulwini, u so sala wena, ngoba u thand'i zono.

Translated: We are going to heaven, but you will remain here because you love your sins.

I loved the song. Everybody loved it and it made people stop and gather to listen and then Catherine would share the Gospel.

She operated more in a Pentecostal/ Evangelical manner as opposed to the way the Dutch Reformed Church was doing things. Rev Moloko didn't like this. He didn't approve of us spending so much time with Catherine, but we did. God has always been the greatest captive power in my life. Where He was, that's where I got more attracted to, way before I officially got saved.

One of the things we did that was not allowed in the house was attending the hospital staff ballroom dance practices or competitions. The practices were every Friday night in the hall. We wouldn't be allowed in but would look through the window. We would watch intently, get back to our room and try the moves. We did this so many times over the three years I lived there, that we could really dance. I remember trying Waltz, Jive, Tango, Quickstep, Cha Cha Cha, Foxtrot, Mambo, Rumba, Samba and many others. We loved them all. We would sneak out every Friday early evening to just go and watch through the window for hours as they practised.

We knew them all.

The Reverend realised what was happening and spoke to Mrs Moloko, asking her to talk to us and stop us from going there. She confronted us and told us not to do this any more. Her words fell on deaf ears.

The Reverend would lock the door and take the keys with him so we couldn't get out. We came up with a plan. The window. The house's windows were low enough for us to jump and wide enough to allow our bodies to move easily through.

The Reverend began to keep an eye on us. This was now really beginning to put a strain on the relationship between him and his wife as he wanted her to stop us and she just couldn't.

We tried to fool them by placing clothes in the shape of a body inside the bed, making them two bundles so they thought we were there. One time, he stood by the room door and called Lucy, but she did not respond as we were out.

He went in and pulled back the bedclothes only to find two bundles of clothes made to look like a body. He was furious.

When we returned, we found him waiting. This time, he didn't ask his wife to talk to us but he did. He then started to put the blame on me. He blamed me for poisoning his daughter, putting ideas into her mind and teaching her wrong behaviour.

He was so angry he didn't mince words that night. He then proceeded to say that he would like me to leave. He stated he would speak to my mother and get her to take me away.

This was the beginning of 1979. I was in Form 3, and Lucy was in Form 4.

The previous year, my mother had informed me that there were constant complaints from Mrs Moloko about my stay there, but not really saying I should leave. She apparently was not satisfied with the type of food my mother was bringing in as contributions as they were mostly basic. It sounded like they preferred to be given money instead of her buying the food but wouldn't say so.

My mother seemed to have picked this up but ignored it.

Now, the Friday evening sneaking out to watch ballroom dance was enough. My mother asked them to have me till the end of the year and said that she would move me out the following January.

The Friday evening sneaking-outs were not happening every Friday though, as the agreement was that I would go home every Friday evening and return Sunday late afternoon. This was so I could help my grandmother with house chores, wash my younger brother's school uniforms, and fetch water enough for the week as my grandmother couldn't do that. Then I had to make sure there was enough firewood for the week.

Lucy and I would deliberately not take the bus home on time for me to catch the bus to Matome. This would cause me to stay over Friday night and leave early Saturday morning. It was now happening quite frequently as Lucy didn't want me to go.

My mother wanted me to go as there were now issues and complaints.

It was in the second year of my stay there, in February, when we deliberately delayed so I could spend Friday night with Lucy to go and watch our favourite dance practice.

My mother got so upset with me for having missed the bus, she told me to see my way home tonight and that I had to find out how to get there. She left me and Lucy standing there and went inside her room.

I believe she was under so much pressure to have me out of the Moloko's house over the weekend, especially Friday evenings, that the thought of having me constantly missing the bus and staying and causing so many problems was too much to bear.

As you can remember, my mother can get upset, and when she is upset you had better do as she says or else.

I told Lucy I had to go otherwise I would be in trouble. We went to the house and I took my belongings and Lucy saw me off up to the end of the main hospital drive. It was now dusk; the sun had just set.

I took the main road, which was a gravel road. It was a large road, enough for two-way driving, which was in the middle of two sides of thick forest. The forest was really thick, with long wild grass, shrubs and all types of trees. There was a barbed-wire fence dividing the road and the forest on both sides, right through from the hospital to Matome. The journey was about 15km or slightly more.

I embarked on it alone on foot. It was now quite deserted. Just when I was about 3km away from the hospital and now getting into the thicker part of the forest, two men emerged from the bushes. They grabbed me and told me to come with them through the barbed-wire fence into the forest. I tried to scream but one of them pulled out a knife and pointed it to my neck without saying a word. I knew I had to keep my mouth shut and do as they say or else, I would die. They meant business. They smelled of weed. At the time, I didn't know what it was.

They half-carried me and half-dragged me into the thick forest. We had to jump the barbed wire fence to get further into the forest. They tore at my dress. I had on a white tennis dress given to me by one of the nurses at the hospital. She was a tennis player there and the dress was a bit small for her now. I adored the dress. It was now stained with dust and covered with grass and leaves.

One of them pinned me down and the other raped me, so forcefully that I bled straight away. When he finished, he gave way to his friend, who didn't need to pin me down any more as I lay there like I was dead. I had passed out. I was woken up by a heavy slap on my face urging me to get up and go.

I struggled to my feet, gathered what remained of myself, and dragged it out of there. The remains of the white dress were now just rags hanging on my body, turned brown with dust and had stains of blood on some parts as I bled so much.

I managed to jump through the barbed wire into the road, dizzy, dazed and confused.

For some reason, they followed me but at a short distance, as if to make sure I was 'safe'. How ironic!!!

Suddenly, a bakery van came by. I gathered the last strength I had and threw myself into the middle of the road, waving my hands, crying and pleading for help. I was just in front of the van when it stopped.

There were two guys in there. One of them got out and asked me what happened. Before I could say anything, he glanced past me to the side of the forest where it happened. My gaze followed his and then I saw them, the two rapists not far from the fence on the other side watching us.

The guy didn't have to ask any longer. He jumped back into the van and off they drove, leaving me there.

I had no more tears to shed, no more strength to make a sound. I cried, but through my heart.

It was now beginning to get darker. I had only one choice, either proceed and go home which was about 12-13km away, or return to the hospital to my mother which was only 3km away. I was sore everywhere. They had kicked me all over, rib cage, legs and face. My private parts were torn apart and I was bleeding.

I decided I would need to have my mother see this as she forced me to go. I was angry with her, with the men (they appeared about 5 years or so older than me) for doing what they did, the bakery guys for leaving me like this, the Moloko family for putting pressure on my mother to get me to go home on weekends; angry with everybody, everyone, and everything.

God? No, at the time, I didn't really know Him. I had heard about Him through the Dutch Reformed Church when I completed that year of basic Christian learning, got 'baptised' by sprinkling, no I didn't know Him enough to even think of Him at this point.

I went straight to casualty and told the nurses who I was. They knew my mother. They got hold of her and she came over. By this time, the doctor was checking me. My mother couldn't even utter a word. Her sorrow was all displayed on her face. I didn't say anything. I was crying through my heart. The doctor suggested we open a case with the police. I didn't know the rapists. They were total strangers to me.

The doctor stated he would take some precautionary measures to make sure I didn't get pregnant. I was only 17 at the time.

The police were called. Everything was so slow then. By the time the police arrived, it was now just before midnight. They took me and my mom, with the doctor's statement, to the police station, 10km away. We drove in their police van. They started off by throwing question after question. I was sore, in pain, tired and exhausted; the last thing I needed was questions.

It was very clear from their questions that they were biased. They were on the rapists' side. It was very common those days to blame a woman for the rape, hence a lot of the time, rape wouldn't even be reported to the police.

They finished taking details to open a file and they brought us back to the hospital.

That was the last I ever heard of the case.

Life had to go on and it did.

A Journey of a Thousand Miles

Photo: Phalalong lower primary school. This is the school where Miss Tladi taught on the subject of the death of Jesus and I just literally got saved at age 12.

Phalalong lower primary

Matome higher primary school

Chapter 4. Matladi High and Early Years in My Career

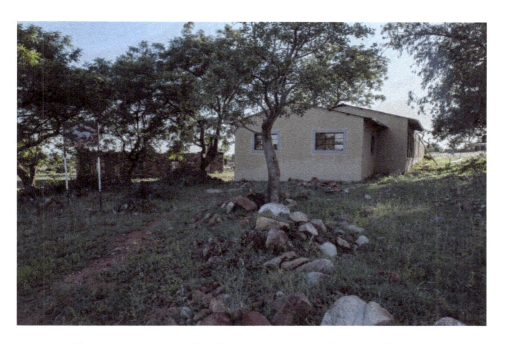

Matome primary school. It has since been moved to a new location.

Matome Mountain

A Journey of a Thousand Miles

The remains of our house in Matome village. Our jacaranda tree very visible (in the middle)

Our neighbour's house. We lived just behind them. The tall Jacaranda tree can be seen on the far left. That's where our house was.

Chapter 4. Matladi High and Early Years in My Career

Tladi's Café

Chapter 4.
Matladi High and Early Years in My Career

The above-mentioned ordeal happened when I was in Form 2 in Matladi High School. I was one of the promising students, bright, hard-working and determined to make something out of my life, to turn the tide and open the door to education and literacy in my bloodline. Very determined, I was. I quickly tried to put all these bad things that happened behind me. I was not going to move anywhere if I allowed them to haunt and dictate my life.

That year, I excelled in the school debate. I was in the junior debate team under Mr Thindisa, a very strict teacher. Coming to think of it, I believe he was bitter, and seemed to somehow show resentment towards, and sounded like he hated, some people from my village.

He taught my class English, and boy, he was good at it. He would spend so much time saying derogatory things, belittling Matome, really getting at it and getting the whole class to laugh. He sounded very narcissistic. He got to be known by the class for this. I disliked him a lot. I really did. I was from Matome and even though it was not my birthplace, that's where I now lived, so how dare he says these things about my village!!

He actually didn't know I was from there. A lot of people didn't as I commuted from Groothoek Hospital during that time. They took me to be from there. Besides, my mother worked there. He wasn't directing these things at me. I just became defensive as I was from there.

Nevertheless, hard-hearted, strict, cold, bitter and unkind as he was, I somehow managed to win him over, not deliberately, but by my hard work and good performances, especially in English and debate, which were his areas of speciality.

He soon took notice of me. It was hard to win this man over in anything. He was a hard man. He couldn't help but realise that I was good and that he could benefit from me as a teacher.

Every Thursday afternoon, the school would hold a debate and the rest of the classes were to attend and be the audience.

We had two teams; the junior team of which I was a member, and a senior team made up of students in Form 4 and 5.

I won every single time I participated. I was so good at bringing my points out, validating my opinions, reasoning and substantiating my statements. I was so good at it. My spoken English was good, I mean in that part of the world, at that time, yes, it was good.

I was fluent and a born speaker.

Common topics to debate on were the ones such as:
- corporal punishment in schools must be abolished
- Women are not to be educated
- Western civilisation is good

However, there were many more topics.

Mr Thindiza gave me a book as a prize for the best speaker in the junior debate team at the end of the year. He told me I should become a journalist.

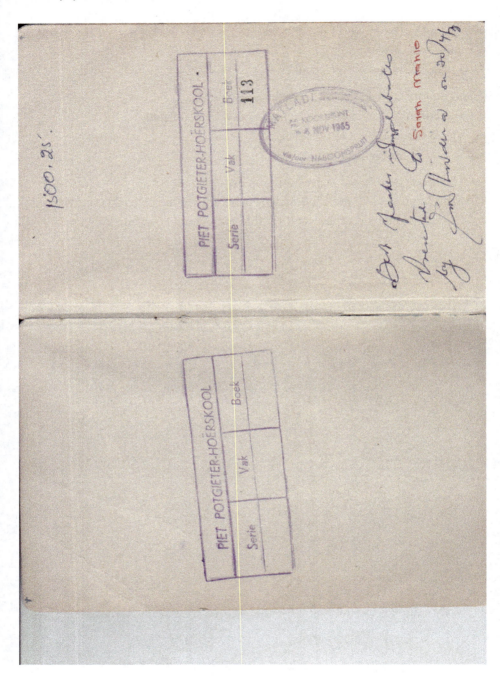

This, coming from someone like Mr Thindiza, was a bonus compliment. No one gets this from him; no one.

I had finally been removed from Lucy's family and my mother had been saving a little towards boarding me in the same school. It was only R42 a quarter. This was a large sum of money for my mother but she managed through thick and thin to do it. This drove me to excellence, seeing her going all out for me.

Even though I was thriving and managing, I became very guarded, and a bit distrusting of adults, especially men. I began to slowly be aware that I was very selective with friends. I had to really feel comfortable with someone before I opened up. It would take me a long time to decide to fully feel free around certain people. I was very shy and reserved. But what was in me would always push me to the fore. Always. This reminds me of this verse;

"A man's gift maketh room for him, and bringeth him before great men." Proverbs 18:16.

I guess because life was going so fast, and I started school late due to ill-health, I wasn't going to waste time working out who was good and trustworthy or what. I had to focus on building my life. That was the priority.

The matter, just like before with Mr Ndlovu's behaviour, was never spoken about. At least with Mr Ndlovu, only my sister Johanna knew, but with this, everybody in the family knew. Things like this were just not talked about. It was not the norm. It was not like the family didn't care, no, it was just how things were dealt with in our society at the time. It's different now. People are knowledgeable about things.

It was during the end of that year that I met and fell in love with a boy who was four years older than me in Matome. I will call him AK. Up to this point, I had never truly been able to open my heart to anyone. I tried but it just wouldn't work and within a few months, it would be over.

With AK, it was different. Very different. He had something magical about him. The only thing with him was that he was drinking alcohol and smoking weed. I knew about the alcohol but not the weed. He didn't drink every day as he was a college student at the time, but it was a common thing for boys in schools, colleges and universities to be drinking and smoking weed at the time.

We fell head over heels. I mean it was love at first sight. The poem I loved to recite in primary school became a reality in my life. I loved him, yes, I did. He returned my love but a piece of him was in love with his two friends, alcohol and weed.

AK was known to be harsh and physically abusive with his girlfriends. At the time I met him, I didn't quite know anything about him. He attended college in another town far from home so he would only come home during school holidays. He was slightly older than me so I didn't get to even see him around when I moved to Matome back in 1972.

We adored each other. Everybody knew about us. We were the talk of the village. He had been seeing another girl at the time when he met me. I was informed by some local girls that he was physically abusing her a lot.

People thought he would do the same with me. He didn't. He truly loved me. He never even raised his voice towards me, let alone say any word that was belittling, insulting or ridiculing to me. He loved me. I remember one day, he said to me, "Do you know that I get aggressive with girls?" I said, "Yes, I heard".

He went on to say, "But I never understood why I wouldn't do that with you". He confessed his love for me that day. He said, "No matter how angry you make me sometimes, I just can't hurt you".

It was common those days in the part of our world for boyfriends to beat their girlfriends. It was known. Even parents knew about it.

He never laid his hand on me.

I loved AK so much that I would spend days on end fantasising about us; having a good life, babies, I mean for hours and hours, I would be thinking about him.

I remember I got to spot his trainers' soles imprints on the ground out on the streets. He used to wear certain trainers with a particular print that was so well-engraved on the ground wherever he walked. If I didn't see him for a day or so, even just a few hours sometimes, I would go to the Main Street where I knew he must have walked and search for that particular print. I would find it and that would be enough. The look of it would feel as if I was with him in person. That's how much I loved him.

Things didn't remain as good with AK. His drinking and smoking escalated and he dropped out of college, couldn't get a job, and just relied on his parents for everything. He was a grown man now, mid-late twenties. I tried several times to make him look at what he was becoming and he just wouldn't change.

He deteriorated, became unkempt, drank daily, anything he could get as he didn't work, so he had no money to buy decent alcohol. He now looked like a real hobo. I still really loved him. Love is blind. But I kept my word and stayed away. This was now 1982; I was finishing my Matric. I could see my future becoming bright in front of my eyes. I looked at him and couldn't see him doing anything with his life. I had to decide to take very painful steps to end the relationship.

I gathered strength and told him. He literally just burst out in tears right in front of me. It was not the norm for men or boys to cry in front of women, even their wives. In my culture, men don't cry. He did. That's how hurt he was. The thought of losing me was unbearable. I was his jewel. His diamond. How could this happen?

He, sadly, through tears, uttered these words which stayed with me for many years. "Is it just because I am not working and I drink?"

I tried to say something but my tongue was rigid. He knew. I had told him many times before.

AK was very creative; he took my photos and photos of us together in happier days, and recreated them again, making different shapes, putting extra stuff on them to add creativity and beauty and put them all in three photo albums. We used to take turns at having the albums. This break up happened at the time when he had them. He told me, "You can go, I won't stop you, but I won't give you back your photos; they are the only thing of you I have left". This pierced my heart. He meant it.

I never got them back. My childhood photos and all. That's the reason I didn't put them in this book. Parents those days were not into taking too many photos of their children. There were very few photographers in the first place, especially in farms.

So, the few I had stayed with AK. I did manage, though, to stand my ground and finish the relationship so I could move on and continue to build my future. It is not easy when you love someone that much. It took me years to get over him.

Sadly, AK went deeper and deeper into drinking and never worked. He lost so much dignity that the village folks began to treat him like a drunk; someone who was once so respectable, coming from a very respectable family. It was really sad.

I then took up nursing in Tembisa near Johannesburg and totally lost touch with him.

We moved from Matome village to Lebowakgomo. This was a new development pioneered by the former Lebowakgomo Bantustan Prime Minister, C. N Phatudi. It was during the apartheid time when people were divided according to language.

Prime Minister Phatudi geared towards developing his region. There were many open spaces in huge fields that were just abandoned and not used. In 1979, plans were laid out to sell sites to whoever wanted some kind of urban life. The house plans and structures would be determined at a central place so the standard of the area would be kept high. If you wanted a house there, you would be directed to the housing office where you would be given various samples of house plans to choose from. That would be approved and made legal, then you could proceed to build. My sister Anna was one of the first people who jumped at the opportunity and purchased the site when they were first announced in 1984.

The area was a forest at the time. You bought that land and had to develop it before you built your house.

It started off with about three streets or so, with empty stands in between as people just bought the stands and did not return to build houses. Some of them later sold them to other buyers.

By this time, I was studying to be a nurse. The site Anna bought was cleaned, and trees, shrubs and grass removed. A fence was put up with a small gate just so it could be seen that someone had taken the place. It was left like that until 1988 when I was now a qualified nurse and earning better. Anna and I teamed up and built the house.

Today, Lebowakgomo is so vast and huge, attracting people from all walks of life, some educated, some not, from all over the country and abroad, who want to live and work in Limpopo province.

In 1980, I was now out of the Moloko's house and boarding at the same school. Matladi High as I mentioned, was one of the biggest, most popular high schools with boarding facilities catering for students from all over the country.

This was a significant year. I was in Standard 9. I got involved with a bunch of born-again Christian students. Something inside of me was ignited. I had not been led by anyone into confessing Jesus as my Saviour even though I was doing everything. I guess those students came from backgrounds where it was just not done.

We started a choir and called it the Living Sound. We had a School Christian Movement (SCM) in our school, run and operated mainly by those who were in boarding. Our schools then, throughout the whole country, were based on Christianity as most of them were built by missionaries. Matladi was not built by missionaries though, but by the community of Moletlane Village. It was just the norm in the country to have all schools teach and practise Christianity.

We had assemblies in the morning where all classes came together in front of the main building outside, we sang hymns and one of the teachers would read scripture and pray before classes started. It was so wonderful. I looked forward to this. To most students, including me at the time, this would be our only 'church' service.

I stopped attending church when I moved out of Reverend Moloko's house. I still attended when I went home to Matome during school holidays, but this would be like four or five times a year. The SCM and these daily morning assemblies helped me a lot and I can say, they sparked a hidden treasure inside of me.

Our group consisted of 8 students. Magdeline, Morgan, Precious, Tungwane, Makgatho, Solomon and myself. On and off, Matilda would join us.

We were on fire. We took ownership of the running of the SCM. In boarding, a lot of students were misbehaving as they were carried away by the freedom they had, living away from home out of the control of parents. Most of them drank alcohol, smoked weed, went to parties, indulged in sleeping around with girls, etc. It was not so in our group.

We were known to be the 'holy ones'. Often, this would be said in a kind of mockery. Some laughed at us, thinking we had lost our minds; we were not normal and were foolish. We got all kinds of remarks thrown at us but we kept on.

We had a service for all students in the boarding facilities every Sunday and it was compulsory. The school authorities left it to the students to run and operate the service. Our group that year jumped at the opportunity. Things began to happen.

Our choir sang every Sunday. One or two of us would give a testimony and we would either get one of the preachers from the community to come and give the Word, or one of us would preach.

Word went round and reached our school principal, Mr Mphahlele, a born-again Christian, a Pentecostal, and a lay Preacher assisting the Pastor in the local church in Moletlane. Mr Mphahlele was a very strict, stern man who never smiled. Every time he opened his mouth, he would frighten everyone. The teachers serving under his leadership were all afraid of him. The whole school was afraid of him. He was nicknamed 'Terror' by the students. When you saw him coming your way, you ducked and went the other way to avoid him.

For some reason, our group managed to melt his hard heart. One day, he announced from the assembly that it had come to his ears that there was a group here that sang Gospel songs. He went on to say he would like us to come and sing at the front. We went and sang. From then onwards, he would get us to come to his office first thing in the morning after assembly to sing for him before he started his job.

This would be two or three times a week.

The whole school got to know about us. Even those who were day scholars. The mockers were ashamed now. We won the heart of the principal.

Debate was one of the activities in the school. As I mentioned earlier, I was heavily involved in it, but things changed this time. My involvement was more to do with our choir singing in between the sessions. Some students would sing solo, some would do proses, whilst some would do poems.

It was so much fun. I enjoyed school. I participated in poetry and sang in the SCM choir which we started. I could do high notes then. Over the years, my voice was affected by recurrent throat infections. I grew up getting them a lot. I was the lead singer for our choir, the Living Sound. When we sang, people cried. I was the high soprano, and leading the group at the same time. Precious was soprano, Magdeline and Morgan were altos, Tungwane and Solomon were tenors and Makgatho was our base. One of our popular songs was "Ezekiel connected them" (dry bones).

Some of our SCM members, with me kneeling down.

Chapter 4. Matladi High and Early Years in My Career

This song would bring the whole house down.

We grew popular and other students began to join us, but the choir remained the same. We began to spread our wings to outside the school perimeters. We began to use our pocket money to hire minibuses on weekends, Saturdays or Sundays depending on which day we were needed.

We visited schools and held services there jointly with the SCM of those schools. We visited old peoples' homes, we visited hospitals and church services in different places.

We literally brought life and sunshine to everyone we ministered to. The sick in hospitals, the lonely, forgotten old people; dead church services came alive and students in schools began to be drawn to the things of God.

Word went round and my mom was told that I was heavily involved in this. One Sunday, we were ministering in Groothoek Hospital, going from ward to ward, and then decided to attend the church service as well. This is the church that Rev Moloko was leading. As I mentioned, most hospitals were built by missionaries and in our country, it was mostly the Dutch people. The most popular church at the time was the Dutch Reformed. There were Methodists as well, almost as many as the Dutch Reformed Church.

I was asked to sing a solo. The set-up those days in the church was that Whites would sit on one side and Blacks on the other side. Segregation was the order of the day. We were so used to it that it didn't really matter. We used separate entrances. We wouldn't shake hands.

This didn't really bother us. I guess it's because we didn't know any different. Things were like this when we were born, so to us, this was how life was.

I sang to both Whites and Blacks and all eyes were filled with tears. Everybody stood up in the end and praised God.

God is colour blind.

A friend of my mother was in that service. My mother was on duty so she couldn't attend that day. The friend ran and told my mom what happened. My mom found me and told me she heard what happened in the church. My mom was very proud.

That was the beginning of a two-year evangelistic ministry. Weekends to us meant a trip. All we did was to figure out where to go this weekend. We spent time practising and praying together. We didn't quite read the Bible as much though. That teaching was lacking those days. Reading of the Bible was left to the preacher. It's better now.

But God was faithful. That didn't stop Him from blessing us with His Holy Spirit and anointing us.

I always exhibited leadership qualities and would be placed in the position of some kind of a leader. In boarding, in my second and final year, 1982, it was the norm that those in final year with leadership qualities would be the room leaders in the hostels. I was the room leader for room 8. They loved me and respected me so much. I loved them too. They treated me like their 'mother', even though some were the same age as me. What happened was the room leader took responsibility for the wellbeing of the occupants, reported to the matron, drew up a cleaning rota, organised birthday celebrations and took responsibility for leading and co-ordinating their team on their turn to prepare Sunday lunch for all the boarders in the two hostels. We did this in turns. Usually, two rooms would team up to man a Sunday lunch preparation at least monthly.

This was the responsibility of the girls only, as boys in our culture then were not expected to be involved in the kitchen.

When it was my room's turn, I asked Magdeline, Precious and Morgan to join us. They agreed and what happened in there shocked everyone including the matron and the boarding Master. As we prepared the food in the kitchen from early morning, about 6 am, we began to sing our Gospel songs. The whole entire kitchen was filled with the presence of the Holy Spirit. Everyone joined in and it felt like a revival in there.

We sang a song based on Isaiah 40:31. "They that wait upon the Lord shall renew their strength, they shall mount up with wings, as eagles, they shall run and not be weary, they shall walk and not faint", with the chorus, "Oh teach me Lord, oh teach me Lord to pray" in between. We would sing this chorus over and over and over, till the presence was so thick that everybody began to comment. The matron came in and said that in all the years she had worked in the school she had never seen anything like this. She called the boarding master. They both just gazed at us. We carried on until all the food was cooked and ready to be served. Hours went by. We didn't realise how close to a full-blown revival we were.

We were saturated with the presence of God. At the time, I didn't even know anything about the presence of the Holy Spirit. I guess none of us had any clue about it, but God with His faithfulness granted us the very thing we were so ignorant of.

Above and below: The school's original block. For years this served as the only building for the entire school. The school was widely known for producing quality, educated people who went on to have high profiles in society. We would have assemblies every morning in front of this block, to worship and pray before lessons started.

A Journey of a Thousand Miles

Above: Matladi High School: Main Gate.

Chapter 4. Matladi High and Early Years in My Career

Members of room 8 when I was the room leader. 1981. Matladi High School hostel.

This reminded me of the time Miss Tladi was teaching about the Cross in Standard 2 and I got so affected by it. The Holy Spirit has always been around and in me.

I then moved on to Nurse training after that year. At the beginning of 1983, I applied for the course. I stated earlier that I passed with Exemption which was a university entrance qualification, but my mom couldn't afford the fees so I had to take a course that would pay me a salary whilst studying and Nursing was such a course. I loved it, though, as I am naturally a caring person.

Whilst waiting for the application, I got a job in a fish and chips shop in one of the townships in Hammanskraal, a town halfway between Pietersburg and Pretoria. Themba was a very quiet township at the time, unlike the ones in Gauteng Province.

The shop was actually a township-style restaurant selling cooked food as well as everything else, but mainly food and beverages.

As it was far from home, I had to live there. I went with two other co-students from Matladi High who were also waiting for further education, Olivia and Pauline.

The job was fast-paced, and the restaurant was very busy. School students ate there during their breaks as well as people who worked in the town centre. I was placed at the till. I loved it there but we worked very long hours, from 7 am to 11 pm with hardly a break in between. Break was when there were no customers wanting to pay at the till. It was very exhausting.

Lots of young people who worked there wouldn't stay long. I stayed. I wasn't gonna leave till I heard about my application for nursing. I made a mistake by telling the shop owners about it. I used their address for the application and I learnt later that twice, the college wrote to me, giving me dates for interview and I never got the letters. They were gotten rid of because they didn't want to lose me.

They trusted me so much that I was involved in counting the money at the end of the day after closing, sometimes with the shop owner, and sometimes by myself.

We had two tills with one of the girls manning one and me on the other one. The next day when the banks open, the shop owner would ask me to go and deposit all the money into the bank. This was a scary thing as the township always had hooligans who were out to mug and rob anyone.

One time, I asked the shop owner why he doesn't go to the bank himself and he told me it's not safe as the hooligans know him and the risk of robbery with

Chapter 4. Matladi High and Early Years in My Career

him is high. He said they don't know me so the risk is lower. It was still scary as these boys would be loitering around there, smoking weed and drinking alcohol, looking at me as I went past. Even though the money was concealed, I felt like they could see it and always feared being grabbed every time I went past them.

That was why the shop owners would not let me go.

I was one of the diligent and trusted workers.

Around July, I asked for permission to have a short leave and visited my family in Tembisa. The nurse training application had been made to Tembisa Hospital as colleges were attached to hospitals for practical purposes.

I went to inquire about my application and that's when I was told they had written to me twice and I didn't come for the interview. They told me the last date was in May. I told them I never received the letters.

They were very good and there and then told me there was another intake in November and that they would write to me but would book me in anyway.

The restaurant was co-owned by two people, one younger man and an older man. The older man was known to be in businesses. He had other shops. The younger one was a starter. Both of them would come and go during the day but the younger man stayed longer as he was not working but looking after his small son whilst his wife was a teacher. The older couple were not working but lived off their businesses. The older man was known for his womanising behaviour in the whole township. He apparently was taking advantage of all women, including married ones, and giving them money from his businesses to pay for his affairs with them.

He began to flirt with me. When I told the other girls, they said he was like that and that one girl was kicked out by his wife after he had an affair with her and she got to know. I started to avoid him. He kept coming to my till and would make remarks about how I looked, my dress, my this and that, winking at me as he spoke. Then he started to come closer when no one was there and he would deliberately brush against me, sliding his hand against my lower back. This made me very uncomfortable.

He began to spend more time in the shop than usual and would always hover around my till. His wife started to be suspicious as she knew what kind of a man he was. She began to show some distrust towards me and a little dislike.

She would make sarcastic remarks about my dress, my looks, saying nice things but in a sarcastic tone of voice, suggesting that I was making myself pretty to attract her husband.

The younger owner liked me for my work ethic and maturity. He found me very reliable and helpful. He started to speak well of me to everyone. The older owner's wife had issues of suspicion about me regarding her husband's behaviour towards me and then the younger owner was now praising me! It was like, what is it with this girl?! Is she here to attract our husbands or what?!

I got to realise that the younger owner's wife was beginning to be jealous of me and started coming to the shop and would behave in a nasty way towards me. She was jealous that her husband found me very helpful to him when she was away most of the time. It seems the two women were now discussing about me and both of them had an issue with me. The younger woman would come to the shop and pick a fight with her husband in front of us and then storm out.

She was hardly there to help him. It was discovered that she had an affair with his best friend who used to come to the shop. Things came out when both of them went on a secret holiday. The friend was also married. Someone saw them and took photos of them and gave them to the husband. It was later revealed that the husband was suspicious of the pair and kept an eye on them. When she lied to him and said she was going on holiday with friends, he then got this guy to spy on her.

Their relationship was rocky at this point and she began to just be nasty towards me, I guess, thinking that the husband would leave her for me as he kept on praising me.

I felt more and more uncomfortable.

I left the job after a few months and went to Tembisa to be nearer for the interview. I got in and began my training on 30th Nov 1983.

The younger owner was so sad when I left. He told me they'd never had anyone who worked the way I did and that they didn't think they could replace me. My heart was also sad as I knew that nothing was happening between us, nor between me and the older owner, but that I had to clear the way.

Chapter 4. Matladi High and Early Years in My Career

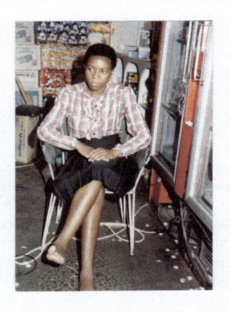

Photo taken inside the shop in Temba township Hammanskraal, when I was waiting for my nursing application call.

My first year of nursing was scary. Seeing so much blood, tubes coming out of patients' noses, legs, stomachs, some with drainage bags attached to their bodies, drips, blood being administered, intravenous and intramuscular injections, babies with all these tubes on their tiny bodies, screaming and crying; it was hard to bear.

Tembisa was one of the notoriously dangerous townships. Those days, it was more about stabbings than gunshots. On weekends, we knew we would be having more stab wound people coming into the hospital casualty department.

We had three or four periods of college then periods of practical work in the hospital to correlate theory with practice.

We saw a lot of stabbed hearts, disembowelment as well as slashed throats.

I remember when I was allocated to work in casualty one time, we had someone come with a badly stabbed heart. I remember both trained nurses and doctors running like mad, and people quickly wheeling the person to theatre for emergency surgery to stop the bleeding. The doctor had his hand clutching at the bleeding heart trying to manually stop the bleeding as they ran, with everybody shouting and running.

At another time in casualty, there was a gun-shot victim and as the casualty crew rushed to attend to him, a mob of hooligans burst in holding guns and saying "uphi yena?" meaning where is he, in Zulu. They had come to finish the guy off having followed him from the scene in the township. Now they were in casualty, running through the floor and the casualty crew quickly whisked the victim away on the stretcher, ducking and running, taking corners and fleeing with him. Meanwhile, everyone, workers, visitors and patients were screaming and shouting, fearful of the mob, running around and trying to escape.

Such were some typical weekend scenarios.

You learned quick.

One of the things I had to come to terms with was seeing someone give their last breath whilst we were trying to resuscitate.

These were severe cases like one where there was a taxi accident and I had a placement in casualty at the time. It was the peak hours of people returning from work. All 16 people in the mini bus were brought to casualty and the crew just threw everyone anywhere in there. Everybody was running around, no time to even worry about aseptic techniques at this time. Wounds would be sutured with minimal cleansing.

You looked around; someone was calling for help on the floor, in another corner someone was bleeding heavily from their head, on one stretcher someone was gasping for breath, and the crew was still bringing more in. Some were being rushed to theatre, and staff had been deployed from other wards to come and help. Everyone was shouting. You looked again back on the stretcher; the gasping person seemed to be gone now. Such were some of the typical scenarios.

Weekends in casualty were worse. Most people were drinking in the township. One night, a woman I knew who lived next door to my uncle's family in Sedibeng Section, was brought in with an axe sticking out of her head. Her partner had struck her with an axe on the head and the sharp end of it got stuck between the skull bones and he called an ambulance after freaking out. The ambulance attendants wouldn't pull it out for obvious reasons. When she arrived, the axe was still in her head, she was groaning, disoriented and smelling heavily of alcohol, so nothing could be done for her. The axe penetrated into the brain; she was taken to theatre but when they tried to pull the axe out, brain gushed out and she died.

You get tough inside.

My practical hospital was Tembisa and the college was in Kalafong Hospital in the nearby city of Pretoria, around the township of Atteridgeville.

We liked the college time. It was relaxed and we got to mix with students from other hospitals. Lebone College catered for Tembisa, Kalafong and H. F Verwoerd Hospitals. H.F Verwoerd Hospital was for the Whites and had a section for the Coloured people. Coloured in SA referred to the Mixed-Race people. This race was created mainly in the 1600s when the Dutch People invaded the country. They arrived by sea in the Cape and formed relationships with the black Xhosa women of the Eastern Cape. Even to this day, most of the Coloured people are in the Cape.

In H.F Verwoerd Hospital, white nurses worked in the white section of the hospital, which was the main part, whilst the Coloured nurses worked in the Coloured section. Training colleges for white nurses were separate from those of black nurses. The Coloured nurses were not many, just like the Coloured nation itself was in minority. They were trained in the same college as black nurses.

There were sometimes issues with them as they wouldn't feel good being mixed with us. They wished they had their own college. Most of the tutors in black colleges were black.

It was just how things were then, but thank God, it has all changed now.

In Tembisa Hospital we had a very strict Matron, a German woman called Miss Schoombee. Even the mention of the name itself would send chills through a nurse.

She never married and had no children. She relocated from Germany many years ago and lived in SA all her life. She was very domineering and ruled those under her leadership with an iron fist.

Many nurses were kicked out for very trivial things in the middle of their training and would never be given references to go and train somewhere else. Their dreams of becoming a nurse would be shattered forever. The reasons were things like gaining weight, falling pregnant or a non-life-threatening practice error.

We were weighed monthly so our weight could be monitored to detect any possible pregnancy. I used to be skinny. I remember in my second year, I gained a little bit of weight, like one and a half kg, and she called me to her office one morning. If you were summoned to her office, you knew the possibility of being kicked out was very imminent.

I nervously knocked at the door and a heard a yell, "Come in"!

I had not been told why she wanted to see me, so I was thinking of a whole lot of reasons, my mind racing trying to find out why I had to go and see her. It felt like a death sentence.

As soon as I stepped in, she said, "Why have you gained weight, huh? Why, what's going on, are you pregnant?"

When she said the word "pregnant", I felt like a stab in my tummy.

I trembled before her and muttered a weak, "No, Miss Schoombee".

Then another bawl, "Don't call me Miss Schoombee, call me Matron!"

By this time, I was shaking like a leaf. "No, Matron Schoombee, I am not pregnant".

I was tall, so the small weight gain didn't even show as it spread all over the length of my body. She was slightly surprised when I walked in as I didn't look fat at all, let alone pregnant.

Another bawl; "Watch your eating. Go and do your job."

I almost ran and nearly knocked over the chair that was at the side of the door.

Apart from that, Tembisa Hospital was known in the whole country to produce good nurses, who were well-organised and with good skills, thanks to Miss Schoombee's strictness. She used to roam the wards during the day. She wasn't the one to stay in her office. She would come in anytime, checking how procedures were done, how uniforms were, how clean the wards were, and she even checked the dining room. She would come in very early in the morning, come and have a look at the breakfast, make comments, and correct mistakes with the kitchen staff. She did that on our behalf to make sure we were being served good food, non-fattening and just big enough portions, not too big. She controlled everything.

Every doctor knew her and most of our doctors then were White. They all hated her. She knew about it and she didn't care.

If you trained in Tembisa, you could get a job quickly anywhere. Everyone knew about Miss Schoombee and they knew she was good at producing quality nurses.

She preferred her nurses tall and slim. I got in easily because of that. When you came for your first interview, she eyed you all over when you walked in. That was the first mark; how you walked, how tall you were and your weight.

The TV room had to be opened at certain times. No one was to be in there after 21:00. Boyfriends were not allowed anywhere in the hospital grounds.

We had about four women who were taking care of the nurses' home. Auntie Betty was in charge of the team. She was big and had copied Mss Schoombee's way of treating us. We feared her as well. She was a tough Zulu woman with a deep voice. She made sure there were no boyfriends anywhere in the nurses' home or hospital grounds, and that the TV room was vacated by 20:45 at the latest.

She was equally strict.

I passed well every year. The General Nursing course lasted three years.

This is where I met and made friends with Irene. We were in the same group. Our group had only 12 students. It was the smallest ever. Each year, we lost some students. By third year, only 5 of us graduated.

Irene and I had a lot in common. Irene was four years younger than me. She started school early as her mother was a teacher and I started late because of ill-health. We adored each other. We just clicked.

We loved books. We would buy secular novels. She would read hers and pass it on to me and I would do the same with mine. Then we would go and buy more and do the same. We ravaged books like Mills and Boon, Danielle Steele, James Hadley Chase, Secret Confessions, even Comics.

When we are off either half-day or full-day, we would be buried in books. Then we would take a break and chat about what we were reading.

Another thing we shared was Christianity. I have to confess that the fire I had in boarding school had gone dormant by this time. I was too focused on nursing education and it demanded all of my attention. Besides, I didn't spiritually find anyone on fire like those high school students.

Anyway, I can't blame anyone but me. No one was responsible for keeping it burning in me but myself.

Irene came from a Methodist background. Both Dutch Reformed Church and Methodist church were popular but they were a bit lukewarm, ravaged by segregation and mostly just religions, really. Nevertheless, I felt very strongly that it gave me the basis of meeting God, knowing about Him, and stirred a hunger for more. By the time I met those born-again students, I already had that in me from the Dutch Reformed Church. Don't undermine what you get from these rather lukewarm beginnings. There is always a remnant of God in there. He will always show up whenever He is allowed.

The third thing we shared was the love of music. We loved Gospel and Country music. There was a programme on TV3 which, at the time, was catering for the white community. It would run every Sunday around 23:00 and finished at midnight. It was run by a guy called Clive. He was so good at it. When we were in college at Kalafong Hospital, away from Auntie Betty and Matron Schoombee, we would get to watch this. There was freedom in Kalafong, unlike in Tembisa where we were ruled with an iron fist.

Everyone would leave the TV room and go to bed, but Irene and I would lie on those chairs and wait for our Clive. When he came on, he would be heard saying, "Siiiiiiinnnnngggg Country"! We would quickly sit up and watch as we sang along. We looked forward to Sunday nights when we were in Kalafong.

The Gospel music we both loved were songs by Jimmy Swaggart. Jimmy Swaggart had been very popular in SA and his songs were widely sung, especially in black born-again Christian churches.

We used to buy his cassettes and would play them over and over. Everyone around us got to know this and they began to like the songs too. One of the songs we played a lot was Sometimes Alleluia".

As Irene and I were from far away, we used to visit our relatives when we had long weekends off. I would visit my uncle's family in Tembisa and Irene used to visit her aunt who worked as a housekeeper for a white family in Lyndhurst, a suburb in Johannesburg.

The problem was, the "matchbox" township houses were very tiny; only two bedrooms with a tiny sitting room and a kitchen. No bathroom facilities. Toilets were outside. They raised their children in those houses and there was no means of getting a house of their own unless they were earning enough to get a mortgage. So, moving out was not happening. Families piled up in those small houses, children, grandchildren and sometimes even great-grandchildren. People would be sleeping under tables and chairs at night in living rooms and kitchens.

As a result, regular visiting was not possible as one additional person added to the problem.

I also befriended Alina, who was also in our group.

Then Alina would sometimes invite me to come with her to the Vaal Triangle, township of Sebokeng whenever we were both on a weekend off.

From left to right: myself, Irene and Alina, Lebone College, Kalafong Hospital. 1986.

Chapter 4. Matladi High and Early Years in My Career

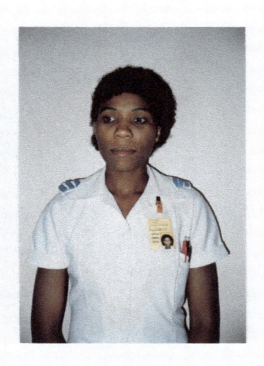

Here, I was in third year, my last year of study. 1986.

Me as a first-year student: Lebone Nursing College, Kalafong Hospital, Pretoria. 1984.

This is where I met my deceased husband Khuli. Alina and Khuli's mothers were sisters. Khuli was third-born too, like me. He saw me one day when Alina and I were attending a family event in the Free State. He took one look at me and knew that I was the one. He had been late in settling for marriage. He was five years older than me. His two younger brothers were already married and had families of their own. Everyone was beginning to wonder if there was something wrong with him.

Khuli was very responsible, almost overly so. Like me, he came from a poor family. His parents lived in farms and his father was an alcoholic and suffered from ill-health. He couldn't work any longer. The mother never worked. Khuli was the one who provided for all of them, younger siblings, two sisters, a brother and parents. He was so kind to everyone; so much so that he was often taken advantage of and would be providing for extended families as well.

At the time, he could manage to do so as he was single and he was good with finances; he had money and he knew how to save.

We met in 1984. He was doing cross-country truck driving work at the time, so he travelled a lot. The distance and his constant absence didn't help the relationship. We split by 1985 without saying anything to each other. He was away too long and I was busy with my studies.

There was a team of born-again Christians which used to come to the nurses' home occasionally and hold a service.

I used to attend those services. This is where I saw, for the first time, an altar call for salvation made. I was one of those who raised their hand and prayer was made; I can't remember if we were led by repeating after the Pastor or it was said over us and on our behalf. My friend Irene did too. The problem was that that was it. Nothing would happen after this. No invitation to their church in the community or mention of baptism, Bible study or anything. We all just continued life as usual. Then the group would come again after a few months, do the same thing and leave again.

I believe if they took a further step of inviting us to church, taught and offered water baptism or any help at all, we would have continued with them.

Tembisa township was situated in the East Rand and near Alexandra township, another notoriously high-crime area. Townships had Shebeens, houses that ran businesses selling alcohol, an equivalent of what would be called pubs in the UK. Most of these places were run by women, very strong-willed, domineering women who could grab a man by the neck and throw them out of the door if they misbehaved. They were known by their customers. Most often, these women were married to weak men who drank themselves to death. They were just as good as not being there at all. Most of the Shebeen Queens, as they were known, were the same. They controlled and bullied their husbands.

It makes you think that weak men tend to marry strong women as if to compensate for their weakness, but it works out to their detriment as these women end up treating them like children.

It's the same as younger men who marry older women as if looking for a mother and that wife ends up mothering them.

Shebeen Queens knew how to handle hooligans. No one would go near them. They fought with their bare hands. They punched like men in a boxing ring.

I finished my nurse training at the beginning of 1987 and stayed on in Tembisa Hospital for a few months whilst waiting for my Midwifery course in another hospital. Tembisa Hospital didn't have the course. I didn't really need or want the course, but in those days, it was kind of like the norm to finish your three years of General Nursing and take Midwifery as a follow-up. I was accepted for this in Far North, Elim Hospital. They needed a reference from my current hospital Matron, who was Miss Schoombee, a German spinster who just acted like the Shebeen Queens. She went mad. She called me to her office and gave it to me, told me that I was secretly trying to leave and that if that was the case, she wanted me to leave at the end of the next month.

That was it. I was kicked out for having applied to further my studies. I thought she would then send my reference, but she never did. I left with no job, no course to go to, no reference and had to start all over again.

This type of treatment happened to a lot of students under Miss Schoombee.

One final year student left only a month before sitting her exams. She was kicked out and had her entire career shattered for being pregnant before exam time.

She was never given a reference to go somewhere to complete the course. She ended up starting all over again but went to do teaching instead.

One trained qualified nurse was sacked for having three children out of wedlock.

Back to the township shebeen life. The Police Force was manned by a majority of whites. They used to target these shebeens and kept raiding them, mainly checking operation licences and sometimes just to give them grief. The Brixton Murder and Robbery Police Squad was notoriously famous for this in the East Rand. The Squad was known for its viciousness. They patrolled townships and controlled the streets trying to deal with gangs and Tsotsis. Tsotsi is a township name for a member of a gang or just a thug, a law-breaker.

They mostly targeted gangsters and rioters. They were known amongst the township residents. If they were seen coming, everyone would dive for cover. They drove police vans that were different from the usual ones. They tended to use small fast cars in place of vans. If they caught a thug or even someone they suspected, they would beat the person to near-death, leaving them crippled or paralysed, and in those days, they would easily get away with it.

They were like animals. If you landed in their hands, you were dead meat. They were known for their brutality and mercilessness.

They terrorised shebeens looking for unlawful weapons and drugs among the customers.

Photo below: Fellow nursing students in 1986 during a fundraising event. We were mimicking the Lady Smith Black Mambazo. From left to right: Irene, Connie, Lombuso, Angie and I. So much fun!!

A Journey of a Thousand Miles

Chapter 4. Matladi High and Early Years in My Career

During fundraising events at our college. 1986, Kalafong Hospital.

A Journey of a Thousand Miles

Tembisa Hospital and a part of Tembisa Township

Chapter 4. Matladi High and Early Years in My Career

Graduation Day in RAU University, Johannesburg. Graduating in Community Nursing.

Chapter 5.
Marriage

After leaving Tembisa Hospital around Easter of 1988, I returned home to Matome village. My mom still worked in Groothoek Hospital. I tried again to apply for the Midwifery course, but in that part of the country, most hospitals had a combined course in General Nursing and Midwifery. They had done away with the one-year separate course. By August of that year, I decided to just look for a job. I struggled to get one as I still required a reference from Miss Schoombee and she wouldn't issue one.

I asked my mom to speak to the then Matron of Groothoek Hospital and ask if she would employ me. She kindly did and from October of the same year, I worked as a General nurse until June 1989.

I had applied for the course I was still pursuing, the Midwifery course in Baragwanath Hospital, Soweto, and I was successful. I started in July 1989.

When I was in Groothoek Hospital in early 1989, I received a letter from Khuli just reconnecting with me and asking me to reconsider getting back together again. He said that he really missed me, that he wasn't playing and meant business with this relationship and that he had never felt like this with anyone.

I wrote back to say we would see how it worked as I was now back in my area far away. He never gave up. He kept writing and urging me to get back. That time, we still had no cell phones in the whole country. Communication was limited to landlines and letters.

When I was working in Groothoek Hospital, I met Bartina, who was also a nurse there. Bartina lived in Lebowakgomo and had rented a room in one of the houses there. This was at the time when our site in Lebowakgomo wasn't developed yet. So, I had to rent a room as well. I happened to be staying in the same house as Bartina. There were quite a few of us; some were teachers and some worked in the new shopping centre.

Bartina took a liking to me. She was born-again. Born-again people just got drawn to me somehow. We began to spend time together in the evenings after work. She used to share the Gospel with me. I didn't tell her I had accepted Jesus in Tembisa with the team that used to come to the nurses' home. I hadn't practised and didn't know a thing about being born-again. So, she regarded me as not saved and really persevered with me.

Bartina had a small box of strips of paper with scriptures on them. She had bought these from a Christian bookshop in town.

She would get me to pick one and then talked about it and explained what the scripture entailed and its application in my life.

A few months after I started work, I began to have sleep disturbances. It happened that when I fell asleep, I would feel something shaking me, or feel a heavy oppressive force come upon me. It would feel heavy, frightening and always suffocating me. This episode would be accompanied by nightmares, terrible nightmares and it felt like something was in the room about to suffocate me. There would be some evil presence and I would struggle to wake up. I wouldn't be totally asleep but wouldn't be able to open my eyes or move. I think they call it sleep paralysis. Then this would be followed by groaning sounds, like someone wanting to say something but the mouth couldn't open to say the word. In my mind, I wanted to shout 'help', but my mouth wouldn't open. This could happen several times a night, depriving me of sleep so much that I started to yawn continuously and feel exhausted during the day.

It had been happening now for some months, especially since I began the job. I told Bartina and asked her to pray for me. She told me it was evil spirits. At the time, I didn't even understand what she was talking about. She just said evil spirits were part of witchcraft and that prayer could expel them. She said mostly this happens when witches are on your case.

She didn't know much herself. One day, she asked me to pick a scripture again and I picked 2 Cor 12:9 "And He said unto me, My Grace is sufficient for you." That was all that was written on that small piece of paper.

Bartina tried to explain what it meant, especially in relation to the attacks I was now experiencing.

She would pray and really tried to help, but it got worse and worse, to a point where I resorted to taking naps during the day in my breaks to catch up. I began to dread the night.

It was when I got accepted onto the Midwifery course around 1989 that I informed Khuli I would be back in the area soon. We then got back together and the relationship got stronger.

We eventually arranged for him to meet my family. I had met his already. He drove for 4 hours to Matome from Vereeniging.

Then talks and meetings began to be held, as per traditional rules, between our families. We have what is called 'lobola'; this is a Zulu term for bride's price or cost. In Sepedi, it is called magadi. The bride's family determines the price to charge for their daughter. The groom's family have no say but are expected to pay as requested, otherwise, no bride will be going to them, period.

Things got settled and we mid-1989, we were married in the traditional way.

It was just around the time I started the course. I fell pregnant with our daughter Dineo soon afterwards.

Khuli and I had only been intimate once at this time. The thought of pregnancy was far from me; besides, I was on a course and wanted to finish.

I used to have episodes of absence of menstruation. My hormonal balance was fluctuating, perhaps due to on-and-off use of contraceptives.

When I didn't get my periods for two months, it didn't bother me much. It was when I started to have some symptoms of early pregnancy which, at the time, I didn't associate with pregnancy. I just thought I must be ill and needed to be checked by a doctor.

The oppression and attacks were getting severe. One of the traditional healers my sister took me to, wanted to give me an enema. It was known that the traditional remedies were often very strong and harmful to the body, especially the internal organs.

Most people used to suffer from internal bleeding from enemas given by traditional healers.

I was a nurse and had seen some of these patients in hospital. I told the woman I would return but I didn't. I was literally in my third month of pregnancy and didn't know it. An enema would have been fatal, not only to the baby, but also myself.

At the end of three consecutive months, I decided to consult with a doctor. I was very slim and tall; I looked nothing like a pregnant woman.

The first thing he did was a pregnancy test. I wondered, 'why would he think I am pregnant? I am prone to amenorrhoea, and my periods always return.' I told him this, so why wouldn't he test for hormonal imbalances instead? I had only been with my husband once, so what is this doctor thinking?

The test came back positive, and not only positive but just over 12 weeks gestation.

The thought that I was meant to have an enema with the traditional healer, and that would have killed me and my baby, or at least caused miscarriage, was too much to bear. I thanked God, the one I didn't even know much about it at the time. I knew He saved me. He made me doubt and caused me to delay and go to the doctor first. I knew it was Him.

I was allowed to complete 6 months of the course and would then return after a year to do the last 6 months and sit the exam. I was so lucky to have had it this way. My pregnancy timing was favourable with the 6 months' rule, otherwise, I would have had to leave and come back to restart again.

The pregnancy brought back the sleepless issue and nightmares I experienced whilst living with my friend Bartina. It was very difficult as I was a student midwife, had to study, do my practical hours in the work setting, and this being my first pregnancy, I was so exhausted, lost so much weight and was just generally unwell.

Khuli was working away from home. He would only come home once or twice a month at the time. Even if he was around, he wouldn't have been able to do much as I was bound to stay in the nurses' home for the duration of the course.

My 6-month period was completed at the end of December 1989 and I was granted one year's maternity leave.

The attacks never ceased; instead, they increased.

My nightmares were filled with things like these:

- Falling from a high cliff or mountains, tumbling down and splashing into deep waters to be grabbed by some creature within the waters, dragging me deeper. I would try to kick, try to beat the thing with my bare hands or fight to wake up to no avail and I would suddenly scream and get up terrified and drenched in sweat, heart pounding and paralysed with fear.

- Sometimes it would be like swimming in shallow waters which suddenly rose to above my neck, threatening to drown me.

- Being chased by a grotesque creature or figures threatening to kill me.

- Being attacked by terrifying beings and people would just look away and become oblivious to what was happening, even when I tried to get them to come and help. I would try to scream and no voice would come out.

- Seeing silhouettes in the doorway.

- A horrible creature would open the door and come towards me, then I would wake up screaming and sweating.

- Being choked, feeling the hand of a person on my mouth and nose and suffocating, unable to breathe, then waking up with a gasp.

- Being bitten by snakes and many more.

They all felt so real, so vivid, it was hard to even believe it was just a bad dream. They would come one after another throughout the night, as long as I was asleep. They began to come even when I slept during the day. As long as I was asleep, whether day or night, they would come. I dreaded sleeping. I began to try and not fall asleep and was extremely exhausted.

It would be difficult to stay asleep, terrified that another nightmare would come.

I went to stay with my sister Anna in Pretoria, where she was working in the Military base. She had rented a room in Voortrekkerhoogte, in one of the Army official's houses.

I lived with her for a few months and then Khuli arranged for me to go and stay with his first cousin in Sebokeng Township to be nearer him. He started to come every weekend, having arranged it with his company.

Anna suggested that I seek help with traditional healers as what was happening to me was believed to be as a result of being under witchcraft attack. Things like these would be associated with witchcraft among the black communities.

I had nothing to lose at this time. I was suffering and, if anything would help, that was it. I was not much of a believer at this point, having not attended church since I started nursing. The little I had was lost.

I accepted the suggestion from my sister and she had been making inquiries around and had been given a few names of the ones regarded as powerful. She took me to the first one. We had to travel miles and miles in the Northern part of the Transvaal to a village where this person lived. He was known around there as being able to show you who was behind the attacks rather than deliverance and healing.

We spent about two days there. The procedure was that you were to ingest some mixtures and then you were taken to a darkened room and watched what was like a film. This would be people or the person that was troubling you. You watched intently and you were supposed to see and recognise faces and then you would know who was doing these evil things to you. Once you saw them, it was believed, they would know and would become disempowered and never trouble you again.

There were plenty of people there who had come to be helped to see who was bewitching them. We would queue up and get to the darkened room to watch in turns.

Chapter 5. Marriage

Anna and I got to our turn and we sat there with our eyes glued to the 'screen', filled with hope that today, Satan would be exposed and disarmed. We saw silhouettes, dark figures moving back and forth but we couldn't see any face or clearly make out whether the figure was male or female, young or old.

After a while, he got us out and asked us whether we had seen what was there and if we recognised anybody. I had to be honest; I told him I couldn't see any face, that it was just dark figures and silhouettes.

He then stated that it was because we had little faith in his work, that's why we couldn't see clearly. I felt nostalgic. I told Anna, "Let's get out of here".

We paid him and left.

The attacks continued.

Anna was more sympathetic towards me as she could see how this was affecting me.

She did everything she could to find me help but, as she was not a Christian, the only help she knew was what the average person believed in.

I was taken to about 5 traditional healers and none of them could relieve me of these attacks. They all worked differently and interpreted the cause of these attacks differently. The only thing they said in common was that I was being bewitched; that some people were jealous of me as I made it into nursing and now I was getting married, I was pregnant, and that all these were triggering jealousy and people were using witchcraft to try and kill me.

The last one was a Zionist Priest. In SA, there is a popular denomination within the black communities called the Apostolic Zionist Church. They wear long colourful robes, scarves and headgear decorated with crosses. They have many divisions and they identify themselves by different colours. Everything else is the same. This was a cult that came out of John G Lake's Apostolic Faith Mission when he went to SA. Over a long time, long after Lake died and the movement had undergone several changes over the years, some black leaders pulled out to form their own denomination. The reason behind this was that they were not happy with Whites being the only ones in high positions and also reasoned that Whites were using their own culture and tradition to worship and run the denomination, and not really following the Bible. The other reason was, as I mentioned in the previous chapter, that during the apartheid period, segregation ruled and reigned even inside churches.

Black leaders were always subordinate and never got to be senior leaders. Also, some blacks felt like they were not free to worship wholeheartedly as they are using foreign ways of worship. They decided they need to pull out so they could employ their own ways and methods of worship. The cult was now formed.

The true Apostolic Faith Mission, birthed by John G Lake, remained. Some black leaders and congregations remained in it. I was later to be truly converted in one of them and was baptised properly.

With the cultivation version that split out from it, there was very little knowledge of the Word and there occurred a mixture of Biblical truths and traditional beliefs. They honoured their ancestors and believed that they were the ones to mediate between them and God.

With them, the Bible is not read much, even during the services. The songs they sing don't really have authentic Biblical messages. There may be a mention of God or Jesus in the songs, but the rest of the lyrics are not really saying much.

Anna had been a member of one of these churches before, for a while. She was not with them any longer. At this point, she was not a practising member of any church. When none of the traditional healers we consulted weren't able to help, she suggested we try her former Zionist Priest.

I agreed. He 'prophesied' to me and told me that I had been given healing anointing by my ancestors and that they wanted me to utilise it. He said I came from a lineage of healers and that I had the gift.

He said the reason I was suffering was because I had not obeyed them.

He said there were witches wanting to harm me. He actually said their aim was to kill me but that they were unable to access me as my ancestors were protecting me.

He said the reason I got woken up every time I fell asleep as if someone was shaking me, and the sensing of an evil presence in the room, was because the witches were actually getting inside the room, but as soon as they tried to come to where I was lying in bed to do whatever they want to do, they were blocked by my ancestors and that's when I got a feeling of being shaken and then waking up. He said this would go on for as many times as the witches would try to access me at night, hence I got woken up so many times. He said the witches wouldn't touch me when I was awake. He said that the waking up was actually saving me and that my ancestors were behind the protection.

His advice was to do with what he said my ancestors were wanting me to do.

The Priest never once referred to God, Jesus, the Holy Spirit or read the Bible, let alone prayed.

One of the traditional healers had said the same thing about my ancestors.

Anna suggested I do what I had been told to do to be rid of these attacks. I refused. Something inside of me asked, why wouldn't he mention God, or read the Bible or pray for me? He is a Priest; surely, he should know God? Something is not right. I couldn't pinpoint what was wrong but I just felt uneasy with the whole thing.

I discussed this with my mom one day, and she told me, "Don't listen to these people; they are liars and they will lead you astray. You are not going to be involved with these evil things; God will see you through this," she said.

One thing with my mother, even though her own parents were traditional healers, she was the only one who was opposed to this. She always believed in God. Even when we lived in remote farms where there were no churches, twice she travelled far with me to attend church.

When she now joined the Dutch Reformed Church, which in itself didn't have the power and was very lukewarm, her faith in God was revived a little and her opposition to ancestral worship grew stronger. She told me to have nothing to do with traditional healers or Zionist Priests. She was not happy with Anna, that she took me to them to seek help.

That was the end of it. I still experienced the attacks.

My pregnancy term came to an end and on Good Friday night, I gave birth to my daughter Dineo. That was in Groothoek Hospital maternity unit. It was a difficult birth and I had some complications. There was a shortage of midwives that night and student midwives were conducting birth deliveries unsupervised. Most of the women who gave birth that night returned to hospital with sepsis through badly managed episiotomies.

We were all in one ward with the same problem. I had to be in hospital for a week, having intravenous antibiotics to clear the sepsis and then had to have secondary suturing. It was traumatic for all of us, but more so to the first-time mothers like me.

The good thing was that all our babies were well.

Traditionally, the first baby must be born at the bride's home. It is believed that as it is the first baby, no one knows as to whether the woman will have difficult deliveries or not. The only people to be with her are her own parents. Subsequent babies are delivered anywhere.

I returned to Matome in February 1990, just after Mandela came out of prison.

It was a time of outspread joy in all parts of the country.

Khuli had bought a small 2-bedroomed house for us in Evaton, a part of Sebokeng Township.

I moved to Evaton in June 1990.

Khuli was a very down-to-earth, caring and loving husband. He was just too good to be true. He never raised his voice, never complained about anything. He was so liked and loved by everybody. His calm, loving, caring nature opened him to abuse of his generosity.

I would be the one often spotting and objecting to some of these incidents of abuse when they occurred. His relatives would take advantage of his good heart and ask him for financial aid all the time. I started to object. He meant well. He wouldn't decline to help anybody.

Khuli married late. His two younger brothers were long-married with children.

His folks were wondering as to whether all is well with him. They had begun to doubt his manhood. I was informed by his cousin that he was never seen with a girl or a woman, he had no child and as far as they were concerned, he was not in a relationship. He said, everyone had given up on him and never thought he could marry, let alone have children.

It was such a big thing when he announced to everyone that he had found someone he loved and wanted to marry. Then, in a year or so, a baby was on the way. To everyone, this was a miracle. His uncle, who was the one who travelled the distance to my home for initial talks with my family about marriage, whilst on the way to my home, apparently kept asking, "When are we getting there? How far is this place, nephew? Why did you have to take us this far? Were there no girls in our region? What is it with this girl who managed to capture you like this? No girl has ever managed to get near you ever." He meant well but was genuinely surprised by all this.

I was informed by my sister-in-law that the uncle would say, "There must be something about her; tell us, what is it she has that others don't have? So many girls have tried to throw themselves at you and you always made it clear that you were not available. Why her, tell us, why her"?

He said that to tease him, but he was serious about it as everyone had given up on him. He was 35, and according to the cultural expectations, he was a little past the age of marriage for a man.

He did confess to me one time and told me he really seriously fell deeply in love with me and that this had never happened with any of the prospective girls he met before.

He was just so kind, he made me feel bad sometimes. He just had a way with me. His love, authenticity, peaceful and calm nature somehow compensated for some of my shortcomings.

Chapter 5. Marriage

Above: Pastor Sibiya of the Apostolic Faith Mission church in Sebokeng Zone 3, married us in the Apostolic Faith Mission church in Lebowakgomo, Zone F.

A Journey of a Thousand Miles

Chapter 5. Marriage

Vaal Triangle townships were calmer and more peaceful compared to the ones in the East Rand and Soweto.

Evaton and Sebokeng were very close to Sharpeville, where people were massacred in 1960 when they protested against the then Pass laws. It was a very small, quiet township just outside the town of Vereeniging.

Then, in November 1990, my mother informed me that there was a man who went around holding tent meetings and he was being spoken highly of, having helped people who were being attacked in similar ways as I was. She went on to say that she had been informed that this man healed the sick, prayed for witches and they brought their paraphernalia into every meeting, giving up on their practices and becoming believers, that he delivered those oppressed by the devil in many ways. The man was in a village near Lebowakgomo. This time, we had moved to Lebowakgomo. He was a tent evangelist.

My mother asked me to ask Khuli for permission to come and have this man pray for me. I told him and Khuli would never say no to anything I asked.

Our baby was about 6 months old now. My husband drove us there but had to get back as he was working.

I stayed with my mother, my niece Florah, and my brothers, Simon and Joseph.

My mother had been in touch with people who had been attending those tent meetings. They informed her that the man had now moved on to another location and that one man who was working with him when he was here could tell us where he was now.

The man was Mr Sako, a teacher in Lebowakgomo High School. He was Acting Principal at the time. We went to his house and he explained to us that the man was a healing evangelist who went around with his team on 2-3 week-long tent crusades. By this time, I had a slight understanding of Christian things. My SCM and Dutch Reformed Church involvements were not in vain, even if they were not that deep.

God had His hold on me and was never letting go.

Mr Sako said the Evangelist was now in the Far North, near Tzaneen. His name was Evangelist Machimane of the 'Come to Jesus' ministry. He was a travelling tent Evangelist, who had powerful anointing in healing and deliverance. I knew no one in Tzaneen. Besides, I had a small baby, I was now very frail and weak. Mr Sako was full of faith and said, "You don't need to be following the Evangelist everywhere and travelling that far; we can pray for

Chapter 5. Marriage

you," he said. "I was on his team when he was here; I prayed for people and I know what to do in your case."

My mother said there was nothing to lose; whatever he said, we would do.

Mr Sako wanted me to come and stay in the house and explained that deliverance often takes more than one prayer and because I was not really saved, I needed to live there where I would be in an atmosphere of God's presence all the time as the ministry was carried out. He said they would be fasting for three days, no food, no water, and we would be having a time of prayer every evening as he was working during the day.

He stated that I would be given relevant healing and deliverance scriptures and be taught how to pray.

I agreed. We returned home to pack then come back for ministry.

I stayed for two weeks with them. I was breastfeeding my daughter at the time and Mr Sako was not playing games with the devil. He instructed everyone to fast for the first three days, with no food and no water, including me.

I had never even heard of fasting. I followed everything he said. He gave me a Bible, as I had left mine at home. He showed me which verses to read, memorise and use them in my prayer against the attacks, especially when they came. He taught me how to command the devil to leave whenever I felt the oppression, or had a nightmare, or disturbed sleep. It worked; it really worked.

After three days of full fast, I was crawling. I looked like someone with anorexia. Miraculously, during that time, my baby never ran short of breast milk. I was not drinking, not even water for three days and three nights and yet my breasts produced milk. I couldn't have cheated as there were two young ladies in the house; the younger sister of Mr Sako's wife, who was looking after their toddler as his wife had gone to her parents to have their second child, and this young woman's friend. I spent the day with them. They were part of Mr Sako's ministry team. He had formed a worship team. He had a friend who was a policeman who was a singer and was a born-again Christian too. They were just such a perfect team. Mr Sako played the keyboard. He was a beginner but was learning fast.

Mr Sako was a lay preacher and he assisted the Pastor in the Apostolic Faith Mission church in Lebowakgomo.

During my stay with them, we attended church on Sunday and he got me to testify in front of the congregation.

On Saturdays, we went on an outreach in the nearby village of Mamaolo in the Mphahlele region. We would just find a tree and unpack our stuff; he would begin to play his keyboard, the girls would start to sing and he would preach a fiery evangelistic message, then the villagers who gathered round to listen would get saved and confess Jesus as their Saviour. It was so wonderful to be with them.

We would go to other believer's houses and hold prayer meetings and services.

I remember, one Friday night, he took us to an all-night prayer meeting in another one of the Mphahlele region villages called Tooseng. A woman from Zimbabwe was visiting and he wanted me to attend that meeting as the woman would be leading it. The woman was a prayer warrior. I had never heard anyone pray like that. All night. I mean, she brought the house down. The whole place shook when she prayed.

Mr Sako was on fire for God. He walked with those who were hungry and on fire for more of God. Evangelist Machimane left a legacy; fire of God was all over the villages. Those who chose to catch it, like Mr Sako, they got it.

God had gotten hold of me, never to let go.

Both girls were singers, and Mr Sako played the keyboard.

The first thing Mr Sako did was to get me to believe afresh in God and confess Jesus as my Saviour.

Every evening, after they came back from work, we had a service and prayer and then they would minister to me in prayer. Mine was not an instant deliverance but very gradual, with distinct evidence. Each night whilst I was there became better than the last one. The attacks and oppressions became less intense and fewer.

I now knew what to say, so was able to pray for myself at night in my room as I couldn't keep on waking people up in the middle of the night to come and pray for me. Mr Sako made sure he empowered me so I could pray. He taught me to cast the thing away, confront the devil and tell him to leave my room, read those verses out loud and worship God. This was something I had never heard of. It was powerful.

I grew stronger. By the end of week two, I was happier, more alive, knew a little of the Bible and more importantly, I could pray for myself. Mr Sako wanted me equipped so that when I returned home and the devil tried to attack me again, which he would try to do of course as he never gives up, I would be in a position to pray for myself, know what to say, which verses to read and increase my faith and confidence in God.

Chapter 5. Marriage

I was on my way to wholeness and healing. It was the beginning, but a great deal had been done; a Great Wall had been broken. I had been empowered. You see, the devil targets people who don't know how to fight for themselves.

My mother visited twice a week during the time I was there. In the last week, she commented on how well I looked.

My friend Bartina visited me once too. Mr Sako was not happy for me to be friends with her. After she left, he asked me to stay away from her so I could concentrate on God and maintain my healing. He stated that she was a weak believer and that she was living in sin. He didn't elaborate and I didn't ask questions.

I liked Bartina. As far as I was concerned, she had been there for me in the beginning when these attacks started. She didn't judge me, but tried to help me. She prayed for me, weak prayers maybe, but she prayed. She was there when none of the so-called strong and holy were anywhere to be found. God used her to give me scriptures at a time when I wasn't reading the Bible at all.

Every time she was with me, she was not talking about boyfriends, but God. She would take out her little box with strips of paper with verses on them and ask me to pick one, then she would explain to me what my verse meant. She also would pick hers and explain what she felt they meant. We talked about God all the time.

Maybe other Christians knew things about her as Mr Sako suggested, but whether those things were true or not, as far as I was concerned, I knew her; she was a good person and loved God and cared about me.

Sometimes, Christians can be very judgemental and harsh with one another. I know Mr Sako had begun good work in me and really helped me and wanted me to continue safely in the walk with God without getting distracted, but I felt this was a bit of an unfair thing to say about Bartina. I never saw her doing anything wrong, talking about other people or anything like that.

It was very common among born-again Christians then to always look out to find fault with one another, point fingers, hurl accusations at each other and so on. They never evangelised; all they did was attack each other. A lot of people left churches because of this. Even some preachers were being really unkind and used to shame people, especially young girls, or those among the youth who fell pregnant outside of wedlock. They would suspend them for a period, announcing publicly in front of everyone that they had sinned and therefore wouldn't be allowed to fellowship for a given amount of time, as per their church policy.

During this time of public announcement, the girl would be requested to come and stand in front and face the congregation as the preacher announced it.

This horrible practice drove a lot of girls out of the church and some resorted to abortions.

It's really amazing sometimes how people forget that the same Jesus who covered their sin and loved them enough to die for them, would like the sin of everyone else covered, love them and restore them back to Faith and right standing, not kill them or drive them out of the church.

As a result of these evil practices, the churches were empty, and only the holier than thous, who were so good at finding fault and spying on others, were left. No one wanted to be part of them. People would come but wouldn't stay.

So sad. Holding those He trusted to account, God would ask, "What have you done with my people? Where are they? I gave them to you and you drove them away."

Then, Sako advised me to continue reading the Bible, and not only the verses he gave me. He gave me a whole list of verses to read. He urged me to attend church, become a member of a church and fast for one day in every week.

I returned to Evaton, Sebokeng, fitter, mentally, physically and spiritually. We were now approaching the end of the year and I was to go back to Baragwanath Hospital to complete my Midwifery course from January the next year.

Chapter 5. Marriage

The new building of the hospital in Baragwanath.

A Journey of a Thousand Miles

The old version of the hospital. This is when I was still working there.

Chapter 6.
New adventures in Christ

I had a friend, Winnie, who was a nurse and lived in Sebokeng. She trained at the same time as me but was not accepted in Tembisa as she was overweight, and Miss Schoombee wouldn't take anyone big.

Winnie was a saint. She was born-again and very faithful.

We clicked from the day we met. Winnie was the key person who made me settle in Sebokeng as I lived far from my in-laws, and my husband's relatives who were nearby were not close to me.

I informed her about my healing and deliverance. She knew about my attacks. I told her that I was much better. I'd been equipped and could now pray for myself and that I had been taught to read the Bible daily. She was thrilled. I went on to say that I had been told to find a church.

She took me to an Apostolic Faith Mission church in Sebokeng, zone 3, which was nearer where I lived in Evaton. She introduced me to a home group in my area and I joined them. I started attending services.

I was baptised a year later. I grew more and more gradually. The attacks were slowly vanishing. They became very occasional now.

The Moloi family were into the Zionist church. I mentioned earlier that they mix traditional things with Christianity.

My father-in-law remained a Dutch Reformed Church member. He refused to convert to the Zionist denomination. All of my husband's aunts from his mom's side and his uncle and cousins, nephews and nieces were involved in it.

When I got married, they held a small traditional ceremony whereby they said, in their Southern Sotho culture, they were presenting a new member of the family to their fore fathers for the purpose of uniting the newlyweds to seal their marriage and get the bride accepted by them to have their blessings and favour.

The Zionists use colourful strings of wool as per each division and would bless them and tie them on their wrists as bracelets and on their necks as necklaces and around their waist, and even around their ankles.

After the welcome ceremony, they suggested I place them on me and my daughter and that I needed to attend their special service where another ceremony would be held to complete the welcome. I was not happy to do this but they put them on my baby nevertheless.

My sister-in-law, the wife of my husband's younger brother came to visit one weekend and I asked her what this ceremony entailed as they wouldn't tell me when I asked and said that everyone discovers it for themselves when they attend.

She told me that she attended it and that it's the policy in this family for daughter's -in-law, to do that to be fully regarded as part of them.

As far as I knew, this was not a Moloi family thing, but was from my husband's mom and her side of the family. The Moloi's were Dutch Reformed Church people. The Father stopped practising a long time ago when he became an alcoholic and left the running of the family to his wife and her family.

I felt uneasy about this whole thing. I asked her to tell me what happens in there as she had attended it, but she refused and said it's never passed on to anyone and insisted that each person find out for themselves. I grew more and more curious and uneasy.

I kept pestering her about it and she agreed to give me some clues.

She said, there are two points to go past before you enter if you are new. The first one, you meet someone who will give you a password and instruct you to say this word at the door when you are asked, otherwise you won't be allowed in without it. She said it's just a word. Then you proceed to the door where there is a doorkeeper who will ask for the word. You say the right word, you go in and then become a member. She said it's a separate type of church to the normal Zionist church but most people who are Zionists are part of that too.

She said it is called ' The Secret Church'. I'd heard of this church in passing before and I didn't think it is right to expose myself and our baby to something like that.

I just knew that I was not going there.

I told my husband, "I am not attending that ceremony; I am sorry, I am a Christian. I can't just do it."

He was not happy as he knew his mom and her family would kick up a fuss about it, but he loved me enough to say, "If you are not happy to do it, that's fine."

He was not invited to it. He just couldn't be bothered by all this.

When they welcomed us the first time, they put those strands of coloured wool on my daughter's waist and wrists. I refused to have them on me. They told me my daughter was their child, and they have full rights to have her wear them.

When I was with Mr Sako, he spotted the strands of wool on my daughter's wrists and said, "Before we begin anything, we've got to remove these things." He knew they were from The Zionist cult and were demonic.

I agreed. We removed them all.

When I returned to Evaton, I found my mother-in-law and her people not very happy with me.

From then onwards, the relationship between them and us was a bit strained. Things became better years later. I chose to forgive them and took the initiative to rebuild a strong relationship with my mother-in-law and her remaining children. We are friends now.

My father-in-law, Mr Moloi, was very kind to me. He loved my husband very much as he provided for them all the time. He stuck with me too. When the others distanced themselves from us, he would come and visit and see how we were doing, see his grandchildren, call them by his own terms of endearment and just loved us.

He was very lovely. I liked him.

In January 1991, I returned to complete my course. I managed to do well, got my certificate and moved to the main hospital. I didn't like Midwifery; it was not something I could make a career out of.

For five years, I was placed in Cardiac out-patients, which specialised in Echocardiography. Things were in my favour, as I had my baby and would have found it difficult to do shift work. In this Department, we worked Monday to Friday, day-duty only. My husband was still doing a long-distance job and coming home on weekends only.

It made my life easy. I continued to fast once a week even when I would be working on that day. I chose Wednesday as Mr Sako and his team were fasting on that day on a weekly basis.

By this time, the attacks were coming very rarely, sometimes once a week or once a month, and it would only be one attempt at an attack as I now knew how to deal with them and how to pray. The weekly fasting was making a great deal of a difference. I wouldn't always find a good time during the day to pray whilst at work, but I would take my lunchtime and find somewhere to pray.

In most cases, it would be in a room that was not being used for the day or, if there was no room available, I would find a toilet or a corner somewhere away from view.

Mr Sako taught me to pray for myself and not rely on anyone, let alone him and his team, as they weren't going to be with me all the time, especially when these attacks came.

I now knew what to say, how to pray and which scriptures to base my prayers on.

I guess what impacted me most was the love, concern and care these people showed me. From opening their house to me, a total stranger, coming into their house harassed and oppressed by strange forces of evil. This entailed taking a big chance, not only of opening themselves to the attacks of the forces, whatever they were, but putting the lives of their loved ones on the line too.

It takes someone who has been with God, someone who has seen God move in mighty ways, someone with great faith in God to do things like these.

This compassion and love anchored me. It was to prepare me for the worst trials ever that came later in my life. They may not have been the same ways Satan employed, but the knowledge of God I gained through these wonderful people gave me the huge foundation required to see me through every single one of them.

Demonstration and action are much more powerful than words. You can give a person a million good words of advice, but without accompanying them with actions, their impact will always be limited.

I saw God move in my own life. My faith in Him keeps growing. I knew He was capable of healing. I knew He was more powerful than Satan. He removed what all the other so-called healers, priests and prophets couldn't remove.

He saved me from death. One of them told me that the aim of those attacks was to ultimately kill me. I believed it as I was slowly wasting away. My mental and physical strength were gradually being drained out of me.

I was much happier, and much healthier physically and mentally now.

I gained a healthy weight and was a regular churchgoer as well as home group member. They called them cottage meetings.

I was baptised properly this time as the Faith Mission church was practising full immersion.

The church leader, Pastor Victor Sibiya, asked me to take the youth on Sundays and teach them. I did for a year but was unable to continue due to two small children. This was after my son was born.

Mrs Montshioa, the mother of one of our cottage meeting leaders, who lived very near me, helped look after my daughter when I started working. I would drop her off at her house and pick her up on my way home after work. God was good. Things were working well.

My husband got into the mini-bus taxi business, bought two mini-buses, and hired one driver whilst he used one of them to take people who worked in factories and firms outside the town of Vereeniging to work, and would then pick them up in the afternoon. All taxi owners were doing this as it guaranteed regular income as commuters paid their fares monthly. My husband was very good at money-making and management. In those years, money was never a problem. We had enough; often more than enough.

I was left to keep my salary and use it as I pleased. My husband had a bit of pride, just like a traditional African man, who was raised up to believe that men are providers and never to take money from women. It gave them status and signified power and good manhood to be able to provide for your family.

We were very happy.

I conceived again in 1992 and had my son Moses at the end of March the next year. He was named after my father-in-law.

By this time, my husband had left the job and started his own business so he could be at home with the family.

My son was born in Vereeniging Provincial hospital which was formally serving only the white community.

This time things went very well. My son was the biggest baby of the day. He was slightly overdue, and his epidermis was peeling off on his hands and feet.

He weighed a whopping 3.9kg. The hospital authorities came to see him. Big as he was, both the Midwives and the Obstetricians were very knowledgeable and professional. He lay at an oblique position and had not rotated to a full 360 degrees with the head facing down ready for delivery. He was moving very slowly due to his size and delaying the birth process. I ended up with a prolonged labour period.

My Midwife got concerned and suggested Forceps delivery as he was now at 180 degrees, and very low; Caesarean Section was out of the question.

I was so tired and exhausted that all I wanted was anything to bring this delivery to an end.

She notified the Obstetrician and he came to check me. He then said, "There is movement and progress, it's just slow, but the baby will eventually be delivered." He was opposed to Forceps. I was too; as a nurse and trained Midwife, I knew the complications the baby can suffer.

Another long wait. He finally arrived, very big and no spontaneous cry as he, too, was so exhausted. The Midwife panicked a little but, after a few seconds, he cried.

My son was later to learn that he has a small degree of brain hypoxia, which could be attributed to the delayed prolonged labour.

It only affects his academic ability, but he has an amazing creative gift.

In 1996, my wonderful father-in-law passed away through uncontrolled high blood pressure, some mild heart disease and liver cirrhosis. I didn't know much about complications of alcohol at the time, even though I was a nurse.

I had taken him to hospital many times when he had a health crisis and his blood pressure was always sky-high. He was told many times that he needed to stop drinking but alcohol services for black people at the time were unavailable. Rehabs were mostly private, very expensive, not well-known or advertised, and located in suburbs and inaccessible to the poor. Few were public but would only be made available to white people.

It was such a loss to us.

Earlier in the same year, I got accepted for the Psychiatric nursing course in Tara Hospital near Sandton, Johannesburg. This was formally one of the hospitals that served the white community only. It had been open to all since 1994.

All hospitals, universities and schools were now open to all.

My sister Maria came to my rescue again. She agreed to take my children to Lebowakgomo and look after them for the year. I enrolled my daughter into a multi-racial pre-school just outside Pietersburg, a small suburb called Westenberg, which was resided mostly by the Coloured community. (i.e. mixed race.)

It was a difficult time of separation and starting a new school. My daughter had been in a similar pre-school in Vanderbijlpark the previous year. The requirement then was that your child should be in a pre-school at ages 5 and 6 to start lower primary school at age 7.

My daughter struggled to adjust. Two factors contributed to it; separation from parents and moving to a new region, different language, my mother tongue of Sepedi (Northern Sotho), as in Sebokeng, we spoke her father's mother tongue, Southern Sotho.

It only lasted a year. I graduated in February 1998 and brought the children home.

I never went back to work in Cardiology but was placed in a medical admission ward, ward 20. We called it "Scutari" after the old barrack hospital at Scutari, Florence Nightingale's base during the Crimean War in a district in Istanbul, Turkey. This was between 1854 -1856. The conditions of this hospital were reportedly very bad. Florence Nightingale was said to have arrived in Turkey with a group of 38 nurses from England in 1854. The war was between Britain and Russia.

Ward 20 was the busiest ward in the whole Baragwanath Hospital at the time. No nurse or doctor wanted to work there. So, there was rotational allocation, especially for those working in the Dept of Medicine which had 6 wards, 3 female and 3 males, plus ward 20, which was an admission ward. It received patients from all areas within the hospital, including Casualty and Outpatient Departments and the 6 wards were divided according to the lead Medical Professor. A Professor was allocated two wards, a female and a male ward.

Intake was done rotationally amongst the Professors, usually once weekly. Intake day was like a war zone but even so, much less chaotic or busy as ward 20. When I returned from study leave, having worked in Tara, The H Moross Hospital, with a relaxed and homely atmosphere, in Hurlingham, very close to Sandhurst, a stone's throw from Sandton, bordered by beautiful towns like Randburg, Hyde Park, Parkmore, Craighall, Illovo, Dunkeld, Sandown, Bordeaux, Morningside to name but few, and come and work in ward 20, Soweto, Scutari, I really felt like, God, what is this??

I wanted to leave. I survived it, though. I was in there for a few months then moved to a medical ward.

Chapter 7.
Another tragedy

I was commuting from Evaton/ Sebokeng to Baragwanath, Soweto daily by bus as I didn't drive then. I got tired of this and asked my husband if we could move to around Johannesburg region, either to the newly built residential areas in Soweto or in the suburbs. Black people were now allowed to live in any parts of towns and cities if they could afford it. My husband was not comfortable with this as he feared for his life. The taxi industry then was very dangerous, with taxi owners hiring hit men to kill fellow taxi-owners just over taxi routes and operations.

There were a lot of such wars that would erupt at the taxi ranks in towns and townships.

It would be in taxi ranks, along the routes, whilst in operation or in people's houses.

My husband lost two best friends in a very short space of time due to this. The four were very close friends.

Both incidents happened at their friend's home. In the first one, the victim was parking his minibus taxi in his driveway when a guy suddenly emerged from the gate and shot him. He didn't reach hospital. He died on the spot. The wife was inside the house and just heard a bang. Those days, these incidences were common in the taxi industry and the police were thought to be involved through bribery and were not doing a thing about it.

In the second one, the remaining three were sitting and having a chat in the house of the victim. Someone knocked and when one of his children opened the door, he quickly pushed past him and entered the living room, pointing a gun at the father. Shot at close range again, he was rushed to hospital but died a few days later. My husband was there among the three of them and was an eyewitness along with the other man. They both rushed him to hospital but unfortunately, he died.

During the negotiation period of moving to the Johannesburg area, we agreed to start by renting in the nearby town of Parktown. We found schools for the children, my son was 3 ½ years old and he was in a nursery.

My daughter was 6 ½ and in the nearest primary school, Roseneath just down the road. It was a very nice, quiet area not far from the now-notorious Hillbrow, which is now populated by drug dealers and human trafficking activities carried

Chapter 7. Another tragedy

out in what used to be very nice buildings and hotels, but which are now just dilapidated and uninhabitable.

My husband stayed in Evaton most of the time as he was still doing business there and the house wasn't sold yet. He joined us at weekends.

My husband was next on the hit list without anyone knowing. He went about his daily routine and took the driver of the second minibus home after work in the evening as usual. This is when me and the children were in Parktown and he would come at the weekend.

The story goes that he apparently dropped the guy at his house as usual. He always drove him home in our small car. Eyewitnesses stated that two cars came speeding down the street in Sebokeng and the other car just overtook my husband and blocked his car in the middle of the street. The guys from the chasing car got out and the witness said gunshots were fired.

Immediately after the sound of shots, the witness said he heard a car driving away. He stated he was watching through the window in his house. He couldn't see properly, fearing death if he were to open the curtain. He feared that if they saw him, they would kill him too.

After the car drove off, he didn't come out of the house. The houses were very small and clustered together. None of the people in the other houses came out either.

This person called the ambulance but unfortunately, it was now after 8 pm and with poor services, the ambulance took over an hour to come. When they arrived at the scene just in front of this man's house, he then came out to relate the little that he had seen and also try and see if he knew the victim.

He found that he didn't know the victim. Our car was left untouched by the killers in the middle of the road, with my husband lying on his back having been shot a few times in the mouth. The witness said there was blood pouring from his mouth and he was making gurgling sounds when he breathed.

He was taken to Sebokeng Hospital casualty department. According to my brother-in-law, when my husband arrived, the duty doctor for casualty was nowhere to be found. Those days, in smaller hospitals like Sebokeng, especially during the week, there would only be one doctor allocated for casualty. The nurses did their bit, then tried to bleep him, calling him through the switchboard, but in vain.

My husband gave his last breath lying there behind the screens, not having seen a doctor. After over an hour's wait in the middle of the road, with his own blood pouring down his throat, he had to wait for another hour for a doctor who was nowhere to be found at the time when he was supposed to be on duty.

His body was labelled 'unknown male' as was normally done with those who couldn't talk and had no one with them.

My husband died alone, under very strange circumstances. To date, no one knows who killed him and why.

We discovered after 3 days what really happened to him. My brother-in-law went searching and found him in the local hospital mortuary. The matter was not reported to the police. I was the one who opened a case after I got the information about what happened. No one could reach him by phone. By this time, cell phones were now in use in the country and everyone had them.

His phone had been off all the three days. I thought he was upset with something as sometimes people can be upset and not say it, but just use avoidance techniques. This was not like him though, but one never knows.

I was just waiting for the weekend as he was due to come to us.

I worked hard at trying to get the police to do their job until I felt unsafe pushing this thing.

My in-laws declined to involve the police. They said they feared for their lives. I was the only one pursuing the matter but getting nowhere as the police weren't prepared to work at it. I got to a place where I began to have suspicions around the police and some people, but by then it was too dangerous to pursue the matter.

There were a lot of things that were not making sense. I suddenly was shown a car-ownership certificate of the older minibus, which was paid off. The ownership had been just changed from my husband's name to someone I didn't know. My younger brother-in-law was the one dealing with this. He said the new owner came over after my husband was found dead in a hospital mortuary and showed him these papers telling him he was the new owner.

He stated the guy said my husband sold the minibus to him a week before his death. At the time, the minibus was still at home. My husband never breathed a word to me of wanting to sell any of the cars. I knew him very well. He would never do anything like this. The car had to be given to the 'new owner'.

The second newer minibus was still under the bank but very nearly close to being paid off too. It survived because of that.

I took it to the bank and explained everything and paid off the balance and changed ownership to myself. I sold it immediately afterwards.

I rented the house after this as, luckily, I was now staying in Johannesburg.

Chapter 7. Another tragedy

My tenants started to get threatening phone calls from the older son of my husband's aunt. He was telling them to vacate the house, asking them who put them in there and making threats to their safety and lives.

The tenant was a younger woman with her children. She got scared and felt unsafe. The brother who was said to be making those threats denied it when I asked him about it. It was obvious, but he wouldn't admit it.

I began to feel unsafe myself.

Our private car that the eyewitness said was left on the street next to my husband on the day of the attack, went missing before I was informed of his death. More confusion came in. Who took the car and when?

My friend Winnie, after a while, told me that the small car had been seen being driven around the township by a strange man. During the time my husband was still missing and during funeral preparations, my younger brother-in-law was running our business. He took over the minibus that was left and continued the business.

He took all the money generated from the business from the time my husband went missing to a couple of weeks after the funeral without declaring any of it to me.

I then decided to stop this by talking to the bank and got the minibus paid it off and sold it immediately. He wasn't happy with this.

There was no time to mourn.

My husband owned a gun for protection as all taxi owners could have them because of the frequent taxi wars. The guns were registered and monitored by law. This was also missing. I inquired about it from the younger brother, who seemed to be the one handling things, but he denied knowledge of its whereabouts. I reported to the police and they demanded that they hand it over to the police station.

They did. The police called me to the police station to come and identify it. They then asked me what I wanted to do with it. I told them to dispose of it.

The tenant eventually left for fear of being killed following the threats from my husband's older brother.

I asked the town council to help find me another one and they did.

I paid off the house too and put it on the market with profit. The Lord was merciful; it got sold in a few months' time. I removed everything from it now.

My husband and I married in community of property and we made a will. No one could bypass the will and do anything. I was the legal beneficiary. That helped a lot.

When they were making threats to the tenant, I was advised to involve lawyers. I found a very good lawyer who started off by calling the older brother in question and giving him a verbal warning and sending him a letter afterwards.

That stopped them from threatening the new tenant. By the time the house was sold, and the new owner moved in, things were quieter.

The younger brother had taken my husband taxi business certificate and was using it for himself. He left his job with the council and was now in the taxi industry. It was easy to bribe the authorities anyway and get any paper changed to what you want.

My daughter was greatly affected by the loss of her father. She was old enough to know what had happened and as I hadn't even had time to mourn, everything was pushed away very quickly.

It did not show till we were here in the UK.

My son didn't quite understand at the time. During the week of the funeral preparations, he kept following his uncle round in the house and calling him 'papa' as he used to call his father. It was so heart-breaking. He was too little to understand what death meant. The brother's voices sounded so similar; hence he was mistaking him for his father.

Despite all this, I forgave everyone, including the unknown murderers, and right up till today, I maintained good relationships with my in-laws, especially my mother-in-law. The children and I always pay her a visit and then the others come to see us in her house. It has not been very bad. I had to swallow my pride and become the fool for the sake of my children and God. I avoided causing total separation between my children and their blood relatives. Their father is gone now, and this is all they have left of him.

My sister Maria came to my rescue again and came to help me with my children in Johannesburg.

By the time of my husband's death, I was a regular church attender in Rhema Church in Randburg, led by Pastor Ray McCauley and his first wife, Lyndie.

I registered myself as a member and loved it there.

My children attended Sunday School and were water baptised as they baptised children in Rhema.

We had home groups and I quickly joined one in my area. It was in Berea, near Hillbrow and within walking distance from the part of Parktown I lived in.

The area was still alright and safer at the time.

I always hungered for more of God. They had a very big Bible college there. It ran up to the third year of study. I wanted so much to join but I was unable to do this as it ran during the day, Monday to Friday, and students had to help whenever there was a conference or special services, as well as on Sundays as part of their curriculum. I was working full-time as a nurse in Baragwanath Hospital at the time and needed to work as I was the only financial provider for my family. I took the Counselling course in 1999, which required attendance only once a week. This was a year's course.

Life was moving on and had to move on.

Chapter 8.
Relocating to the UK

In 1999, nurses were going to the UK to take work opportunities that arose following a gross shortage of nurses The exchange rate attracted nurses and they began to see it as a way to boost their financial situations and do what they wouldn't have been able to do before, which was travel overseas.

Many of these nurses, especially blacks, had never travelled anywhere beyond the borders of SA. This was a miracle.

I also started thinking hard about it. Then by the end of that year, I began inquiring with agencies that were helping with the recruitment.

I got all the information and started the process. It took me till early 2002 to get through to my first interview. The interviews were conducted through Skype and were based in Sandton, Johannesburg.

My first one was in January and I didn't get through that time. God knew what He was doing. It disappointed me at the time, but the area and type of setting were not going to be the best for me. The desperation made it look like a disappointment. In my own power, I would have taken anything that came by. God had to choose for me by allowing a momentary disappointment.

I was to later learn from this that many times, what seems like a 'No' from God, is a way into the best thing that God has for us.

I was given another chance for interview with one of the UK's leading private Healthcare Groups. Two people were sharing the interview for the group's two sites, one in South West and the other in North London.

This was what God had for me. I slid through the process so easily. I was informed a few days later by the agency that the South West London site had picked me.

At the time, I didn't even know where that was, what difference it made, etc.

I left home on Sunday 7th July 2002 and I arrived in the UK on the morning of the 8th.

I got such a warm welcome. My first impression was very good, and I guess that really made a huge difference in my decision to stay in the country. A lot of my colleagues were unsettled in their jobs and areas and many stayed in the country for short periods and quickly returned to SA.

Some of them were employed by the employers whose interview I didn't get through. I heard from them how terrible things were. They were in remote parts

Chapter 8. Relocating to the UK

of the country, with very few black people there, and that made them a bit isolated. And, they had difficulties transitioning into the new culture and lifestyles, and things were not going well for them at work either.

I felt very lucky to have not gone through with the first interview, that God somehow knew it wasn't going to work out for me.

I fell in love with the hospital. There were already 5 other nurses from SA, one of whom I had worked with in a psychiatric ward in Baragwanath Hospital in 1999-2001.

I immediately felt at home. They were informed of my arrival and told to come and greet and welcome me. I was given a room in the posh building in the hospital grounds. It was a bit small but I couldn't have asked for more.

The nurse I worked with in Baragwanath Hospital had been given a room next door to my one. She had arrived a month before me. The other four nurses arrived a few months earlier and stayed in the hospital facilities at first for a couple of months, and then management helped them find their own places.

They shared a flat just outside of the hospital. We were very lucky as we were left to stay in those rooms for six months.

We moved out at the end of February 2003 to share a flat not far from the hospital.

I was allocated to an addiction ward. I had no idea what addictions entailed. I knew what it was about but had no experience of working in that type of setting with that type of patients.

When my colleagues heard, everyone was warning me how difficult and dangerous addicts were, and how they would never work in that unit, etc.

Everywhere I went during my induction period around the hospital, I got told the same thing. I began to be a bit concerned. Again, it was just a set-up by God.

The reason I was allocated there was that the 5 nurses who came before me were distributed each to the other wards and the addictions unit was the only one left short of a nurse. I was to replace a nurse who was leaving at the end of that month.

Amazingly, I settled so well in that unit. I loved the staff, and I loved the patients. It was an internationally highly acclaimed addictions rehab facility and attracted very wealthy dignitaries from all walks of life. It admitted celebrities from all over the world. Most of these people were very respectful of the staff, behaving nothing like one would expect of a drug addict or alcoholic. I was amazed. I enjoyed it very much there. There was one nurse from the Philippines in particular, who unfortunately passed away in 2008, from breast cancer. She made my stay a very pleasant one and helped me settle so quickly into the job.

Our unit manager was the best manager I ever had. A bit laissez-faire type of leadership but nice.

The Philippino colleague was a saint. It was as if God provided her for me. I adjusted so quickly to the new health system and procedures as well as policies in my workplace.

I got constant feedback from everyone, including my manager, on how well I was doing and how good my performance was. Of course, it was made possible by their help.

I remained in that unit for the next 13 years and moved to a general psychiatric unit for the next three years, making it 15 years all together.

Now and again we would get difficult patients. Within my first six months in the unit, we had one. It was a celebrity woman from abroad. Very well-known and renowned in her sphere of work.

The normal period of treatment was 4-6 weeks. It was normally 4 weeks, or 28 days, as was normally referred to. Those who worked a bit harder and seemed to require more input, and were able to fund the extension, would be allowed another two more weeks.

This woman stayed for three months. She was someone who was greatly damaged from childhood and learnt early in life that in order to survive, she had to control everything around her. She was unable to adhere to the rules of the programme and kept getting into trouble with counsellors. In a nutshell, she had narcissistic traits of grandiosity and self-importance. She got suspended a few times and the last time everyone gave up on her. No one wanted her. She had the most wonderful, caring, warm and loving consultant, but even he gave up on her but remained her consultant throughout, due to mere tolerance. She seemed to have twin personalities; one minute she could be smiley, sweet and sociable, and the next, she was swearing, raging and fuming when things were not going her way.

It happened that I managed to get through to her. She found me different. She would be very vulnerable with me. With everyone else, she was this tough, strong, resilient woman and she often used verbal aggression and passive aggression to defend herself. Everyone avoided her. I somehow didn't. The consultant became aware that she was a bit more open with me and listened more to me. He would often ask me to talk her into doing or agreeing to things they wanted changed or done. And it would always work.

During the periods of her suspensions, I would spend time with her in her room. These were the times when she would display feelings of rejection and verbalise them to me. This seemed to jolt her memory to her traumatic childhood experiences. I would just sit there in the chair as she sobbed and sobbed. She would go on and on venting out and I would just sit and listen to her, not even sure what to say at times.

She wouldn't break down like that in the presence of anyone in the team. She did a few times with the consultant.

All she seemed to need at those times was just someone to listen, someone to hear her out and just be there.

I have to say that she was very difficult. You needed the grace of God to tolerate her. I got a bit tired myself but somehow, I kept in with her. When she was angry, she lashed out verbally and her face took on a scary countenance.

I totally understand where the team and everybody were coming from with her. She had broken all the rules, became disruptive and was now affecting other patient's recovery causing others to break the rules too and sabotage their treatments like her. She wanted her way in all that was being done. It was against the programme model and treatment operation. It was difficult. They had to do something or else it would reverse everything they were doing.

But I found that I couldn't resist the pleading eyes of that hidden silent child inside of her. I just knew something would work. I wasn't sure what it was, but I knew something would work. The empathic me got stirred inside. I wasn't aware at the time that I was an empath, and always have been. I discovered early this year. Now I understand why I managed to put up with her and why she was 'attracted' to me.

If it wasn't because of the grace of God, I too would have run away from her.

That helped not only her but the consultant. He told me several times and thanked me for my ability to contain her.

It happened that the whole team wondered what it was with me that was making her mellow down. It was even suspected that she was manipulating me and that I was not strong enough to be firm with her as it was believed that part of the treatment was to be a bit tougher with patients.

That wasn't the case. I was also, at times, getting what they were getting from her, but my gentle compassionate response made all the difference and it attracted her. She was used to having people run away from her due to her personality and behaviour. In fact, she was a troubled little kid inside who yearned for love and acceptance but was full of anger and hurt which her behaviour would display. That would not give her what she wanted most, but the opposite.

She almost expected rejection. I was different. She could be angry and nasty towards me today and I would be in her room first thing in the morning asking her how she was, when she expected me to have run away like everyone else.

That attracted her. It was something new. She relied on me, almost treated me like her family. She came from a broken family and was not in touch with any of her family members. She had no friends. I became family and in her own little child-like heart, she saw me as a friend.

She somehow stayed for three full months, in and out of the programme due to behaviour issues, but she eventually did it.

One day, my manager asked to have a word with me. She informed me that the team had a meeting with her and were a bit concerned about my 'relationship' with the patient. They said everyone in the team, nurses and all, found her very challenging and had stepped away from her; all except me. She stated that there were questions of what it was with me and the woman, why she was so drawn to me. She went onto say that the team asked her to interview the woman without my knowledge to find out what it was she saw in me.

She did and she expected to find some unprofessionalism in the way I was interacting with her.

The manager said the woman answered in one word; "compassion".

She reportedly went on to say that, "Sarah is very compassionate".

And that was all.

The manager went to feedback to the team and when people were hoping to find some discrepancies in my professional conduct, they were shocked to hear what the woman said was the key to the whole thing.

My manager expressed her thankfulness for having managed the most difficult of all the patients they had ever had.

It was very scary as I had only been in the UK for six months, and here I was being questioned about my practice. I thanked God for this, and I never forgot about it.

What I learnt was that people are on different journeys and that their life-walks are different from everybody else's. Their experiences from childhood are different from everybody else's. How they learnt to cope with the effects of those damaging experiences is also different from everybody else. Some, like her, use a false facade of strength and control, and display anger and passive aggression

Chapter 8. Relocating to the UK

which, in turn, pushes people away. It takes a bigger heart, a selfless attitude, an ability to see through their behaviour, and know what exactly it is they long for, what exactly they are trying to convey, to see the deepest of hurts, hidden so deep, the cry for love and acceptance.

That was my first real discovery too. For the first time, I found I had that type of tolerance and compassion.

Lesson learnt:

Give everyone a chance. Never give up on anyone. Just as much as God loves them and wants them well, love them; no matter how unlovable they may be, give them the benefit of the doubt that they can change. However, sometimes full-blown narcissists can be best left alone, as they never really change.

In God's eyes, no one is too far gone to be reached and brought back. No one is beyond help. Just as much as we all, each one of us, would like to be understood, would like people to be merciful to us, others want that from us too.

My plan was to work in the UK for only two years and return home. I left my children in the care of my mother who was still very able, just retired at 60, and still very strong.

End of 2015, I left private setting and joined the national health service. This was my first time working for the NHS.

I was appointed as the first mental health nurse in that particular hospital to work as part of the liaison psychiatric service based within a general hospital to help with people who are admitted to the hospital as a result of the negative impact on their health by alcohol. This had become such a demand for the service that they needed an additional staff member to cater for it alongside the mental health service provision part of the service.

My extensive thirteen years of experience working in addictions came in handy.

Early 2016, there was a media release about the service.

See, below, part of the article from the local newspaper, The Evening Standard.

50% rise in alcohol admissions sees new service at St Helier

The number of people admitted to St Helier Hospital with alcohol-related illnesses and injuries has jumped by 50% in the past two years – prompting the launch of a new specialist service to support patients with problem drinking and those suffering from alcohol-related conditions.

Figures show that in 2013, 247 people needed to stay overnight at St Helier Hospital because of alcohol consumption, rising to 332 in 2014 and hitting a high of 370 patients in 2015.

Additional support for patients with alcohol misuse issues is now available, thanks to the hospital's new Alcohol Liaison Service – an initiative that has been commissioned by the London Borough of Sutton, developed in partnership with South West London and St George's Mental Health NHS Trust, and will be led by recently recruited specialist nurse Sarah Moloi.

Sarah said: "Hospital records show that over the last two years we have seen a significant increase in the number of people referred or admitted because of harmful or hazardous drinking and alcohol-related problems. Excessive drinking and dependency on alcohol can have a significant impact on a person's health and wellbeing, not just physically but mentally as well. It is incredibly important that we are able to offer these people the right kind of help at the right time.

"Often, individuals are not aware of the damage alcohol can do, so a big part of my job is to raise awareness and help people understand the impact their drinking is having. It is important that people are able to make the connection between their drinking habits and why they may have ended up in hospital – in order to treat their health issues and achieve the best possible outcome, we need to provide the right support and treatment to address their use of alcohol.

The new service, which will provide support to those drinking above recommended weekly limits, those with alcohol dependency and patients with alcohol-related physical illnesses, has got off to a busy start. As staff have got to know Sarah, the number of referrals of patients with problem drinking has increased, with up to 10 new cases each week. Sarah also advises staff on how to treat patients with alcohol-related problems. She explained: "In order to provide the help that is needed, it is essential to understand individual cases, including that person's history and relationship with alcohol, and to work closely with them to help them recognise what is happening and what help is available.

"Although the journey may begin with me in the hospital, it is also about signposting to and linking people with the support that is available in the community to ensure that they continue to receive the help they need, even after they have left the hospital. One of our key aims is to encourage and empower people to take control of their own health, and to provide them with the awareness and support that they will need to keep this going in the long term."

I had been told whilst still in SA, by those who came to the UK before me, that there were not many churches in the UK and that the ones that were there were quite weak and boring.

I began to pray to God to lead me to a church just like Rhema. I prayed very hard, every day. I said, "God, there must be a church like this; there has to be, please, lead me to it."

I remember making a deal with God. I said to Him, "If you get me to a good church, I will give 10% of my first six months' income as a gift to advance your work in the church".

And I kept my word with God. My first holiday was in December 2002, six months later. I went to SA and gave the Light of the Nations church, which was my home church then, under Pastors Deric and his late wife Belinda Linley, the whole six months' worth of tithes. I was a member there from 2001 until I relocated to the UK.

I had moved back to my birth town of Pietersburg, now Polokwane at the beginning of 2001, as part of the preparation for relocating to the UK. This was to let my children bond with my mother, find them schools and get them settled in those schools before I left.

I had a friend called Regina, who was in Matladi High School at the time when I was there. We were not friends then. Regina was a qualified primary school teacher and had returned to complete her Matric, the last 2 years of high school, to qualify to teach secondary and high school students.

She was very quiet and reserved. I never saw her with anyone. She was saved but I didn't know it at the time.

In 2001, when I returned to my small town of Pietersburg, Lebowakgomo, I met with her. She lived there and was a teacher in Matladi High School.

She was now a very grounded, established believer and Minister. She didn't have her own church but had been going to prisons on a regular basis, preaching the Gospel, and had fantastic results.

She was also into prayer and intercession. I immediately loved her. We started meeting regularly, mainly in her house or mine for fellowship. She was into books and so was I. We started to exchange books.

She introduced me to Benny Hinn by lending me two of his books, 'Good Morning Holy Spirit' and 'He Touched Me'. I didn't know who Benny Hinn was at the time.

She told me a lot about him. I got hungry to know him more. She then gave me those books to read and I lent her my TD Jakes' ones that I bought in 2000 when he came to Rhema as a speaker for the yearly conference;

'Woman Thou Art Loosed' and 'Can You Stand To Be Blessed?'

She liked TD Jakes too.

I read those two small books of Benny Hinn in a week. They were old and covered in dust as she had had them for many years and had put them away in storage.

Something happened within me. I began to feel my heart melt when I read the books. I began to experience spontaneous emotional expressions. I felt that the deepest core of my heart seemed to be touched. I would feel the urge to pray. At the time, I wasn't a prayerful person. I would feel being pulled to kneel, literally drawn to a kneeling position. This continued throughout the period I was reading those books. I began to lock myself in the room when the kids were at school or playing and just read over and over again, getting emotional out of the blue, my heart softening more and more and I would experience this enormous hunger to know more of God and pray more.

I started to isolate and bury myself in books and prayer. I always loved music, and when I became a Christian, it became Christian music, worship songs.

During these times of reading, I would be constantly listening to worship. Prayer became a breath away. It was spontaneous and unplanned.

I was seeing Regina almost on a daily basis now. I fed back to her how her little books are affecting me tremendously. I found myself retelling the book, especially 'Good Morning Holy Spirit'. Regina had read it quite a few times and knew more about it than me, but here I was ranting to her about it. I just couldn't help it. I heard and discovered something I never quite knew before.

She would just let me talk. She could tell that something was happening. Our conversations changed.

I remember my eyes filling with tears and my voice breaking when I told her about the book. I told her I really didn't know what was going on with me.

Regina continued to disciple me. She gave me more books and worship videos. I would also give her what she asked for in my library.

One of the worship videos she lent me was 'God is able' by Ron Kenoly.

Whenever I wasn't reading a book or listening to worship, I would be watching this video.

There was a song that captured my spirit; 'I See the Lord.' This song touched my heart so much, that I wept while listening to it. Tears just rolled down my face spontaneously. I would keep on rewinding it and playing it repeatedly. The whole living room would be filled with the presence of God.

By the time the children came back from school and I had to attend to them and prepare dinner, I would be saturated, immensely saturated.

This was early 2002, February till June. I knew God and Jesus and something about the Holy Spirit, but I realised I didn't know I was discovering more about them. I met the Holy Spirit with the help of two little books that were packed away, forgotten about and came out to me full of dust and with some pages falling out.

Worship became very real. It brought me an intimacy with God. Desire to know God more increased within me. Nothing mattered more than spending time alone with Him.

Benny Hinn talked a lot about Kathryn Kuhlman in His books and a bit about Smith Wigglesworth. It was Kathryn he mentioned a lot of the time. I didn't know who she was and had never heard of her. The way these books impacted me and roused such hunger to know more about the Holy Spirit, I felt I had to get a book that spoke about Kathryn or one she herself had written. I didn't know where to get it. Even Regina didn't know her. She didn't seem to feel the way I felt about knowing her more.

I embarked on a 'shopping spree', looking for any book about her. I ravaged our town, all the bookshops even non-Christian ones. Finally, I checked in the small bookshop in the church I was part of at the time In Pietersburg, Light of the Nations. At the time it was called the Christian Community Church. I searched the whole entire bookshop, shelf by shelf, and just when I was about to give up and leave, I felt a nudge from the Holy Spirit to look in a far corner of the top shelf. There it was. A small old-looking pink book entitled, 'A Spiritual Biography of God's Miracle Worker'. I was excited. I chuckled like a child. It was old and worn-out, full of dust. It didn't look like anyone had ever read it. I read that book, in tears, about five times, I guess. I would take it to work with me and every time I got a minute, I read it. My break time consisted of me going into one of the empty rooms, locking the door and reading it again and again.

Worship had become my constant companion. I didn't have a portable CD player at the time and mobile phones were not the type to store music like they do now. I was working in a long-term psychiatric hospital and it served as a permanent home for those patients. Most of them had attained a functional state and there was one such patient in the previous ward I was allocated to. He had a radio with a CD player. I used to borrow it and he would then charge me R1 for the use of it. It became a daily thing for as long as I was at work. I had just purchased the latest music CD by Michael W Smith from Rhema Church bookshop in January 2002 and would be playing it all day long. I remember one time, I was on my break and, as usual, locked myself in an empty room and was reading Kathryn's book whilst listening to 'Let It Rain', a song by Michael, and the presence of God fell upon me in that room; I began to weep uncontrollably, non-stop. My break time was done but I was still weeping, shaking and kneeling on the floor praying, unable to compose myself or stand and go back to the ward. It took about 15 more minutes of my break. Fortunately, God protected me; no one was looking for me or realised I hadn't returned from my break. That was my new-found life.

Chapter 8. Relocating to the UK

The next month, I accidentally came across another book while looking around the bookshop. This was a paperback about Wigglesworth with the students of the Bible. All the people Benny Hinn mentioned in his books, Kathryn Kuhlman and Wigglesworth, I had now found their books.

It was November 2001 when Rodney Howard-Browne visited the church and held daily meetings for three days. I attended two of them.

I hadn't heard of Rodney at the time, even though he was South African. I had no idea of the type of anointing he carried out. I had never seen or heard of Holy laughter. The first day, I sat there in the middle of the church hall with a friend. People were getting touched everywhere. Some laughing, some weeping, some falling under the power. There was a guy who captured my attention and awareness with this Holy laughter. He was a pastor of a church in Venda, in the far north region of the Northern, now Limpopo province. He began to laugh from where he was sitting. The laughter was getting louder and louder but not too much. Rodney asked the ushers to bring him over to the front. He instructed him to stand and lift his arms up to receive more. The guy became uncontrollable. He laughed so much you could tell his tummy hurt.

Rodney kept asking him questions, like who are you, what do you do. He had difficulty answering these questions as the laughter was so uncontrollable that he barely paused. It was so genuinely divine; no man could have faked that. In later years, I saw some faked Holy laughter, but this one was very genuine.

He tried to answer, though, in between the bouts of hilarious laughter that got so infectious that we all joined in and laughed, but his was still utterly divine. That's how I got to know he was a pastor.

After all this, he fell on the floor under the power of the Holy Spirit and lay there for hours. Rodney never touched him all this time. He just asked him to raise his hands and receive. God just did it. It was so splendid.

I yearned for this. Everyone did. Nothing happened to me or my friend that day. On our way out, I told my friend, "Tomorrow is my day. I am coming to receive".

This was the last day. The service was like a Kathryn Kuhlman, Benny Hinn kind of service that goes on for hours. People were receiving just like the day before. Some were lying on the floor, some laughing, some weeping, some rolling, some running around, some shouting in tongues. It was a Holy chaos.

I sat there watching and wondering, why am I not receiving?!

Then suddenly, I felt something drawing my knees to the floor. A feeling of a force. Something I couldn't resist. As it happened, I felt my heart getting warmer, gentler, and I was getting weaker physically, to a point where my legs couldn't support my body even though I was sitting in the chair. My body was being pulled to a kneeling position. I couldn't stop it. Whatever it was, it was too powerful for me. And then, it began. I started to weep, uncontrollably. I barely heard Rodney say, "Bring that lady over here, bring her over here." I felt ushers trying to help me to my feet, as by then, I was literally kneeling on the floor weeping. They couldn't get me up that far, as I went very limp. They then just half-carried and half-dragged me to the aisle and lay me there. I was gone. I lay there rolling and weeping till the end of the service. It happened just towards the end of the service, but time was of no concern; the service would just carry on if God was working.

My friend didn't get touched in a visible way, though. When we left, she reminded me that the day before I had vowed, and said, "Tomorrow is my day; I am getting a touch from God".

My time to come to the UK drew near. Everything required had been provided.

When still new in the UK, in my second week, when I was still living in the hospital premises, one day I went to the shops in the High Street in East Sheen, and on my way there, I saw a small building with a board by the gate stating, "Elim Pentecostal" and below that, was the name of the Pastor, which didn't mean anything to me as I knew no one here, and the service times. The services were on Sundays at 10:30. I was so happy. I had found a church. God led me to a church as I had asked.

On the Sunday, I went there and was a bit disappointed to find 8 people, including the Pastor and his family.

Being an immature Christian at the time, I felt disappointed because when I prayed and asked God, I specifically said a church like Rhema. This was nowhere near it. This was way smaller than Light of the Nations in my town of Pietersburg, which was itself about 10 times smaller than Rhema.

I didn't know anyone except the nurses from SA in the hospital that employed me and none of them was a practising Christian. So, I had nothing but this church, this very small, almost-empty church. I decided I would stay here, after all, I would be going back home after two years.

I had a very warm welcome there. Everyone was so nice. They had found an addition.

Chapter 8. Relocating to the UK

This was the third week of July. I continued to attend for the next three Sundays and on the second Sunday, after the service, I picked up a magazine from their literature and free resources table.

It just appealed to me.

I took it home.

It was a church magazine for the month of August 2002 and the church was big and looked very vibrant, just like Rhema. It had all the church activities and programmes in pictures as well. My eyes bulged in admiration. I heard myself say to God, "Now, this is what I asked for, thank you, Lord".

There was a problem. I didn't know where the church was.

Something in my spirit told me to go and ask someone from that small church; they would know since this magazine came from there.

The next Sunday, I hurried there. After the service, I showed the magazine to someone and asked them how I could get to that church. I could see the disappointment on their face. They knew I was not intending to stay there.

They reluctantly pointed to the piano player and said, "She is the person who brings these magazines. She's the best person to ask."

I approached the lady, who spoke with a very nice UK English accent. She was Afro-Caribbean. She was born in the UK. At the time, I was just about learning to pick up the English accent properly but I loved it. It sounded very different from the SA one.

The lady said to me, "Oh, I am going there now. I drive. You can come with me if you want".

I really wasn't ready to go that afternoon as it was my day off, and I had planned to spend the afternoon with God, reading my book, praying and worshipping as it had now become the norm with me since the beginning of the year.

I had no choice but to go with her as I wouldn't dare miss the opportunity to be taken there and learn the route so I could then go by myself.

I quickly said, "Oh, yes, that's very nice, thank you. Yes, I can come with you".

Long story short, we hopped into the car. On the way, she introduced herself as Marcia Campbell. She told me she lived in Southfields. At the time, I didn't know where Southfields was. She said she was a nurse by profession but that she was also a music teacher and currently teaching small children.

She knew Pastor Ray McCauley, and said he was a friend of the Pastor of this church we were going to and that he preached and visited their church on several occasions over the years.

My ears pricked up. Wow, here I was again, on what seemed to be familiar grounds.

Now, she told me that she was a member of that church and not really of the small church we had come from. She said she was just helping them out with worship as they had asked her to.

She said she went there to do that every Sunday morning and then attended her own church from 2:30 pm onwards.

She told me that, in this church, there were several services throughout the day, so one could choose which one they wanted to attend.

She told me that she liked the 2:30 service as it was dedicated to African service. She said it was very vibrant and lively and assured me that I would surely like it too.

We arrived and indeed, it was beautiful. The Preacher was a big Nigerian man with a booming voice. His frame almost filled the whole platform. The service was more prayer than anything. They sang a mixture of songs, some African Gospel. I immediately felt at home. Not that I didn't like songs sung in European languages, but you know, when you've just arrived in a foreign country and found that they do something in common with your country of origin, it kind of reassures you, doesn't it?

I thought to myself, God is good. How He orchestrated this!! How He just answered my prayer!!

The thing is, I was lucky to have stayed in the small church even if I didn't quite like it there. That was the doorway to what I had asked for.

Lesson learnt:

Many times, God doesn't give you what you ask for straight away or in the way you expect Him to. And also, He usually doesn't answer in the time you expect.

We can often miss God's best gifts by our preconceived ideas of how or when it will come and what it will look like.

Maybe, if I knew anywhere else, I would have left prematurely, I sure would have. The fact that I didn't know anywhere helped, as I got stuck there.

The church was around central London and carried a very rich Spiritual history background.

Marcia informed me that, in the month of August every year, on the bank holiday weekend, the church embarked on a mass outreach alongside what she said was carnival celebration in Notting Hill Gate, which takes place around where the church is situated. She said this celebration is to do with the first Afro-Caribbean's who relocated to the UK many years back and who experienced segregation. She said they later fought against it and won. The majority of those people lived around Notting Hill Gate, hence, the marches and protests were carried out there.

Carnival outreach 2018

It so happened that the next weekend was that event. Marcia informed me she always participated in the church outreach which culminated in a concert on the Sunday and Monday evenings.

Chapter 8. Relocating to the UK

She urged me to come and experience this.

She offered to come and fetch me on both days. I agreed as I was off that Sunday.

She came and took me to the concert. She didn't take part in the outreach though. I thoroughly enjoyed the concert. I felt like I was back in SA. The stories I was told by those who came here and returned to SA, saying that the UK was very dull and boring, were proven wrong. This wasn't the UK I had heard about. This wasn't the church in the UK I had heard about.

Marcia continued to pick me up whenever I was off-duty on Sunday and would go with me to church. This went on till I was confident enough to travel by myself. She showed me how to get there by tube and bus from my place. She got me a tube map and bus and tube tickets, showed me where to buy them, which ones to buy and so on. She really took care of me.

Everything was just being orchestrated by God for me. I then began attending with or without Marcia. I loved it there.

It was announced one day that the church operated in small groups ministry. It was explained that new people needed to fill in a form and get allocated a group to be part of. It was in October 2002, when I filled in a form for that and was placed in a group by the end of November.

We had a small group meeting in her house near where I lived. She was a lady in her early 30's and lived at home with her brother and parents.

She helped provide more information about the church. I managed to invite one nurse from SA in my workplace and she attended the service with me. On that day, she gave her life to Jesus, as altar calls were made at every service. I invited her to the group. She joined it too.

In the August church magazine that I got from the small church, there was an advertisement about a Benny Hinn crusade coming to the UK in November.

Having just gotten acquainted with Benny Hinn earlier in the year through Regina's books, and how they impacted me, I made up my mind, I was going to attend this. I was thrilled that finally, I was going to see the author.

It was going to be in Manchester. I had no idea where that was, but I was determined I would find out. Marcia came in handy again. She was a follower of Benny Hinn's ministries and was going to this crusade. We then bought our tickets; in those days, one had to buy a ticket to attend. It was in Manchester Arena. Tickets were sold at different prices depending on where you would be sitting.

Marcia had a friend in Manchester who used to live in London. The friend had agreed to accommodate us as we needed to sleep over since it was very far from London.

I invited another nurse from SA in my workplace. She was a Methodist from back home but was not practising here. She agreed to come. Marcia went two days before us. We met with her in the house of her friend on the day of the event. We attended the crusade that evening and spent the night there.

On the first day of the crusade, we were told by Marcia's friend to leave early so we could get better seats. The event was ticketed, and tickets sold in advance on a first-come, first-served basis. She also warned us that Benny Hinn crusades were packed and that if we didn't get there early, the chances are, we may not get in at all.

She couldn't have been more accurate.

We were three hours early but already there was a queue. We joined the queue which was not moving yet as the doors were still closed. The queue got so long that it went as far as the town centre.

It was November and very cold. Not only that but it began to rain. I saw for the first time, desperate people, hungry and thirsty for more of God and His divine touch, standing for hours in freezing temperatures, in the rain, waiting and waiting. I thought to myself, "Is this the end? Are we going to heaven? I had never seen anything like this except in big soccer stadiums or political rallies and marches. Never for church-related or Christian events.

I heard my spirit say, "This is Benny Hinn, the author of those two little books that brought tears to your eyes, that evoked a deep desire for God, that melted your previously hardened heart, that brought a deep revelation of who the Third Person of The Trinity is. All these people had more or less a similar experience and they want what God has given him to impart to His people. "

I asked the lady and Marcia, "Guys, is it always like this when he comes to the UK?" They said to me that this was nothing as he filled stadiums, where this was just an arena.

I spent those three hours with my mouth open with amazement. I thanked God repeatedly for bringing me to the UK. Benny had been to SA many times, even to Rhema Bible Church. He is a friend of Pastor McCauley. I bought one of the videos recorded in one of the services he ministered in 1988. That was almost 10 years before I joined the church.

I just never knew him nor got to even attend any of his crusades.

Chapter 8. Relocating to the UK

This was like I was asleep, dreaming and had just woken up to find it was real; it was not a dream.

The queue was now moving. Along the way, a commotion started by the entrance. We heard screaming and shouting and as we looked, even though we were still far back, we saw people pushing to go in and security guys trying to stop them.

People were overpowering the security and pushing forward in numbers causing so much chaos that everybody from behind us to where we were, ran forward pushing and trying to go in. Ticket inspection and collection at the entrance was not working any longer.

We had to push along too. By the time we got to the entrance, the police had been called and taken over control from security.

What the police did was to close the doors and turn everyone who was still outside back. We were just by the door when that happened.

I was so disappointed, so heavy-hearted, I nearly cried. Capacity for Manchester Arena is 21 000. Only about 10 000 managed to get in. The place was half-empty and the police said no more people were going in.

The ten thousand or so left outside began to protest angrily with the police. Someone stopped that by getting a few people to sing. We all joined in and for the entire time of the crusade, we held our little crusade outside.

Tickets were £25 each for the two-day crusade.

We heard later that what caused the commotion was some people having the paid tickets and some having free tickets. The order was that those with paid tickets would get in first, then the rest afterwards.

The people with free tickets were not willing to wait their turn and began to push their way in.

This is what hunger for God does; desperation to meet with Him, feel His presence and somehow get His touch.

We eventually returned home to spend another night in Marcia's friend's house, then came back for the last night.

It was the same procedure, getting there three hours early, but unfortunately, we were way at the back of the queue.

There was much more order this time; the police took control from the beginning and there was respect for them from the crowds.

By the time we got in, the arena was packed on the front, lower and middle balconies.

Marcia and Mary found a seat somewhere in one of the lower balconies and the two of us went to the very top one as it was the only one now with seats.

God has a sense of humour. Please read on.

We sat down. There were few empty seats scattered in between the rows.

We were so far away, that the stage looked like a small space down there and Benny Hinn looked so tiny that we could barely see his face.

The ground floor was packed with wheelchairs and stretchers as well as all kinds of disabled people and the very sick and elderly.

It was very sombre, with every one of those people over there, looking very tiny due to the distance between us and them, and yet so desperate for a touch of God.

The service began and the choir started singing. They sang two songs and then sang 'How Great Thou Art' and Benny Hinn stepped onto the stage and quickly began to conduct the choir and led the worship.

The whole place exploded with worship. This was new to me; very new, except of course for the few times in Rhema when we had the yearly conferences.

The presence of The Holy Spirit quickly filled the entire place, even up to where we were in the top balcony. I was a novice. There was no need for me to pretend or lie.

I began to sing with all of my entire being. Everything within me sang; every part of me worshipped God.

I suddenly felt the urge to take another look at the ground floor, to the very sick, elderly, wheelchairs and stretchers. A wave of compassion filled my heart. I began to softly talk to God. I asked Him to heal every one of them, that none would return home in a wheelchair or stretcher, that none would go home disappointed. I cried out to God for them. Benny Hinn was still leading worship, moving around the stage in front of the choir. Everyone in the arena was singing. Some praying, some praying in tongues, some crying, some dancing, some clapping. It looked like God had arrived and everyone could see His Face.

Up to this point in my Christian life, I had never spoken in tongues. I wouldn't even say I was baptised in the Holy Spirit. I didn't even know what that meant. I had never heard of it.

I had my arms lifted up, singing to the bottom of my heart, eyes closed and suddenly felt a swift but gentle brush of what felt like wind softly blowing on my cheeks, then on my whole right side from the head to the legs. It felt very much like wind. Then I opened my eyes to check if there were open windows in

Chapter 8. Relocating to the UK

the area where I was. Marcia's friend was still singing, swallowed in the presence of God.

As I checked, I found that no window was open. I wondered where this wind was coming from. It was as if God allowed me a bit of time and strength to look and check so He could have me assured there was no open window to let that kind of wind in.

Then I began to sing in a strange language. I spoke words that made no sense. I went on and on, and the more I spoke these words, the more of the wind was blowing on me. The blowing became intense, and I felt my knees giving way; down I was going, helplessly so. I tried to resist, but in vain. I felt my face being gently pushed to the left side and my body slowly swaying to the left and further down I went. Tears began to roll uncontrollably down my face.

I sobbed in between the strange talking and singing. The sobbing increased and I became more and more powerless. I slumped in my chair as there was no floor to fall on. Seats were joined together, and you only had enough space for your feet. Marcia's friend noticed what was going on. By this time, I was crying loudly, talking in that strange language loudly. Ushers must have thought I was in pain, or trouble. Two of them came running to me. By this time, I was slumped in the chair, my head tilted back, floods of tears rolling down my face. God took over. I lost awareness of my surroundings. I was in another place.

I never stopped talking in this strange language. This happened when the worship was still on. The service started, Benny Hinn preached, healing time came, and people were prayed for and testimonies given. All this took place with me slumped in that chair, still talking in this strange language, praying and sobbing.

I barely heard Marcia's friend when she told the two ushers to leave me alone and said, "Can't you see God is doing something? Please leave her".

They stopped touching me and trying to get me to pull myself together. One of them stood closer to keep an eye on me.

Eventually, I 'returned' to reality, and sat up straight. By this time the service was closing. I saw nothing of it. I had to buy the video to watch at home.

No one, except those up where I was, saw what happened to me.

We were too far away from even the cameras and photographers.

No one laid hands on me. Benny Hinn was not even aware himself. So many things were happening in there and people didn't really pay much attention to everything.

God took me up there, to the last and top balcony for a purpose. He had work to do. My prayers during and after reading those little books, the hunger for more of the Holy Spirit; it seemed they were being answered.

We went out and Marcia's friend told Marcia and Mary what happened to me. Marcia and her friend were seasoned Christians, so they knew what it was. I still didn't know what it was, but I knew God had touched me. That was very clear. But the wind! I asked myself, what was that all about, that wind blowing on my right side and literally forcing me to my knees and turning my body and face to the other side? What was it? I asked myself over and over, trying to figure out what it was. The only thing I knew was, it was from God; it was supernatural.

We travelled back to London by coach and it was a six-hour journey. I sang all through the journey, just softly under my breath, making sure not to disturb other passengers.

My worship life continued to grow more serious. Lyrics came alive. They ministered to me. I sang with understanding. I bought more and more worship CDs. The Holy Spirit guided me specifically to Hillsong worship. I bought their yearly album every year from the beginning of 2002. Their worship brought a tremendous blessing to me.

My heart continued to soften. It was easy to feel touched and tears would freely and very easily fall when I prayed or worshipped.

I didn't seem to be able to control this. My heart had softened so much, and it seemed that I was closer to God and felt the presence more tangibly than before.

My desire to know more of God and fellowship with The Holy Spirit grew. I prayed more, mostly alone in my room as, at the time, I was still living in the hospital premises. I would lock myself in that tiny room whenever I got a chance or off work, read a book all day and alternate this with spontaneous prayer. My prayer time was more spontaneous than planned. I would be reading a book and listening to worship and suddenly, I would break into spontaneous prayer that could go on for any length of time, from five minutes to an hour.

I started reading and studying the Bible more for the first time ever, feeling a desire to read and know the Bible. I hadn't done this before. My Bible reading up to this time had been when I was reading a book and the author quoted a verse, or when the author recommended a certain verse or chapter. I would then read that verse fully from the Bible.

I always had been a book-reader, always. Up to this point, God used books to get me to read the Bible. It was February 2003 when I started reading the Bible from cover to cover, just three months after my encounter in the crusade back in November.

I started with the New Testament. Scripture suddenly became alive. I understood better, and it was much clearer. I loved the Bible. I wanted to read it. I had the desire to know it. I had the required discipline. I didn't only read; I studied and took notes. I began to isolate more and more. My colleagues wondered what had become of me. I would find excuses not to go out with them whenever they invited me to come with them. I loved my times with God. I looked forward to these times.

When I stepped into my tiny room, just when I unlocked and opened the door and stepped in, I would feel a wave of the presence of God come upon me and would spontaneously begin to weep, close the door quickly behind me and talk to God.

Up till this time, I hadn't known how to pray. When it comes to prayer, knowing what to say, knowing the right words and flow in prayer, I always counted myself out. I stayed as far away from it as I could. There were those people, I believed, who knew how to pray, what words to say and that I didn't have that and wasn't one of them.

These spontaneous moments of prayer cancelled all that false belief. Because I didn't consider myself to be a praying person, I wouldn't even plan a prayer time. God used these spontaneous prayer times through the Holy Spirit to bring it out of me.

Among the books I bought was The Generals series. I got my own copies of the two books I read back in SA by Benny Hinn. I bought 'Daughter of Destiny' by Jamie Buckingham. I devoured these books. I bought more and more books. Kathryn Kuhlman's 'Glimpse into Glory', 'God Can Do It Again,' 'Nothing Is Impossible with God,' 'I Believe In Miracles,' 'The Greatest Power In The World' and many more of Benny Hinn's books. I was hungry.

I remember one day, as I was in one of my times with God, reading and worshipping, I suddenly felt an urge to preach. I felt very strongly that I was being called to preach. This was in the same month of February 2003. I had never thought of myself or even imagined myself as a preacher. All my future revolved around taking care of my children, being a good mother to them, giving them a good life and bettering my career. That was it. Now this!!?? Preaching, me? No!!

That day, it came so strong upon me that I felt like climbing a mountain and shouting to the whole earth, "I am going to preach".

I really did. I didn't climb a mountain, but I had to tell someone what I just felt God was saying and how I felt so convinced that I was going to do it. I sent a text to my friend Winnie in SA.

Later, after the Benny Hinn crusade experience, I still couldn't spontaneously pray in tongues. I had no clue that the strange language I was using that night in the crusade was tongues. I became ignorant of it and no one told me as no one really listened. Marcia's friend was aware God was working in me, but she thought I spoke in tongues already.

The church had what organised retreat weekends. People would go outside London, away from the busyness to a remote quieter place from Friday evening till Sunday afternoon, seeking God, worshipping and praying. Among other things, there would be Bible teachings and ministry.

I heard a lot about the impact people get in these retreats but I never made time to go. My group leader would urge us to go.

In May 2004, I registered to attend. Again, it seemed I was just doing it to please my group leader. The thing was, I had never gone to a retreat before. I didn't have any experience with retreats and wasn't really interested in them.

We got there on Friday, early evening. We were told to avoid unnecessary disturbances and distractions with the outside world. Contact was only allowed with immediate family, and again, it was emphasised that they should be informed to avoid unnecessarily disturbing you.

This was so you could maximise time with God, give Him all your undivided attention and be in a better place to hear Him and receive what He has for you.

I did just that. My children were still in SA with my mom, so I had no concerns.

God really came. My heart was so open that everything that was done there meant a lot to me. I had a constant touch of God throughout the entire time.

Things came to a head at the Saturday evening service which was dedicated to cleansing and deliverance. This is when people are given the opportunity to forgive, renounce, confess and have soul ties broken.

After this, there would be an opportunity to be filled with The Holy Spirit. This entailed an altar call where people got prayed for individually for in-filling, on a one to one basis by the ministry team people, as everyone else would be loudly praying in tongues at the same time.

One of the ministry team ladies was praying with me. She prayed in tongues in my ear and encouraged me to pray the words that were coming to my mouth.

Nothing happened for a few minutes, then 'bang', my mouth suddenly opened and spontaneous strange words came out. At first, I was a bit guarded that I would say things that were not tongues. The longer I spoke those words, the more words I received in my spirit. I began to slowly flow.

The lady kept encouraging me and saying, "That's it, more, more, more, Lord, keep speaking, keep speaking". She was so encouraging. In a split second, it was like a bomb exploded inside of me. I began to feel more of the presence of God come upon me. As it happened, I became emotional and heard myself praying loudly in tongues, saying strange words that made no sense to me. I went louder and louder, faster and faster to a point where, for a few seconds, everyone stopped and looked to see what was happening. Then, 'bang', everyone exploded in tongues; everybody that had come for impartation of tongues exploded. The whole place was ablaze.

By this time, tears were uncontrollably rolling down my face, I was walking around as I prayed in that language, very loud, unashamedly, as if I had been doing this for years.

I felt such a wave of love envelope my heart. I loved everything. At some point, I hugged a pillar. I just felt so much love in my heart that I had never felt before.

The Preachers in the church used to now and then ask people to pray in tongues. The next time it was asked of the congregation, to my surprise, I was able to do it and not only do it, but flow.

It was since that time that I began to be able to pray or speak and even sing in tongues.

I wondered why I couldn't do this after the Benny Hinn crusade. I was still, at the most, a baby Christian. God was working and doing things in me that I didn't understand, and no one knew exactly what was happening so they couldn't help me understand.

It later became clear to me that there are two types of tongues. There is the baptism of The Holy Spirit with the evidence of speaking in tongues, like with the disciples in the Upper Room in Acts 2. This type happens only once. It evidences the baptism of The Holy Spirit. The baptism of The Holy Spirit happens only once in one's life. It's different from the gift of tongues in 1 Corinthians 12. This one is one of the nine gifts of the Holy Spirit. One gets baptised in The Holy Spirit first to receive the gift of tongues or any of the nine gifts.

It made sense now. My questions were answered. What happened in the crusade was baptism and that's why I couldn't speak in tongues as I willed, as I hadn't received the gift of tongues yet. The gifts can be given by God to whoever He chooses, at whatever time, but there must also be a conscious awareness of their existence to a believer so they can ask for them from God.

I hadn't asked for the baptism, but God chose to baptise me because this is His promise to every believer. Acts 2:38. The disciples received the gift because Jesus had said so to them.

The gift of tongues in the first book of the Corinthians is the one that comes into manifestations when we sing, pray or speak in tongues. We usually would have been baptised in The Holy Spirit before.

In this retreat, it was the norm that on the Saturday evening, delegates were led and encouraged to make a list of known unconfessed sins, and there would be a time for confessing them and then manually burning those papers in the fire outside made specifically for the purpose, to symbolise Christ's forgiveness of one's sins now and forever. I've got to say that I was so overtaken by the presence of God in this retreat that I felt I needed to have a clean slate. Once and for all. After the burning, there was ministry time and delegates were asked to come forward for more prayer for anything we still needed to give to God.

I went and was asked what it was I wanted to confess. I spoke out with tears rolling down my cheeks. I felt like I had never really confessed a certain type of sin I committed years back before I met my husband. This happened only once but I had never confessed it in the presence of anyone except God. Now that there was this opportunity, I felt deeply called to do so. Little did I know that this confession would be a thorn in my flesh for years to come.

Soon after the retreat, it came to my knowledge that there was gossip going round about what I disclosed in the retreat as advised and requested for the purposes of leaving there with a clean slate with God.

It kept increasing in intensity over the years to a point where it now sounded like I was actively indulging in the sin. I was now regarded and treated as one who was living a double life, of Christianity and sinner. Unfortunately, it kept going on to the point where Satan kept adding more flavour to it, so much so that it was now being spoken of as not just a 'normal' sin but a horrible pervasive version of it. with. It was not only shocking but hurtful to discover that people are people, no matter what position they hold or how long they have been a believer for, they can be available for the evil one to use against other believers, to bring them down. But there you go. We live in a real world with real people.

God forgave me the first time I went to Him about it, even before the confession in the retreat. I know that for sure. God truly forgives but man will hold you accountable for life, throwing it in your face every time they see you, making sure they gather as many people on their side as possible to torment you. If there is a call of God on your life and they are aware, they allow Satan to use them to try and prevent you from answering the call by constantly reminding you of what you did many years ago as if you did it yesterday or you are still doing it. It becomes a weapon or a tool to fight your progress in the Kingdom journey.

I now know that the enemy truly seeks to destroy. But I thank God that, as with Job, He won't let Satan destroy you. Nothing will, unless He permits it.

There is a saying that says, "What doesn't break you, makes you."

Satan takes advantage of things like this by using them to put obstacles in your progress on the Spiritual journey and blocks access to the door of your call.

It is important to know God for yourself, His character versus that of man. His love for you versus that of man.

You will be in a good place to not fall into the traps of Satan to overthrow you.

I want to let you know that I have since forgiven those responsible for this. I am only saying it here because I believe it will help encourage someone who may have or is currently experiencing a similar thing.

Chapter 9.
Coming Out of the Upper Room

The time of isolation, alone with God, continued for some time. I began to attend church more regularly. I developed a hunger for prayer and intercession. Up to this point, I had been praying a lot alone in my little room. I heard that there was an all-night prayer happening once a month in church. I was still fairly new, and people didn't really talk to you unless they knew you. So, I was just going to church and coming back. Fellowship was only during the group in my area which was mostly the group leader preaching on the message that was preached on Sunday. I asked someone at reception in church about it and they referred me to the church magazine which had a list of contacts at the back. I contacted the person mentioned, who was one of the leaders in the church. Despite calling many times, they never picked up. Each time I left a message and they never got back to me. I didn't give up. I was hungry. I felt like I had to take a further step than just praying alone in my room and pray with others and learn from them. I had never been a part of any prayer group or prayed in a group, for that matter. This was new. God was working fast in me.

I resorted to asking my group leader who wasn't interested in prayer at all. She had been a member for a longer time so I assumed she would know where the prayer meeting took place. My aim was to just go there, even if I couldn't speak with the leader first.

She gave me directions and times. It was Friday nights into Saturday morning. I attended that Friday. It was the end of September 2004. I got a bit lost but finally found the place. I was determined. Indeed, there was a group of people, many of whom I didn't know yet. The leader I tried to call was leading it. I didn't ask him about not responding to my messages on the phone. He didn't say anything either, but suspected he knew I was the lady who had left messages on the phone. In a way, I regretted having done that as it felt like my attempts and hunger to attend the prayer meeting were taken out of context, as if I was pursuing the Pastor, not really the prayer meeting. The experience of how my confession in the retreat was handled got the better of me.

The prayer went on till morning. This was my very first time with all-night prayer, except the one I went to with Mr Sako and his team back home in 1990. That time I was asked to attend. This time the Holy Spirit Himself got me to attend.

It was a good experience, with people praying in tongues and singing, and doing all kinds of prayers and praying for different things.

I learnt a lot that night.

A week later, we heard that the prayer meeting couldn't continue in there any longer as the venue was taken away from the church. The prayer was moved to another location the following month, October. All-night prayer was happening only once a month at the end of the month.

I didn't know the area it had moved to. Another issue occurred. I had to find out where they were meeting. I called the main church line and the receptionist told me where they would be and gave me an address. It was not far from the church.

I would become a regular participant from that September of 2004 to around 2011.

I grew way so much in the area of prayer. I began to have confidence to even lead it.

In February 2005, I enrolled into what was a course to train small group leaders. It took two sets of 10 weeks each. The course went on till Summer of that year. Then there was another 10-week course for the purposes of learning about the importance of being set free from issues of life that people can carry from childhood into adulthood and have them removed by prayer and deliverance. This was to give people an extended opportunity to become aware of issues in their lives that had not been addressed and were posing a hindrance to their walk with God. It was conducted in a group setting, once a week over 10 weeks, at the end of which there was a weekend away, the same as the encounter weekend, to give participants a chance for them to receive one-to-one ministry and more intense time of prayer, breaking bondages and getting a fresh infilling with The Holy Spirit.

The church location was near where London's yearly carnival festival takes place. I mentioned this briefly in the previous chapter when I spoke about how Marcia first took me there. It was during the month of August, the month of the celebration by the descendants of the West Indies' immigrants for winning the battle against segregation and inequality.

The whole church gets mobilised to participate in outreach, reaching out to the lost during this weekend of celebration as multitudes go past the front doors of the church.

A lady who had been in the church much longer and always participated in these special outreach events invited me to join. I signed up and participated that year. I quite enjoyed it but the way they did evangelism was a bit daunting to me as it entailed approaching strangers and not only to offer them a Gospel tract but speak to them about God and share the Gospel.

The first time, I just hid behind my friend or just silently extended my hand to people and offered them the tract.

After the event, I was contacted by someone in the church evangelism team who invited me to their regular weekly evangelism time on Saturday afternoons. I responded and my lady friend was a participant in that team.

I took part in this now and then. I couldn't do every Saturday as I was working some Saturdays.

My adventure with God continued. I began to feel led to know more about aspects of God and Christianity. First, it was worship. I collected resources, books, CDs, tapes; you name it. As I did, I found that my knowledge in this area grew more. I was then led to explore prayer. In the same way, I collected resources on prayer, intercession etc. I bought Cindy Jacobs's 'Possessing the Gates'. It set me on fire on prayer and opened my spiritual eyes about types of prayer. I bought my first Generals book, the one about Kathryn Kuhlman and Smith Wigglesworth. These two were the ones Benny Hinn had spoken a lot about. They were the first people I wanted to read about. I went on to buy some more books by the same authors, such as Kathryn Kuhlman and Smith Wigglesworth which I bought when still in SA. I was drawn to books.

I was also led to explore healing and deliverance. I continued to collect resources for this ministry and felt very much drawn to it, maybe because my childhood was filled with illness and poor health.

I experienced deliverance from those strange attacks and got helped by Mr Sako and his team.

As I explored and searched for more resources, I came across Francis MacNutt's book, 'Deliverance from Evil Spirits'. My eyes bulged when I read this book. I felt a huge hunger to know more in this area. I ordered an entire conference pack, a set of cassette tapes and videos. The conference had happened in 1988. I didn't care. I found these materials very interesting and powerful. I gained a better understanding of some things that I experienced during the time of the spiritual attacks I'd had. Since the time I read Benny Hinn's book back in SA, my desire for worship had been constant and I would always be singing and worshipping.

Chapter 9. Coming out of the Upper Room

In the summer of 2004, I got my children to visit. That time it was still easy to get visitors from abroad. This was just a couple of weeks after the powerful time I had at the encounter weekend.

I took them around some parts of the city, just to see London. One day, I was travelling with them to the London Eye on a train to Waterloo. We found our seats and sat opposite a man who was travelling with a small girl of about 6-7 years of age. We sat facing each other, my children and I on one side and him and the girl on the other. I had worship music on as usual with one earphone inside my ear and I had the other out as I was travelling with my children and needed to talk to them on the way as I showed them things in the city.

I had no idea how worship places your heart so connected to the Holy Spirit that you carry the presence of God wherever you are when you are constantly worshipping.

Suddenly, the man began to cough. The cough was an irritation kind of cough and nothing was coming out. It seemed to be more of an effort to dislodge an object that was in his airway. The coughing became worse and worse. He started to clutch at his throat. The little girl was beginning to be afraid and I guess thinking that he was dying.

I had no idea at the time what was happening. I stood up and tried to offer him water to drink to try and moisten his throat with the hope whatever it was would get dissolved or dislodged.

The closer I got to him, the worse it got. When I spoke to him and asked him to drink the water, he gave one last bout of cough, and his eyes were now watery and bulging out in distress.

It stopped.

He kept looking at me in a very strange way. The look was more like blaming me for that ordeal. I couldn't understand why he would blame me. I didn't do anything to him except try to offer him water. He grabbed hold of the little girl and moved further to the far corner of the seat, avoiding looking in our direction. It was strange. I didn't understand his behaviour.

At the next station, he took hold of the girl's hand and off they went out of the train.

I was puzzled by his behaviour. He totally acted as if he was terrified of me, as if I caused what happened to him.

I kept asking God why, what is this? By this time, I was very close to God. He said in a very audible but soundless voice, "How ignorant are you?

Yes, you caused it. Don't you realise the presence you carry? No demon or evil spirit can withstand it; they will have to leave".

That was my first lesson and realisation that when you put your heart and soul into constant worship and prayer, learning more about God, searching His scriptures regularly, you become filled with His presence and you carry it with you everywhere you go. Only God chooses to use it however it's needed and however He desires.

Random manifestations of all kinds started to happen without me praying for people.

People seemed to be convicted when in my presence. One Saturday at work in 2003, a lady who was working with me that day, told me she was going to take a 5-minute break for a cigarette and went on to apologise and said she felt evil and unclean for smoking. I had never said anything before about smoking at all. I wondered where this was coming from! I reassured her and said it was ok, she mustn't feel so bad, that I have no problem with people who smoke. I know it sounds like I was compromising but what do you say when the Holy Spirit has gone before you!!?

I never spoke about my faith or even church as it was not allowed at work. Despite this, everyone just knew that I was a Christian. Every Christmas, the organisation would have all employees go for Christmas lunch and managers would agree a time and venue. In 2003, it was the London Dungeon. I didn't know what it was, as I had never been there before. When my line manager asked me to come, one of my colleagues said, "Oh, no, Sarah won't go to the Dungeon, she's a Christian." I wondered what this place was like; why wouldn't Christians go?

A recent testimony:

I am involved in mental health

One time got to see a lady who was seeking help with what was troubling her.

I asked her why she is here and how we can help her.

The lady started to make jerking body movements as she tried to explain to me why she was here. Her body jerked in a way that appeared to be like it was being pushed forward from the back by a powerful force.

She then looked at me and said, "This. This is the reason I am here." I was a little confused, but I knew she was referring to the jerks. I just didn't understand. She went on to say, a 'force' came into her room one night, three days ago and that since then, she had begun to experience weird things. Among the things she mentioned was that she never felt suicidal in the past but that since this 'force' came into her room, she had been feeling like doing something harmful to herself.

As she was talking, the jerking movements became more frequent and more forceful and it seemed she couldn't stop them voluntarily.

I looked straight in her eyes and our eyes locked and held for a few seconds. Then, my intuition led me to realise this was not a case of mental health but of demonic attack.

You see, it's all in the eyes. Eyes are windows to one's soul. Demonic entities reside in the soul and when they operate through a person, they can be seen or detected through the person's eyes.

As soon as I felt that way, I began to say, "Come out of her in the Name of Jesus." My voice was barely audible as I was wearing a mask and speaking in a whisper making sure I don't scare her.

As I said, "Come out in the Name of Jesus," the jerking movements increased.

I felt compelled to help this lady and I took a chance but bore in mind to be tactful about it.

As soon as I said the words, "Come out in the Name of Jesus", even though no one could hear them as I just literally whispered them she said, "Yes, that's it, Jesus, say that again please, don't stop." I got a little encouraged and continued to say "Jesus" over and over and then suddenly the situation changed.

I found myself face to face with demonic forces that had come into this poor woman. She began to go into gross demonic manifestations, voice changing into shrieks and groans, screams, hands clawing towards me, mouth and lips forming into a snarl like a dog, spewing obscenities at me in a soft tone of voice but words filled with sheer hatred, a kind of hatred that penetrates your entire inner being, eyes rolling back and only the white part visible and her whole body jerking like it was put under electric shock. Very scary.

I started to cast under my breath.

For a few seconds, I felt scared and intimidated by these demons. Remember, our eyes were locked the whole time. I quickly realised that if I allowed myself to be intimidated, I would lose my faith in God and I would be in danger of severe attack from the demons. Demons can sense fear in you, and they will know if you are geared and well-equipped to kick them out. They operate by intimidation. Whatever you do, don't you ever allow fear to come into you, no matter how fierce the manifestations are.

I went in now feeling a holy anger against these demonic spirits, and a surge of faith came upon me. I discerned spirits of death over her and as soon as I said, "You spirits of death come out of her", it got worse. I had seen manifestations of all kinds before but nothing like this ever. She was snarling, hands and nails clawed, body and face contorted like some animal, and she made different sounds in different tones of voice. One minute she was shrieking in a high-pitched female voice, and the next, she was screaming, then she was growling like an animal and with clenched teeth, spewing obscenities at me as I prayed.

This was a clear demonic issue. This was remarkable; demons just literally taking over someone and clearly changing features and countenance and behaviour and then changing back into their usual self in front of you!!

She was coming in and out of this state. Sometimes she was crying, meek and begging me to say 'Jesus' and when I asked her to say Jesus herself, she would say it a few times and then the demons would surface and take over again.

It went on for some time till she slumped on the bed, sobbing and all manifestations were gone.

God seemed to have taken over the situation. Doesn't God have a sense of humour?!!

He sure does.

I learnt later that she had mentioned that she was looking for a priest as she was having a 'kundalini awakening'.

I didn't know what this was till that day. I searched for it on Google and learnt that it is to do with the yoga meditation stuff and heavily connected to Hinduism. This happens when someone gets involved in these spiritual meditation techniques and summons certain 'gods' and spirits to dwell in them in seeking peace and a renewed sense of control in their souls.

This kundalini, I discovered, is a serpent spirit that gets into someone and fits itself along their spine, hence the jerking movements she was displaying.

She unknowingly sold her soul in exchange for what she deemed peace and inner stability. Now the god that she summoned had come into her and taken control of her whole body and soul.

It is so amazing how the demons reacted to the mention of Jesus, even when I just whispered it. Believers, we carry so much power and we are not aware of it. The Name of Jesus is powerful, just as the Bible tells us.

My hunger to explore further in this area grew more and more. I bought a book by Carlos Anacondia, an Argentinian man who moved powerfully in deliverance in his city. It was in the early 80s.

God raised him from a business background to use him to deliver the people of Argentina, especially in the squatter camps, which were filled with all sorts of demonic forces and things. That was the issue there at that given time.

This book added to what I studied from MacNutt's resources.

I talked about these things to every Christian I met, trying to make them see how God has more for us, not only to go to church on Sunday, sing and hear a short preaching, tick the box and leave and wait for the next Sunday. There is more.

There was a lady at work who was from Brazil. She was the only person who seemed to know what I was talking about. She knew about deliverance from her home country. I didn't know much before I came to the UK, except that Mr Sako and his team tried their best to have me delivered that time but I never manifested or anything. They seemed to have assumed that I had some demons that needed to be cast out and they tried to cast them out every evening during those two weeks I stayed with them with no outward obvious manifestations coming from me. I believe, in my case, it was a matter of oppression as opposed to possession. Oppression is when evil spirits harass you from the outside, whereas possession is when they have an evil presence residing inside you, either fully, or in a part of your body. With possession, there are always outward manifestations as the spirits leave. With oppression, they are already outside still looking for an opportunity to come in.

It was during this time, when I read and explored more in this area with these materials, that I got to know the different ways evil spirits work. It's not that everybody is inhabited with evil spirits. In some cases, it's a matter of being oppressed by them. That is, they come upon you and oppress you. They work from the outside, hence, when people cast them out, the person doesn't manifest.

At times, and commonly speaking, evil spirits do gain access into someone's body or part of their body and then, when they get cast out, the person is likely to manifest and show some signs of them getting out.

In my case, it was a matter of getting me stronger so I could resist them when they came to oppress and harass me. I didn't have them inside me or any part of my body.

I needed ways of prayer for myself, knowledge of particular relevant scriptures to quote and base my prayer on, and strength to tell them to leave. Once that was accomplished, they stopped harassing and oppressing me and the same is correct to date.

This type is easy as they are on the outside.

My Brazilian colleague was in a Brazilian church and they tended to invite guest speakers from Brazil or Portugal as they spoke Portuguese.

She told me that the ministry of deliverance was very common and popular in Brazil. We didn't have a lot of it in SA then. If it was there, I guess I didn't get exposed to it.

In September of 2004, they were being visited by such a person from their country. She spoke very highly of him and said I needed to come and see what happened when he prayed.

My hunger to witness this grew more. At the same time, I was a bit scared that I didn't know what was in me for sure; what if I had a demon somewhere and I went to this service and I manifested?? What would my colleague think of me? I was still a bit immature spiritually.

The desire to see this for the first time, on a larger scale than the one I saw in the train, grew more than the concern of me having a demon and manifesting.

The service began, and the church pastor gave the guest the platform. He preached in Portuguese and a young lady sat next to me to translate. I didn't get much that day. I was just waiting for the ministry time.

And then it began. They asked everyone to stand up, leave their chair and stand against the wall, leaving a large vacant area in the middle. All chairs were packed away.

He began to pray as he saw by the Spirit what to call out and cast among the people.

I got really scared. What if I manifest?? I could tell that lots of people seemed to be a bit worried too.

He continued to call out and cast and one by one, people began to manifest. It was beginning to look scary but interesting at the same time, as what I read in those materials was becoming a reality.

People were falling on the ground without him touching them, rolling, screaming, foaming at the mouths vomiting, coughing and kicking out.

There was a younger guy who was more interesting. He began to growl like a lion. His face changed and his features became distorted. His head was half-bowed as if to hide his eyes. He began to walk towards the man with hands outstretched and fingers clawed as if to grab the man by his throat. He continued to charge towards the man, as he growled. His demeanour was very threatening and frightening. He sounded and looked like an animal. You couldn't see his eyes properly as he had his head slightly bowed. His neck was slightly twisted to the side in a contorted manner.

This was real. I had my hand on my mouth with amazement. My colleague kept glancing at me and smiling. Everyone who wasn't dealing with their own demons was now watching.

It grew more intense. The manifesting guy was fast approaching the man, so the man was praying more intensely and commanding those demons to come out.

When the preacher took a step to meet the approaching guy, the guy began to retreat. The man prayed more. The more he prayed, the more the guy stepped back, away from him. The guy seemed to be in some sort of trance. He began to turn around and round. By this time, the preacher was taking control more. He went for his face which he seemed to be trying to hide. He was going around trying to avoid eye contact with the preacher.

I was going around the hall behind the preacher at a distance, trying to see what he did, how he prayed and so on. It was very interesting.

Whenever the preacher got his eyes locked with the guy's, the guy would try to grab him by his throat. The preacher would duck a little but intensify his prayer.

I got a glimpse of the guy's eyes. They seemed to have rolled upward, where only the whites could be seen. His face was contorted as if he was in pain.

After a while of that drama going on, the guy gave a loud cry and began to sob like a human being. The growling stopped. His face became normal. He wept like a baby and slumped onto the floor and went limp.

The preacher knelt beside him and continued to pray. The guy stretched out his arms and hugged the preacher. He couldn't stop crying. He was totally delivered.

By this time, all the people who were manifesting were all delivered without anyone touching or praying for them individually.

It was amazing!!

This was all new to me.

My colleague had been reading Watchman books over the years and she was still reading them. She saw my hunger to know more of God and introduced Watchman to me. She started lending me some of her books, and one by one, I devoured them. They were full of deep revelations of scriptures I had never heard of or found anywhere. This was between 2005 and 2009.

The first one she gave me was 'The Messenger of the Cross'. It brought a whole new understanding about the Cross, it's work, purpose and meaning. I must have read this booklet five times. Then I went and bought my own copy. I began to search for more books by Watchman.

>Among them:
>Latent Power of the Soul
>The Character of the Lord's Worker
>The Release of the Spirit
>Spiritual Authority
>Sit Walk Stand
>The Normal Christian Life
>Spiritual Man
>Salvation of the Soul
>The Word of the Cross
>A Balanced Christian Life
>Secrets to Spiritual Power

In those years, whenever I stepped into a Christian bookshop, the first thing I looked for was the name Watchman Nee.

It was around April of 2005 that I noticed that I had become an undesirable being to some humans. I didn't know exactly what it was I had done but it increased over the following years.

It was just things like constant put-downs, sarcasm, ridicule, belittlements, sometimes even mere insults, pure hatred, slander, mistreatments, injustices, you name it, it came.

It was really becoming a bit unbearable. Given that I had just entered a divine realm with God, there was no turning back. I had found God and He had found me. I still was an immature believer to a greater extent, and unfortunately, my deep hunger for more of God, my searching for materials to resource my knowledge, my discoveries of God's power to heal and deliver, my depth of worship in spirit and truth and deep desire to pray had all made it obvious, to some people who had walked with God longer than me and maybe knew Him better than me, that there was something in me more than just an ordinary believer. The call of God upon my life had been noticed and it didn't take long before the enemy stepped in trying to kill it before it went anywhere.

You see, God uses people and Satan also uses people. Many times, both God and Satan use the same people for their purposes. God will use someone very powerfully for the work of the Kingdom, and the person will succeed and bear fruits, beautiful fruits. But the same person can be entered by Satan at a given time, or even multiple given times, through their weaknesses in areas such as hatred, jealousy, envy, fear of losing out and someone else taking over etc.

They can see the hand of God on someone who is still immature spiritually, who may not even be fully aware of what God is doing in their own life. This mature person, who may even have some authority, will quickly see this and because of the things we just mentioned above, they allow Satan to use them as an instrument to kill that which God is doing in this other person's life.

I mentioned that I was growing faster in the many aspects of Christianity with God, but I was immature in dealing with the enemy. I had never been exposed to such attacks. My view of Christianity was pure, perfect love of God in everyone's heart and desiring goodness for each one of us. I never thought that opposition could come from another believer, let alone authority figures.

It was plain shock, and I had to say, it derailed me. Because I couldn't stand by myself, I was not strong enough in the knowledge of warfare, not even associating warfare as part of a Christian's life. I had just discovered God, and I was happy and in my immature opinion, life was now going well. I thought the journey was going to be smooth.

It was as if God had allowed this to happen so I could have my eyes open before the worst came and I got shut forever.

I tended to look up to people for encouragement, assurance and sometimes even commendations, to be sure I was doing well and was heading in the right direction.

This was something that Satan aimed at. He seemed to know this part of me and dwelt on it for years. He made sure that those from whom I expected to get these, would withhold them from me, and not only withhold them from me but throw attacks, as mentioned above.

I learnt that it hurts more when those from whom you expected certain good things seem to be the ones being used to do the direct opposite.

I believe that I needed assurance, and somehow, feedback about what God was doing in my life. I guess I expected or thought that in Christianity, those who had gone before you and knew better would help you along the way; they would guide, reassure and tell you to carry on if you are going in the right direction. I learnt this at school and my mother was a good encourager.

I thought everybody was like that. It was a wake-up call. I began to hurt. These constant attacks were taking their toll on me.

But a believer should not rely on people for commendations, affirmations, assurance or even guidance. Yes, as human beings, we are inclined to live life this way. We are humans and humans always need other humans to live life. It doesn't always go this way. It is good to have someone by your side who believes in you, tells you how to go about things, helps you to make good changes and adjustments in a loving way, who sees what is happening in your life, even the things that are hidden from you. This person can come and make you aware and when they realised you have a blind spot to certain things that will later deter your journey with God, would be loving enough to make you aware and help you sort it out.

I didn't have such a person. And God knew. He was going to do it Himself, His own way.

It was as if God knew that I was naturally inclined to rely on and look up to man for help, and He being a jealous God, He caused this to be withheld from me so that I would be forced to look up to Him for everything. This was vital for my faith in Him. If man was always there for me, my faith in God would have been very little and my need for Him even less.

I have to say that, as of writing this, I have totally been delivered from the hurt. I totally forgave and I love everybody. Even you, the reader.

This was made possible when slowly God showed me that He allowed it and the purpose of why He allowed it; to make me aware of Satan's existence, his aim to thwart the work of God and to stop His people from advancing it.

Where He was taking me was going to attract a lot of the enemy's oppositions and attacks, and He knew that the sooner He opened my eyes to it, the better. The instruments used were not a big issue in all this, they were just available.

One day, around the end of 2006, I met a lady I had never seen before. She had come out to evangelise with us that Saturday afternoon. As we were walking back to church, we began to chat. One thing led to another and we started talking about healing and deliverance, how it is important for all believers to get a deeper level of ministry in these areas.

She then told me about how, in the last year, she had been helped with her childhood issues, whereby she hadn't forgiven her father who left the family when she was still very little. She stated that she had discovered that she struggled with seeing God as a father. She said her relationship with God was rather distant and she was unable to connect fully with Him due to the desertion she experienced by her own earthly father. She stated that she loved God and she believed in Him, but just couldn't fully open to Him and that she had trust issues.

Chapter 9. Coming out of the Upper Room

She told me she heard of a place in the UK, Ellel International Ministries, which specialises in healing and deliverance. She informed me that she had booked into their retreat and got some real help. She told me it's not just being prayed for and delivered but also teaching and empowerment.

My ears pricked up and I felt I needed this time of ministry and this empowerment, especially around warfare.

I told her I needed to attend this type of retreat.

She then said they had a yearly magazine with a programme where I could attend courses they run and also retreat dates to book myself.

She agreed to bring me the magazine the next time she came to church.

She did, and although it was for the previous year, I then had their contact number. I called the office and inquired about the next retreat and how I could attend. I was given the necessary information and told I needed to apply in writing, give a detailed description of my needs and the reasons why I need healing and deliverance.

I didn't waste time. I sent in my application by October 2006. I was told that it could take up to six months to get confirmation of my attendance as it was free, even for three whole days, with extensive personal ministry where a person is allocated three counsellors over the three days. Board and lodging were also offered free. As a result, they were getting a whole lot of applications and the waiting list was long.

It did take six months.

I was accepted in May 2007. I also enrolled in one of their short courses at the end of January 2007, in one of their branches in Lancashire. For short courses, there was a fee to pay. I attended with one of my friends from church. She didn't really like it but I found it very helpful. It was just not what she needed, I guess. The course was about teaching and ministry on Acceptance and Belonging. This was very good. It helped me differentiate between the unconditional love of God versus the conditional love of man. Man can dislike or even hate you and reject you, even those who profess to be at the forefront of service in ministry. People's love and acceptance tends to depend on what they do for them. God is different. He is the same yesterday, today and tomorrow. He changes not. He has loved you enough to save you when you didn't deserve it; He accepted you into His family and that will never change. Your doing or not doing things for Him won't change His love for you.

Just because those who may be representing Him are behaving in certain ways doesn't mean God is doing it.

I had difficulty separating God from man, especially if the person was an authority figure.

This is where I was at the time.

My turn came and I attended the retreat in the East Sussex branch at Glyndley Manor.

The format of ministry was writing down in advance what were your prayer needs, areas of ministry needs in your life, and anything else that came to mind. This was sent around the time of application. The reason for this was that the ministers allocated to you would have a look beforehand and start to pray for you accordingly.

When you came to the retreat, prayer would have been going on for months.

The main sections covered were confession of sins you had committed, knowingly and unknowingly, then renouncing sinful acts and things you had got involved in knowingly and unknowingly. Then it covered forgiving those who had sinned against you, one by one, where possible and most desirably, mentioning them by name and telling God you had chosen to forgive and release them. Then, soul ties were broken, first by you with your mouth, cutting ties off with those you may have formed unhealthy relationships with and those who had sinned against you.

Then ministers concluded it by tearing down those ties once and for all in prayer. The last step was a fresh infilling of the Holy Spirit, now that you were free.

It was very powerful.

If need be, with your ministers' discretion and how you felt things had gone, you were allowed another one to one session, a couple of months or so later with one counsellor. There may be more than one session, depending on the need.

I had one such session after three months. What happened in there was amazing. I just sat down opposite my counsellor. They asked me how things had been since the retreat, and the conversation went on for ten or so minutes. Then, I felt like something was breaking inside of me and I spontaneously began to cry. I cried so hard, so much. I sobbed and sobbed and sobbed for what seemed ages. The counsellor just kept praying softly, barely audible. I cried. I never ever cried like that before. It was needed. Something indeed broke and I was completely free after this. The sobbing stopped. I heaved a sigh of relief. I was relieved. I lay there on the floor for almost two hours. The lady just left me there. She knew what God was doing. She'd seen this before in her work as a counsellor. She just kept an eye on me. It was needed.

Something new began to happen in my life. I got to a place where I was getting messages from God mostly in dreams and sometimes through the still small voice. My spiritual sensitivity became very heightened.

I began to write these down. I have two notebooks full of these. At times, He would talk when I was praying, or listening to worship, or worshipping in a church service or reading the Bible or reading a book.

Some of these have come to pass; some are yet to come, good ones and the not so good ones.

I had, and still have, a heightened sense of knowing. My intuition is very sharp. I am an empath. Naturally, empaths are gifted in intuition, a clear sense of just knowing, an ability to see hidden things in people and places. They have an ability to sense what's going on in an environment or situation and an ability to tell if someone is happy or sad, no matter how hard they try to conceal their feelings.

I can tell good from bad by just entering a room or a place. I can tell good from bad by talking to someone for less than 5 minutes. I can sense good or bad or just have knowledge about a person, not everything about them but as God permits it, by meeting them or being next to me, sometimes by just looking at them.

I pick up very quickly, in any conversation, things that the other person is not verbally saying but thinking about.

This takes me back to my childhood at age 2 (if you remember in the first few chapters in this book), where I mentioned that my mother's best friend had to leave as I sensed something not good that seemed to be associated with her dress. It could have not been the dress itself but maybe something she had on her body or somewhere. Whatever it was, it was evil, and I picked it up with my spirit. As a 2-year-old, I just cried and kept glancing at her in a frightened way and clinging to my mother, running away from the woman. It grew very intense, to the point where the two women couldn't pretend any longer and the friend opted to leave.

One of these significant times was while I was at Glyndley Manor for the three-week course. We used to have longer lunch breaks when we would take walks in the beautiful countryside. I made friends with an older lady there who was retired. We used to talk and share stories. We identified with each other about a lot of things we had experienced. We took these walks every day and would ask each other how things were going, how we were finding it here and how God was coming through for us.

The route of the walk entailed tiny little footpaths in bushy parts of the surroundings which would open out onto fields of green crops and a gravel road that went all round to the main gate of the centre.

It was so peaceful and beautiful.

That year, 2007, we had a very warm autumn.

One afternoon, we took our walk as usual and got to the footpath in the bushes. It was so tiny that we wouldn't be able to walk side by side. One had to walk in front while the other followed behind. I was in front. When we got to the middle of the footpath, my right foot had been raised ready to step onto the ground to walk forward, and suddenly my spirit said, "Look!" I held my foot for a few seconds in the air and I saw it. A brownish, thin but long snake coiled up right in the middle of the path facing me, just a step away from where I was. It had its head sticking up and the whole part of it coiled up in a heap. The position was that of readiness to strike. A step away. Had the Holy Spirit not told me to stop and got me to hold my foot in the air, I would have placed my foot right on its head, and God knows what would have happened.

I didn't scream. My African village upbringing came in handy.

I just gasped. My friend had to stop behind me, and she asked what the matter was as she couldn't see what I was looking at.

I couldn't talk but just pointed and immediately, as I looked properly, I locked eyes with the creature and it quickly uncoiled and fled into the thick forest. That's when my friend saw it. It had the colour of the soil on the path and this made it hard to see. It was the Holy Spirit that saved me.

I was shaken but I managed to compose myself and we proceeded. We quickly put our experience behind us and continued chatting and enjoying the beautiful scenery. We got onto the gravel road that was surrounded by fields. The whole area was green and so serene.

We approached the entrance of the centre and suddenly I heard the still small voice saying to me, "So and so (Name withheld) has set out to destroy you".

There was no further message, explanation or advice as to what to do now. Nothing. Just like that. I quickly stopped my friend and told her what I felt God was saying. We trusted each other so much. We confided in each other. She became a true friend to me, at least during that time we were there. She was English and from Cornwall, and much older than me at the time.

She said to me, "Sarah, that's a warning; don't take it lightly". I said to her, "What am I supposed to do now to stop this from happening?" because for a few years now, the individual in question had started behaving in not so very nice ways to me and it was really getting a bit worse, but never to the point where I could say they were aimed at destroying me.

You must understand that it wasn't them wanting to destroy me, but the enemy wanting to destroy what God had placed in me. They were just an available instrument to him. At the time, I was immature, and took things literally.

My friend said to me, "Ask God; ask Him, and He will clarify to you and tell you what you are to do." I tried to ask God so many times, but it didn't seem He was answering. Then, one day, long after the course was finished and we had all left and returned to our homes, I was taken to the day of the walk in my mind and re-lived the moment I nearly stepped right on top of a snake's head. I went over the whole scenario, where I heard the warning from the Holy Spirit, and held my foot in the air long enough to be able to avoid stepping onto it, to the minute I locked eyes with the creature, and it fled. God said to me, "That's the answer; that's what the enemy is going to do. He will eventually realise you have seen him and will flee, but not without a fight first".

This was still 2007. Little did I know that I still had more than a decade to battle with the enemy. God brought this verse to my mind: "But, beloved, do not forget this one thing; that with the Lord, one day is as a thousand years, and a thousand years as one day". 2. Peter 3:8

You see, when God speaks, it sounds and feels like it's going to happen right now or tomorrow, or the next year, but in most cases, it's after years and years. It's always a test of our faith, to know that if He said so, it is so. Wanting to know more than what He has told you or pushing to know in detail is a waste of time and energy, as He often speaks in part and in parables.

Faith helps, because even when you don't fully understand, at least you know He said something and you can cling on that as a promise, knowing He will never fail you, nor forsake you.

You, see, many times, the gifts of God are in us from birth just waiting to be fully activated and utilised properly when we are born again and receive the Holy Spirit. Oftentimes, there are hindrances to the proper operation of these gifts due to unresolved issues in our lives or warfare.

I began to realise that God was constantly talking to me, giving me messages, sometimes even warnings.

Back to my retreat. It was indeed as the lady told me. I was allocated three counsellors. Over the three days, I received teaching around childhood issues, inherited sins, unforgiveness, renouncement, confession, the unconditional love of God, heart issues, generational sins and curses, trauma and a lot more.

I received prayer in all these areas, and on Saturday, that was when the main work was carried out. This was where you dealt with issues that had come to hinder your relationship with God. You referred to your previously written list of your life story and issues as you could remember, and one by one, you were guided to take them to God.

Ministry starts from conception. If the counsellors sensed that, according to your story or issues, it seems problems began in conception, you start there.

It was intense but much-needed.

You were led to a fresh infilling of the Holy Spirit at the end of the retreat.

I was so impacted that I went back later that year, in September/October, to do a concentrated course that ran for three weeks. It was a stay-in course.

You get a certificate with this one and could minister to others.

In 2008, I learnt that in another branch in Pierrepont in Surrey, they run three sets of courses that equip people to fully minister healing and deliverance to others. I felt very much called to do this.

I inquired and got through. I was given the grace to skip the first set and begin with the second set, as I had already completed the three-week course in Glyndley Manor.

Each set comprised of three months' duration and one full weekend attendance each month.

I completed that by the end of 2008 and applied to be part of their ministry team to help with retreats and every event that required ministers for praying for attendees.

I was registered as a Christian Counsellor with the UK Association of Counsellors.

I would get invitations to come and participate in various events, including the one in partnership with Premier Radio. I had one of those in Westminster Central Methodist Hall in October 2009.

I was much better now, able to help others, even though healing is an on-going process. You don't usually get completely healed and get rid of issues or habits, but you gain knowledge and awareness, empowerment to deal with things and gain wisdom and understanding and ability to fight.

My first retreat as a prayer minister was a bit daunting, but God was faithful. I was the third minister and most third ministers were still shadowing and observing.

Chapter 9. Coming out of the Upper Room

Most of the candidates at these retreats are Christians who are in churches and feel like they are burdened by whatever things in their lives are unresolved and creating problems with their Christian walk.

We had one such person in our team, and on Saturday, during the actual ministry time, they began to manifest. They had traumatic childhood experiences and were exposed to dark deeds and activities of evil as a child.

They were having flashbacks and often being attacked by demonic beings in their house.

They had to confess, renounce, forgive and have a breaking of soul ties and then receive healing and get a fresh infilling of the Holy Spirit.

It was in the middle of this process when they needed to renounce the demonic strongholds. Their head slid back, eyes tightly closed, the face began to contort, and the body was twisting in what looked like a painful way. they began to make noises and we started to pray. The lady who was our lead minister in the team seemed to be struggling as this was getting out of hand. I wanted to cast out as I felt led, but I felt I had to respect the leader. It was at some point when the situation was really getting worse and none of the experienced ministers seemed to be getting a hold on it that I jumped in. I too didn't really know much and didn't follow a set pattern or way but just cast out as I felt led in my spirit, and the war began. The more the casting, the more the manifesting. We pressed in and realised that their eyes were closed, and I went for them. I commanded 'the candidate' to open their eyes. They couldn't at first as the spirits wouldn't let them do it. We pressed in and they slowly opened them, but they were turned inside. Only the whites could be seen.

We pressed in more and commanded the candidate to fight this thing too. We got them to say the name "Jesus" over and over. I knew that demons couldn't say this name. They struggled at first too, but slowly and barely audibly, they said it. Just a mere whisper in the beginning.

It was getting better and better till the stiffness and contortions were being loosened and they were now saying the name bolder and clearer. As they did, their head came back to the normal position, their eyes returned and there they were, set free and delivered.

They were so thankful. They said that they knew there was stuff in them, but no one could help them. They had been to various retreats and many healing sessions and services but to no avail. They loved God but knew they needed deliverance to clean up the stuff within them.

Later on, as we all got together to reflect and pray to thank God, the lead minister confessed and said it was good that I was there as I seemed to know what to do. She said in all her years as a prayer minister she had never come across anything like this. She was honest and said she wouldn't have known how to go about helping the candidate in that situation. Both confessed the same thing.

It was as if God was trying to show me or communicate to me that this was the type of healing, He had bestowed upon me and that He would like me to help His people. Honestly speaking, I didn't really know what to do but just followed the promptings of the Holy Spirit.

Chapter 10.
Getting the Human Soul Saved

The Holy Spirit enlightened me along the way that, just as I needed healing and deliverance from all sorts of things, everyone needs that same touch. People often come to church because they need a touch from God, especially the ones who did not grow up in church, whose parents were not believers.

For those whose parents were believers and often took them to church all their lives, it can be that their continuing with church is a part of their lives as that would have been the only thing they knew.

Others, like me, whose life experiences had a negative impact on their lives, often turn to God as a perceived source of help, as the one who hold all the answers.

The picture of church with these types of people can be like a heavenly place where there are no hardships, no hurts, no ill-treatments, no favouritism, not even racial segregation, so to speak, no opposition or any negative thing that can befall anybody in life.

What we often forget is that many are those who came in looking for answers from God, seeking for His healing hand, His unconditional love and acceptance. Now, when a place is full of people who are hurting or needing help in some way, with no one among them to help anyone because everyone is looking for help, it can be a dodgy place to be.

Many people have experienced traumatic events in their lives, be it in childhood or in adulthood. Their personalities are often shaped by these events, especially if these happened in their early life. They learn to protect themselves, and they develop defences that aren't healthy. Oftentimes, they shy away from people, perceiving them to be potentially dangerous. They know they need love and acceptance, but they never learnt how to receive it or, at times, even how to give it. They tend to send wrong messages without awareness of their behaviour, then they are surprised when others respond to them in certain unpleasant ways. They just don't know. They need help. Sometimes they don't even know they need help, as for some of them, life has always been like that.

The way they process information may be different. They may hear something different from what was said. Their interpretation of words or phrases may be different too. They get easily hurt. They become very sensitive and have trust issues. This is due to betrayal by those they may have trusted, especially if it happened in childhood.

These people would still be very carnal in some of the ways they live. They would have very minimal knowledge of who God is, and minimal knowledge of who they are in Christ. The way they deal with things would still be very much like those outside. They have real needs. During all this, they accidentally, unintentionally, trample on one another's toes, hurting one another, afflicting one another, mostly not because they choose to do so, but through lack of self-awareness and their own unresolved life issues.

This then gives out a negative experience to new ones who come in for the same reasons. They expected to find heaven on earth and church life as being like paradise, only to be met with the opposite.

Through immature eyes and unrealistic beliefs around how church people should be, they wrongfully liken God to church people and authority figures. This tends to mislead them in how they perceive God and this can create resentment towards not only the church but God Himself, feeling like He doesn't do what He says He will do, or He is not that which He said He was in the Bible.

This happens a lot in church settings, in every denomination and in non-denominational churches. It is very common; as a result, many have turned away from God and gone back to the world in despair and with great disappointment. It is because those who are enlightened have paid very little attention to healing and deliverance. They underestimated the need for proper healing and grounding of people for however long it may take for them to be set free, be enlightened and taught on how God works, and have a proper grounding of the Word. Oftentimes, people are rushed into maturity. They get unrealistic expectations imposed on them and comparisons among people set in, about how it only took so and so a short while, or it took me two weeks from salvation to maturity. Yes, it can be so, lucky to those who had it that way, but remember there will always be those who are a bit slower. God loves them too.

At times, people can even be placed in positions of leadership, leading the flock of God, when they themselves are still burdened with their own unresolved issues. Can you imagine the disaster?! That is the reason why people are hurt and damaged inside, as opposed to outside the church. It's even worse when it comes through those in authority. It can do a much greater amount of damage as to how the person will end up perceiving God and this can be detrimental to their ultimate relationship with God.

Everyone must have the opportunity to heal and be made whole. If they are struggling in any area, mercy has to be exercised upon them to allow them a smooth transition from carnality to spirituality, not get constant mockery and condemnations thrown at them. They will end up seeing God as an impatient God, who put demands upon people and placed unrealistic expectations on them. People do this, but God is merciful.

Some people may be lucky to transition with the supernatural help of God, get supernatural self-awareness and change and make the necessary adjustments, whereas some may need help.

People will often develop defence mechanisms to protect themselves from what is perceived as attacks on their persons. These types of defences are often unhealthy in themselves and cause more harm, not only to others but to the person themselves. They can either lash out in any way or manner or become passive/aggressive, or become avoidant and coil up inside, retreating to their own world to avoid further hurts.

This shouldn't be anywhere where God is supposed to be. Everyone needs to be given an opportunity to have His touch, be whole and lovingly be guided into the right path without judgement or scorn.

You see, when the hand of God touches you, and He wants you to serve Him and His people in a more significant way, Satan begins to find ways to stop you. If you had all, or some, of the traumatic experiences mentioned earlier and they had not been dealt with in prayer, deliverance and inner healing, he then uses them to pose blockages and hindrances. He will target those areas to try and create havoc in that person's life.

Ministry entails working with and for people. It requires healed vessels, or at least those in their journey of healing.

Preaching does work but it depends on the state of the preacher's human spirit, whether the Holy Spirit is the one transmitting the message; for if it's the Holy Spirit speaking, there will be comfort, there will be compassion, there will be love, there will be consolation, and these will result in the hearer being convicted and not condemned.

Pointing out people's flaws or weaknesses through human effort and power will increase their wrong beliefs about God; they will shut down and coil inside and even if God intended for them to step out and serve Him, this will not make it possible. There must be a nurturing ground where the broken can be mended and allow God to use them.

Healing and restoration are a journey. Salvation is instant. Patience and understanding are vital on the part of those less broken. Love opens closed spirits, it softens hardened hearts, it disarms defences. It always wins, it never fails. 1 Corinthians 13:8. It makes a way where there was no way, enabling a previously damaged person to see things differently and see themselves as God sees them, all with the help of a messenger of God.

If believers badmouth one another, lack forgiveness and lack confidentiality, it reverses the work of God on one another's lives. When one brother or sister falls short in any way, however big or small, and they come to seek guidance and prayer only to end up with betrayal, it pains God big time. It puts shame on God in the face of the enemy. He laughs at God and says, "Look what your children are doing to each other; just look".

When we fail to lift them up, but instead, each time they try to rise, we keep on reminding them of their shortcomings, we fail God. We put Him to shame and have not fulfilled this commandment:

1. "Brethren, if a man be overtaken in a fault, you who are spiritual, restore such a one in the spirit of meekness; considering yourself, lest you also be tempted". 2. "Bear you one another's burdens, and so fulfil the law of Christ." Galatians 6:1-2 KJ 2000 Bible.

That's the reason Jesus said, "Father, forgive them; for they know not what they do". Luke 23:34. This is the reason you need to forgive them. They just don't know what they are doing.

The sad thing is that the world is watching. How then can those who are still living in the world be convinced to come and join in with believers? How can they believe?

It's so very, very sad.

Some people are really damaged but God still loves them. He still has high hopes for them. He is waiting for a messenger, a vessel that can say, here I am God, use me to minister your nature to them, not only by talking but by my actions too.

People who had no father will always have difficulties relating to God as a father. Those who have been hurt by their fathers, or any male authority figure, will see God as a cruel father. Those betrayed by their fathers, or any male authority figure, will have trouble trusting. Those rejected by their fathers, or any male authority figure, early in their lives, will have problems connecting to God.

God relies on those who are healed and those in authority to help these ones, reverse the lies of the enemy, give them God's kindness, unconditional love acceptance and positive regard, not to be deemed difficult, boring, slow to grow in the things of God, unhelpful, unteachable or even bad people. Not to heap blame on them for their slow progress or what seems to be no progress at all. God is always behind the scenes working. He loves them, He wants them well and they will be healed.

This attitude towards them only reinforces their negative thoughts; "I am not good enough; I am stupid, and always have been; Mom, Dad or my teacher always said so." It increases self-doubt, low self-esteem, feelings of inadequacy, guilt and shame. It serves only to push them deeper into their misery.

Non-verbal communication plays a significant part. Someone may not say the words or phrases, but their demeanour, behaviour and expressions say it all. The person will see this.

If you seek to correct someone, don't belittle, ridicule, shame or call them names. It will never work.

People tend to employ methods that were used on them by others. People do unto others that which was done to them.

If you are to correct someone, make sure you are the person God has chosen for that task.

Check with God first.

Examine your heart.

Are you doing it to be spiteful?

Are you genuinely concerned about them?

How do you feel about them? Compassion or disgust?

How close are you to them? If you have no form of a loving, trusting relationship with them, you had better leave it for someone to do it.

It can be more hurtful and damaging to try to help someone without checking these things out first.

Those helping, mentoring or pastoring these ones need to have self-awareness of their own unresolved issues, or else there will occur a counter-production and a clash.

There are no quick fixes. People are different. Unrealistic expectations can be detrimental to the journey of such a person.

God loves us too much to leave us as we are.

If those in authority, this is authority of any nature, are people who have problems hearing a "no" from their subordinates or those under them, they can push people to accept responsibilities they're not ready for or even equipped for. This happens when expectations on the part of authority are such that you never say no; if you say no, you are a bad person. In these types of situations, people who said no end up being ostracised, marginalised, treated badly, or unwanted. A healthy environment is one where people are free to say what they believe to be the truth at a given time.

Sometimes, in church settings, people may be made to believe that a no to authority is a no to God. This drives people into guilt trips. God knows the hearts of His people. If someone honestly and truthfully, with good valid reasons, says no, God will see that, and He surely will understand and accept it. Humans are not capable of seeing this most times and can end up labelling people with all sorts of judgemental beliefs of what they think is the reason they're saying no. We don't want slave masters and slaves, but fathers and mothers filled with the love of God.

By this, I don't mean people shouldn't respect and obey authority; no, what I mean is there has to be a healthy balance. There must be freedom of choice.

I can hear the reader say, "What about submission"?

Yes, submission is vital and should be practised by those under authority. It's not the same. There is a slight difference between curving towards slave master- ship and being a person in authority, a leader, a father or a mother.

How you treat those under you will tell. People will submit more easily, with love and joy, to a good authority figure and will obey with fear, resentment and dread to a slave master. It's just like that.

I came across this somewhere by Craig Chroeschel:

The difference between a leader and a boss:

"A boss instils fear.
A leader inspires confidence.

A boss assigns blame.
A leader takes responsibility.

A boss demands loyalty.
A leader extends trust.

A boss controls people.
A leader empowers people.

A boss is often guarded.
A leader is transparent.

You will never be a leader that others love to follow if you aren't a leader that loves people."

People can easily sense that all you care about is getting them to get you where you intend to go and that you don't care about them as a human being. You see them as tools for your benefit, very much like narcissism.

I was helped by Watchman Nee's two little books, 'The Release of the Spirit' and 'Salvation of the Soul'. I got to know that when one gets saved, it is the Spirit man that usually gets saved first and instantly, but the body and the soul have to be given attention with much education and teaching of the Word, prayer, knowledge of God, knowledge of who they are in Christ, what Christ accomplished on the Cross etc.

They divide the spirit from the soul. It's very deep but very valuable and a much-needed resource for those new in the Faith especially.

It teaches lessons about things; "facing a servant of Christ—the breaking of the outer man by the Lord for the release of the spirit. The only work God approves is that of the spirit, and the breaking of the outer man is the only way that the spirit can have full freedom."

Watchman Nee based his teachings in this booklet on the following scriptures:

John 12:24 - 'Most assuredly, I say to you, unless a grain of wheat falls into the ground and dies, it remains alone; but if it dies, it produces much grain.'

Hebrews 4:12-13 - 'For the word of God is living and powerful, and sharper than any two-edged sword, piercing even to the division of soul and spirit, and of joints and marrow, and is a discerner of the thoughts and intents of the heart. And there is no creature hidden from His sight, but all things are naked and open to the eyes of Him to whom we must give account.'

1 Corinthians 2:11-14 - 'For what man knows the things of a man except the spirit of the man which is in him? Even so, no one knows the things of God except the Spirit of God. Now we have received, not the spirit of the world, but the Spirit who is from God, that we might know the things that have been freely given to us by God.

These things we also speak, not in words which man's wisdom teaches but which the Holy Spirit teaches, comparing spiritual things with spiritual. But the natural man does not receive the things of the Spirit of God, for they are foolishness to him; nor can he know them, because they are spiritually discerned.'

2 Corinthians 3:6 -'Who also made us sufficient as ministers of the new covenant, not of the letter but of the Spirit; for the letter kills, but the Spirit gives life.'

Romans 1:9 - 'For God is my witness, whom I serve with my spirit in the gospel of His Son, that without ceasing I make mention of you always in my prayers.'

Romans 7:6 - 'But now we have been delivered from the law, having died to what we were held by, so that we should serve in the newness of the Spirit and not in the oldness of the letter.'

Romans 8:4-8 - 'That the righteous requirement of the law might be fulfilled in us who do not walk according to the flesh but according to the Spirit. For those who live according to the flesh set their minds on the things of the flesh, but those who live according to the Spirit, the things of the Spirit. For to be carnally minded is death, but to be spiritually minded is life and peace. Because the carnal mind is enmity against God; for it is not subject to the law of God, nor indeed can be. So then, those who are in the flesh cannot please God.'

Galatians 5:16 - 'I say then: Walk in the Spirit, and you shall not fulfil the lust of the flesh.'

Galatians 5: 22-23 - 'But the fruit of the Spirit is love, joy, peace, longsuffering, kindness, goodness, faithfulness, gentleness, self-control. Against such there is no law.'

Galatians 5:25 - 'If we live in the Spirit, let us also walk in the Spirit.'

I devoured this booklet, reading it through tears. I discovered a lot of things in it that I identified with in my own life and knew that I needed to work deeper in my knowledge of God.

I knew that my soul needed saving.

No one told me or taught me this. In all the preaching's or teachings I had since salvation, I never got it like I did in this booklet.

This happens with every believer. When we get saved, the soul and the body, especially the soul (as the body often gets directives and orders from the soul) remains carnal and raw, till abiding in the law, causing more error in one's life.

The journey is very long after salvation. For some, it may have been shorter, but to many, it's usually long and requires proper teachings like this one, coupled with patience, mercy and love on the part of those who have travelled before. If someone gets it wrong, there has to be understanding and mercy so as not to push them further into the pit but that they can be allowed to try again till they get it too.

If the church was healed and delivered, there wouldn't be so many casualties.

In the end, the scripture in James 1: 2-4 made sense. 'My brethren, count it all joy when you fall into various trials, knowing that the testing of your faith produces patience. But let patience have its perfect work, that you may be perfect and complete, lacking nothing.'

It's not nice to be going through trials and difficulties. It can be very dark and gloomy. It's only after surviving them that one emerges out more enlightened and stronger. You trust God better. He saw you through it all as He promised. During the trials, it felt like He had deserted you and lied to you. After the trial, or maybe even during the trial, you get to know that only Him alone saw you through it all or was right there with you in the midst of it all and this benefits your faith in Him; it softens your heart towards the instruments that were/are used in the trials, it helps your growth in loving your enemies, it helps you see who your real enemy is, that it is never the instruments, but Satan. And God sometimes allows it to help get your spirit uppermost and bring your soul into subjection.

Salvation of the soul often happens when a saved person attains the ability to control their soul and body. Saved life is foreign to all humanity. Humans are born sinful. Romans 3:23 – 'All have sinned and fall short of the glory of God.' NIV.

All we know is sin. When we get saved, new life in Christ requires a change in how we live our lives. Our spirits are often in the right place, but the soul will always be inclined to the old ways of living. Our mindsets, emotions, thinking patterns, even dispositions, predispose us to acts of sin and error. Self-awareness and knowledge of God is vital. Even Paul, in Romans 7, spoke of his own struggle with the flesh. He described that his spirit wanted and desired to do good but his soul still fought to do that which he hated to do. It feels like war inside a person. The spirit and the soul are fighting. The spirit must win and get the soul in order.

This, in most cases, is accomplished by dying to self. Dying to self doesn't always come naturally. It is made possible by trials and tribulations.

Most of the time, many people talk and even teach about the fruits of the Spirit in Galatians 5. Some even boast about how they think they have acquired them, but when faced with situations, they fail horribly. It could be things like when someone isn't what they would like them to be, or they don't seem to be listening to them, or they feel disrespected by them or the person may be too slow in some ways. They get upset, hurt or offended by it and begin to act in ungodliness towards the person. Simple things like this often reveal that someone is still short of a certain fruit of the Spirit, even though they are boasting about having mastered them. What seems to be as simple a thing as patience and loving unconditionally are often lacking in most people.

People often like or love those they can get something out of; those who can benefit them. It's like a pay-back; you do this for me, I will like or love you. If you don't, I will hate or despise you.

In his book 'Salvation of the Soul', Watchman Nee spoke of these:

- meaning
- the means
- the manifestation of the soul's salvation
- the meaning is SELF-DENIAL
- the means is the CROSS
- the manifestation is the KINGDOM

Which bring the secret of a victorious life, and the faith by which such life is lived.

Dying to self.

The soul always strives for its needs, its benefits, it's rewards, good feelings, good things, to be treated nice and fair, to be done well and good. As good as these are, unfortunately, in this broken world, it's not always possible to get them. We live in a broken world, among broken people where sin is rampant, the enemy is reigning and ruling and all sorts of evil happen to good and bad people alike.

Dying to self is vital as it will enable you to live like Christ lived; to love your enemies, to do good to those who don't deserve it, to have a Kingdom mindset, to put God first in everything and to think of Him and His Kingdom before you think of yourself.

This is possible by nailing the self on the Cross.

The result is a visible Kingdom manifestation through one's life.

I've got to be honest here and say I have not yet arrived at such a place. I am not where I was before; each year I take a step forward with it. It's not easy, but momentum is being gained bit by bit.

The first step in the right direction I can say I have taken is to have my eyes of understanding and wisdom opened to know about the need to have my soul saved. It is wisdom; wisdom that Satan doesn't want any believer to know that, after salvation, they need to work on their soul; to know that the soul is the worst enemy to a believer's journey and growth.

My beautiful reader let's carry our cross and seek to complete our journey in Christ Jesus.

Chapter 11.
God's Faithfulness

When people go through a lot of painful experiences, especially from childhood, and then it seems things have continued along that path even in their adult life, it can be difficult for them to see God as He really is. They look at other people who seem forever happy; they have good childhood memories, their adult lives are going smoothly, and we think, maybe God loves them more. Maybe there is something wrong with me. Maybe I am more of a sinner than them. All these, of course, are a pack of lies from the enemy, but when someone is in real non-stop difficult times almost all of their lives, sometimes they can't help but believe these lies. Remember that, at the time of having these thoughts, they are not aware it's all lies. They read scripture, they read about God loving everyone, and Jesus dying for all people, but the enemy throws these lies at them and make them think that those scriptures apply only to certain people and not them.

If not quickly dealt with and the person gets the revelatory truth of who God is and who they are in Christ, they can really end up giving up on God and that's what the enemy wants, especially if there is a call of God upon that person's life.

From the beginning of time, Satan has reversed the truth of God. He got our forefathers, Adam and Eve, to disbelieve God and do what he, Satan told them to do. Satan always aims at doing the opposite of what God does. His aim is to destroy God's people.

I was now getting out of my "locked door" and sought to serve God.

I was so joyful and upbeat that I filled in a volunteer form for stewarding in 2006. I was invited to a one-day training. I never heard from anyone after that. It appeared like God didn't want me to do this at this time; maybe so, maybe not, but nevertheless it didn't happen. After many inquiries as to what happened, or what to do next, there was simply no straight answer.

I filled in a form for consolidation a few months later and attended a one-day training for it, but the same thing happened. For those who don't know what this is, when an altar call is made for salvation, those believers who attend to these new converts pray with them and take contact details for follow-up; we call them consolidators.

It was the same as the struggle I faced regarding finding out about the all-night prayer back in 2004. The reader can imagine how, after just finding out the truth of who God really is, His love, my self-awareness regarding the soul and the spirit which led to a feeling of deliverance and joy, wanting nothing but more of God, then to be confronted by these negative impacts, I was indeed greatly disappointed to tell you the truth.

Luckily, it didn't cause much harm. I didn't leave church. I didn't give up on the all-night prayer.

I joined the all-night prayer meeting around November of 2004 after finding out where it was now being held through the receptionist in church. I have attended the prayer meeting every month since, up until 2011.

The first leader of the prayer meeting left, and the assistant leader took over. In 2007, the new leader wanted to try a 24/7 prayer chain. We had to fill in the slots to lead. I put myself out to help but I was working full-time and my availability was not good. My heart wanted to do this. God knows how much I did.

We started off by just doing what we could, as most of us were working full-time, including the leader. I remember the times I managed to be there. One time, there was just me and a friend whom I had invited. The place was locked, and it was difficult to get hold of the leader who had the keys or knew where they were kept. I called everyone I could to help, and it was only around 11 pm that the leader sent someone to come and open the door for us.

We stayed there all night, the two of us praying. My friend was already a Christian but was not a member of my church. She was so tired as she had worked all day. She kept on falling asleep. Eventually, I told her to get a few hours' sleep and I carried on by myself.

We tried this for a year and realised that availability was a problem for all of us, due to work, and it was stopped. It carried on like it was before, once a month.

It was later decided to do it twice, on the first two Fridays of the month. Attendance was still an issue but this Arrangement has survived to the present day.

I was now a regular part of this prayer group and an on and off part of the weekly evangelism team. The evangelism leader used to organise local outreaches. They were called city missions. He was very zealous, young and on fire for evangelism.

In 2007, around May or June, the leader was training the church Bible school students in evangelism and missions and had a week's practical outreach in East London among a Moslem community. There was a couple who had converted to

Christianity some time ago and the church wanted to help them start a church there and reach out to their fellow community members.

He appealed to the congregation to sign up for a few days of outreach there alongside Bible school students. I signed up and asked the lady who got me involved in this in the first place to sign up too so we could be there together as I didn't know any of the students. I was not very familiar with reaching out in other towns. I had been concentrating on the local area around the church so far, but on an irregular basis.

I had no idea where the town was. It was called East Ham. The first day I went there around 1 pm as agreed and before I left, I tried to get hold of my friend to arrange where to meet. She didn't pick up the phone several times, nor did she respond to text messages or voicemail and I got concerned. I debated as to whether I should really go. My spirit told me to go whilst my soul was telling me, "Who are you going to be with there? You don't know anybody, so you can't go there." Eventually, my spirit won, and I went. It was a very long journey by two buses and a longer train journey. I arrived and didn't know who to call to find out exactly where the place was. My friend was still not picking up her phone.

Luckily, I had the address from the advertising leaflet. I went around asking strangers after I got off the train. I found it and it was just the leader and the students. No one from the congregation was there. I joined them, we prayed and paired in twos and did a door-to-door evangelism.

I paired with a young lady from Europe who had just come for Bible school. We got one couple to accept Jesus in one of the houses.

I was so happy.

Later on in the evening, there was a service planned in a hall to which people from the community were invited. The prospective pastors were there for the planned church plant and most of the Bible school students were there too. It was a good service.

This experience helped me to come out more and gave me some confidence.

We had many more local missions.

My evangelistic zeal and passion from the time I was in boarding school seemed to have been stirred and returning.

In 2008, we went to the town of Stockwell in the South West of London. It was an attempt to reach out to the youth there who were getting involved in dangerous activities.

Chapter 11. God's Faithfulness

The outreach was also planned for a few days. I attended all of them. I was beginning to catch it. We went house-to-house in the neighbouring council estates, inviting people to the evening concert.

We had many more local missions and weekly outreaches. I had become a regular part of this by then.

The church evangelist began regular Saturday evening events. The aim was for the team to go out late in the afternoon, and not only get people saved, but invite them to the event. He started a Saturday evening event in the church that was more evangelistic, and the team would be inviting people to attend. It carried on from 2005 till 2010. It was powerful. Younger members of the church liked it. Later, we carried out baptism services during these events. I was in the baptism team too. This was once monthly.

Towards the end of 2008, the leader asked the team and other church members to form a special choir dedicated to evangelism and missions. I became part of it. I was full of energy. I've always been hungry and very zealous.

We sang at the Saturday events.

Then, in 2009, the church organised an overseas mission to Mali in West Africa. I had never been to an overseas mission before. I had just started enjoying the local ones here. The church had been working with churches in Mali for some time and teams had been going there almost once yearly.

It was April. Preparations were intense. We had to build a rapport with one another as most of us were strangers to each other. We held prayer times together, praying for everything pertaining to the mission, including the work in Mali, the churches and their leaders. Mali is highly Islamic. Christianity was weak and marginalised. The mission's purpose was to support and strengthen the churches there.

We had two weekends away together to get used to one another and get to know one another, as well as praying and fasting. It was powerful.

In Mali, on the actual mission, we had a powerful time there. It was just eight of us including the leader. We would pray from after breakfast till late afternoon and then, often, had one trip to an area to minister and reach out in the early evening, returning late at night, always close to midnight. We then had to meet and debrief and pray before we went to bed. By then, it would be 1:30 am or even 2 am. Each day after breakfast, we gathered together in a room to pray and prepare ourselves spiritually. I loved it.

Most evenings, we had crusades. We had about three crusades in a stadium. Miracles were happening like nobody's business there. We were saturated with the presence of God through spending all day in prayer and worship.

The leader and local preachers would preach and then we prayed for people on altar calls. The whole stadium queued for prayer. People were rolling on the dusty ground, being delivered of evil spirits. One of the nights, there were so many deliverances and manifestations, it seemed everyone I touched had something in them.

One evening, I prayed for a man who wore dark glasses and asked for prayer for his eyes saying he was blind. He was with someone else who was guiding him. He testified afterwards, took his glasses off, his eyes opened, and he could see.

The whole stadium roared. I was really surprised that God could just simply use anyone, including me, in that way. The Holy Spirit reminded me that spending time in the presence of God brings about power.

God can use anybody. Preparation is key. Separation is key. Focus is key. Our leader was very good when it came to this.

We would go to the very remotest of areas there to reach out. Roads were almost non-existent in some areas. There were no streetlights. We would minister in the dark. The people would come, hear the Word, receive prayer, get saved and then we would break into a huge dance and celebration with them. I loved it. The people there were lovely. Very lowly of heart.

We visited churches on Sundays and were asked to preach.

One day, we went to a large playground, so large it was more like a park. They had made a makeshift seating area and platform. The churches brought their worship teams to lead us in worship. In that area, there were streetlights, as it was in the city of Bamako. The problem was electricity was mostly supplied through generators and was never reliable.

Just when we began, and the worship was getting hotter, the lights suddenly went off. We thought they would return but nothing happened. We were in pitch-black darkness and the African people embarked on warfare praise. The worship team began to stomp the ground, beat the drums, sing louder, clap and we all joined in. My God!! I never saw anything like that. The warfare became hot, very powerful. Warfare prayer broke out, every demonic spirit and evil force being commanded to leave. It went on for around 30 minutes or so and suddenly the lights came back. Africa!! They pray. They praise.

Chapter 11. God's Faithfulness

We returned early in May, so encouraged and empowered. The leader encouraged us to get more involved in evangelism and missions. Most of us did. I've never looked back since.

It was July 2009; I managed to enrol in Bible college.

You will remember that I mentioned I always felt a deep hunger to know God more and that, when I was in Rhema back in SA, I couldn't attend as I had to still work full-time.

The hospitals there were not flexible. The rotas were rigid.

I prayed hard to God to make a miracle, a way for me to still work but attend Bible school this time. I always wanted to attend, but due to shift work, even here in the UK, I just couldn't. I remember making inquiries when I got the first church magazine in which the Bible school was advertised in 2002. I was told how it ran and, at that time, I was on permanent day duty, so there was no chance I could manage it.

In September 2004, I got an opportunity to replace a retiring colleague who was on permanent night-duty. Then, when the time came for me to enrol in the Bible school in 2009, I thought night-duty is more flexible, I can do this.

God moved and, at the time, the new manager was someone very understanding. I asked to meet with him and explained my situation, asking that I be allowed to work one night in and one night off for my weekly hours, which were three nights a week, so I could get to rest in between. In most cases, when things involve Christianity, the chances become slim, but God moved on my behalf, that was granted, and I registered for September 2009.

It was just from 09:00-13:00 anyway. That worked. Long story short, I enrolled and completed two years there.

My growth in the Lord took off on a new level during this time.

The new Principal brought a lot of diversity to doctrines, with more emphasis on the gifts of the Holy Spirit, healing, prayer, Faith and knowledge of scriptures.

All these were rather new to me. Healing was not that new as I had attended quite a few of Benny Hinn's crusades and teaching sessions three years prior.

The gift of tongues was very much taught and practised daily, first thing in the morning, for half an hour before we started classes.

It was during this time, in late 2009, that the church evangelist asked me to lead and co-ordinate the teams. There were three teams at the time. I was to lead one of them and co-ordinate and oversee all three of them with leaders of the other two reporting to me and then I reported to the church evangelist. This was new, but I had tended to display leadership skills all through my life. If you remember, when I was in primary school, the principal would get me to step in whenever a teacher was absent.

When in high school, I was not even born-again yet but I led a choir of born-again students and embarked on outreaches.

This made me take a step of faith and come out of my comfort zone.

It was in February 2010 when the evangelist organised a city mission in West Yorkshire. It was just one of the many city missions that the church had organised since I joined the teams.

Little did I know that, like the overseas Mali mission, the Lord had a hidden agenda.

We finished Bible school classes as usual on the Friday afternoon and I took four other ladies with me and drove for five hours to the north of the country. It was winter and it can be very cold up north. When we got close to the area, it was now very dark and foggy. There was so much fog, that the car lights were almost useless. I had no experience of driving in that much foggy weather. It was a struggle and very scary as I couldn't see an oncoming car and kept straddling the lanes on a two-way road.

We proceeded and when we got closer to Sheffield, I began to have problems with my car. It was having difficulties moving and making weird noises. The gears were not engaging very well, and the car was moving slower and slower, making a horrible noise. I pulled over and called the breakdown people. We were in the middle of the highway and very far from London, just slightly over an hour to our destination.

The breakdown man came and examined the car, which was now barely moving, and said it was a problem with the clutch and it needed to be taken to a garage. They took the car and all of us to the nearest garage and I had to leave it there. We proceeded on our journey by train. We got there just on time for the 7:30 pm meeting in the church that was hosting us in Huddersfield. Luckily, I had registered with a breakdown company, and they agreed to bring my car to London to my mechanic, who then replaced the clutch. This was in the next week, though.

We were put up by a friend of the team leader. On the Saturday, we went out to the town centre with the church people there; the weather was so bad, cold and raining but people still got saved.

It was just before midnight on the Saturday that the evangelist informed me that he wanted me to preach in the church the next day which was Sunday. This was their normal Sunday church service with everyone present, unlike on the Saturday outreach, when only a few came.

I was so afraid. Apart from in Mali, I had never really preached so far. I had no idea how to prepare a sermon as I had just started Bible school. I didn't sleep very well that night with anxiety. The evangelist didn't seem to be giving me a choice to say yes or no.

The morning came, but I had nothing prepared. I had been asking God all night to help me out; He seemed to be keeping quiet.

I literally had nothing prepared.

On our way to church that morning, I kept asking God repeatedly, "What am I going to say to those people?" It was just before we arrived that the Holy Spirit said to me, "You have a story." I said, "What?" He repeated, "You have a story; tell them your story." He gave me Joseph's story in Genesis.

The service began with worship as usual. Our leader was introduced onto the platform with us standing from the congregation as his team. He preached a very short message on the importance of evangelistic aim and reaching out. This lasted about 10 minutes or so.

He then called me and our team worship leader, who has now gone home to be with the Lord and announced to everyone that the worship leader would share his testimony and Sarah (me) would share a short message. The worship leader went first and took about 5 minutes, sharing about his journey with the Lord and both he and our leader left the platform.

Now, everyone looked at me. The only person on the platform. When I finally faced the people and discovered that the hall was packed and I had no prepared sermon, my knees were knocking against each other. I was shaking like a leaf. My voice shook.

I opened my mouth. I introduced myself. I told them where I originated from as anyone could tell by my accent I was not born in the UK. I spoke a bit about our teams, what we do back in London, what my role is, etc.

Then I informed them that I was going to tell them about my own personal testimony and based it on Genesis 50:20.

As soon as I started, I could see the faces of people identifying and relating to my story. The interest was more than I imagined.

I talked about my own life story, the trauma, everything and how God saw me through it all and had brought me thus far. I made an altar call and men, women and the young people came to be prayed over for emotional healing, deliverance and guidance in forgiveness of all those who sinned against them.

People were sobbing, getting in touch with their feelings and brokenness, some of them for the first time. They had to come clean of normal Christian stiff upper lip culture, where in most cases after salvation, people are expected to just get miraculously healed, know the Word, have Faith and be whole. Life must go on.

Afterwards, people came to me thanking me for having brought this up and providing a platform for healing. Subjects of abuse and trauma are often avoided in normal church settings and, as a result, many people are forced to pretend that all is well. They come to church as a last resort to have God touch and help them, only to find that most of the time in church, they are expected to hide their pain and just get on with church life. The majority of the population in West Yorkshire are English. The church was packed. When I later asked how many people were there, I was told 200 plus. They were 90% English and got so impacted by a message spoken in a heavy Sesotho accent by someone who is not even a preacher, who had never really preached anywhere except a few times in Africa.

This was the first time I ever opened up about my childhood. I had buried it so deep that it was almost forgotten. I always felt ashamed of it, felt like I was the only one on earth who experienced that. It brought so much relief to see how God used it to impact His people and bring healing to so many that day.

When God says, "go", you go. He knows that you will have everything you need. He will go before you. Isaiah 45.

It was soon after this that this book was born in my heart. I felt very strongly that God wanted me to write it for those who would find it helpful to their own unresolved life issues or to bless someone they know.

The devil seemed to be fighting the writing of the book.

In May of that year, the Bible school was taken to a book exhibition in Surrey. I got a whole lot of materials there and spoke to writers, printers and publishers.

I still didn't begin to write. In July 2012, I had completed two years of Bible school and was helping one of my former Bible school classmates who came to the school just after she started a church. It was still very small, about 10 people. She asked me to come and help her out after my Bible school and I did. I stayed with them for 7 months and then returned to my church. She got a book published in 2013. When I was with her the year before, she asked me if I was writing the book, I had told her about. I said no, and she urged me to start writing it. I started in 2012 but, along the way, I got discouraged and put the manuscript away.

Chapter 11. God's Faithfulness

When I returned to the church I was in before in 2013, one evening, the pastor called out people who had started something and stopped before completing it. I responded to the prayer line. I told the prayer minister about my unfinished book.

They prayed for me, but I still didn't write it.

Then in 2018 in March, I signed up for a three-day book-writing seminar held in North Carolina. One day, I received a personal message from one of the ladies that I met there. She had posted me her new book and urging me to write mine. I told the lady that I was going to write my book.

When I got back from another conference I attended in January 2019, I began writing straight away. I never stopped till the book was completed.

God began to place His hand upon our work of evangelism and missions.

The whole church got mobilised to participate in local missions. In April 2010, the evangelist organised a mission in Luton. It was a blast. 70 people from the church came out to man the streets of Luton on that Saturday and over 70 people were saved. We never had so many people from the congregation desire to participate in evangelism or missions.

In 2011, we had a mission to Marseille, France. We taught in the Bible school there, took the students out on the streets for evangelism and shared our testimonies. France is another country that is hard on Christianity, but people got saved.

Earlier on in the summer, along with the lead evangelist, we had missions in Peckham, Kingston, Portsmouth and other towns.

In 2014, the lead evangelist pushed us further to take courage to man an area and lead missions there. We were four team leaders. I led the Wimbledon area as it was where I lived. The lead evangelist was the one who would organise missions from beginning to end. This involved getting a license to use the outdoor area from the council, materials required to give out to the people, musical instruments, power generators, worship team, a small tent (gazebo) in case of bad weather, furniture e.g table, few chairs and mobilising a team. We would just help mostly with mobilisation of a team. He handed all this over to each team leader to begin from scratch and get the mission up and running. This was daunting but it helped me a lot to step out of my comfort zone. It was not a small thing. God proved faithful. Everything came together and the mission was very successful.

We had missions four times a year, one every quarter. This went on till 2015.

We began to experience issues with the local Government and had to move to another nearby town. We teamed up with a network church there that was a part of our church. They were in Clapham. We had one mission there in Stockwell, a town very close to Clapham. Another blow came our way, as on the very day of our mission, the church was asked to vacate the venue they were using. The new owners were there just as we arrived for prayer before we went out. We had nowhere to pray but the Lord was good. We did not lose heart. We went out and saw a significant number of people get saved.

The Lord's hand was upon the church as the lady preacher was led by God to find a building in another town not far from there and the building was for sale. They purchased the building in conjunction with other churches in their region. All those churches were network members of our church. It's still there today.

In early 2014 and the end of 2015, we had a mission to Romania. Our church was working with a group of churches there. We did all sorts; home visits, hospital visits, preached in churches, engaged in manual work, and helped with street children's ministry led by an American missionary. Romania is still suffering from the negative impacts of communism which attempted to eliminate Christianity and destroyed every Christian, church buildings and Christian leaders. The people don't have much knowledge of God but were very receptive and God always responded positively and blessed them greatly. Church plans are occurring all the time.

We carried out home visits as per requests by our host church. We visited people in the most remote of the remote areas. We encountered the most poverty-stricken areas, where a whole family and extended family members with grandparents all lived together in a one-roomed makeshift house, with no electricity, no wood for fire in extremely cold weather, children not attending school, no food, and no one works as the country's economy is poor itself with no jobs.

We visited areas where a group of young girls, who were already mothers, gathered for us to come and share the Gospel, pray and bless them whichever way possible. We learnt that the girls give themselves a way to men, get pregnant early in their young age with the hope they will get married to escape their poverty-stricken homes. Education remains an issue. Children never finish school.

We visited someone in hospital, and it was a shock. There was literally nothing there. There was a gross shortage of medicines and supplies. Staff were over-worked and grossly under-paid. The whole atmosphere was so gloomy, you could shed a tear. Appalling situations, so heart-wrenching, you broke down afterwards.

In one of the home visits, my team saw a miraculous healing of cancer in a young man who had been bed-ridden, unable to do anything for himself, who was cared for by his grandmother. The grandmother was informed we were coming to pray, and she bathed him and sat him propped up against the wall on his mattress that was on the floor. When we got in, he looked ashen, pale, lethargic, so thin and gaunt, he was literally dying. He could barely speak. He couldn't move a limb by himself. When we asked what the matter was, the grandmother burst into tears. The church member who came with us had to explain to us.

We didn't know where to start. I was the leader of that team. Everybody looked at me. Our worship leader began to play his guitar. We sang and worshipped. All this time, my mind struggling to engage in the worship, thinking where to start, what to do. The worship time helped a lot. Some faith came into me. I was reminded of James 5:14:15. 'Is anyone among you sick? Let them call for the elders of the church, and let them pray over him, anointing him with oil in the Name of the Lord. And the prayer of faith will save the sick, and the Lord will raise him up and if he committed any sins, he will be forgiven.'

I learnt about this scripture from Smith Wigglesworth's teachings. It was his favourite reference for healing.

I took out the anointing oil I had bought when I went to Israel with the Bible school. Power seemed to be coming upon me. I asked the team to carry on singing and asked 2 people to pray in tongues. I went for the young man. He was about 14-16 years old but looked like a 10-year-old. Wasted. I called unto the God of Ezekiel, the one who brings back dead dry bones to life. Something came upon me. I asked the boy to rise; he staggered up, so weak to balance. I took his hand and slowly walked him back and forth around the room. A boy who hadn't left his bed (mattress) for almost a year, was now on his feet, still wobbly but gripping onto my hand and walking. I increased the intensity of the prayer. A picture of A A Allen came to my mind. This took me to the memory of the worst cases of infirmities he prayed for and how they all recovered. I became wild, just like what A A Allen did with someone who was brought to the service on a hospital stretcher, with drips and tubes all over his body, accompanied by two nurses and his wife, just in case he were to need emergency intervention.

AA Allen intensified prayer, filling himself up with faith. I saw him gently pull the man's legs and stretch them, commanding the infirmity to leave. I heard him tell the wife to prepare his food (the man had cancer of the stomach and was being fed through tubes). I heard that man making a sound, life coming into his body, I saw that man rise from the stretcher dragging the tube from the drip, dragging the hospital gown he had on, wobbling out of that stretcher, walking slowly, staggering and beginning to run all around with bones sticking out all over his body as he was just wasted.

I called on the God of AA Allen, the God that healed that man. I reminded God of every healing promise that came to my spirit. I got wild.

I slowly started to walk fast, still holding him. He began to keep pace with me. I increased the speed, and before I knew it, we were running up and down that floor. I let go of my hand, and the boy continued to run up and down by himself. We watched in excitement as strength crept into that boy's body. He had a big smile on his face, and the grandmother crying and laughing loudly at the same time. It was wonderful, just so wonderful to see God in action. This never left my memory.

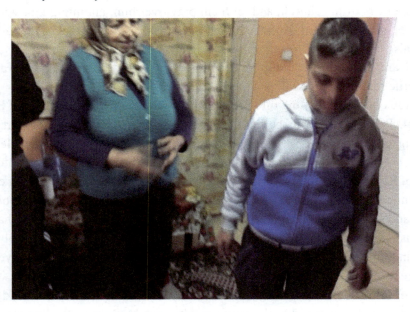

Above: The boy who was healed of cancer. This is him walking up and down after a long period of being bed ridden. The grandmother standing and watching here, had to prop him up against a wall for us to be able to pray for him. He could barely sit up on his own.

Chapter 11. God's Faithfulness

We also visited a remote area where Gypsies live. Most of them were homeless. Children as small as infants were living on the streets with their parents. Alcohol was a major issue. Fights and injuries and sexual exploitation of young children was the order of the day. We preached the Gospel, prayed for them and encouraged the churches to continue reaching out to them.

In mid-2015, I joined a French-speaking outreach ministry led by one of the former pastors who had retired from full-time ministry pastoring one of the network churches that served French-speaking people.

She and a few other people, mainly from her church, had been going on missions to French-speaking countries like Mali, Ivory Coast, and Togo and they had just started going to the DRC Congo. This was when I joined them.

We got involved with the churches there as well, mainly introducing discipleship. As usual in all the missions I have been to, we get invited to preach in churches, share testimonies, and engage in any work the churches are doing there. I was asked to carry out training in evangelism and leading teams for the practical part of it. In one of the churches, a lot of young people turned up for the training and outreach day. We saw 108 people saved on the streets in the space of an hour. People are very open there, just like in Romania.

Poverty in African countries is affecting the spread of the Gospel a lot. Congo is rated as a Christian country, but knowledge of God and the Word is shallow.

In mid-2016, we returned. We continued empowering the churches there under the guidance of the mission leader. One day, we embarked on a wild outreach.

One of the evangelists there took us to a far remote area. We drove halfway, as roads were non-existent further on in our journey. People use small one-passenger scooters to commute as taxis. These scooters travel through very rough and scary paths, full of potholes, hills, sharp curves, valleys and pools of unclean water in some areas.

The evangelist got us to ride on those scooters. You pay a fare as the drivers earn a living from them. You are to sit at the back holding tightly for your dear life to the waist of the driver. They are so rough that, at one point, I closed my eyes but made sure my arms and hands were holding tight lest I fall.

We got there and we went to the streets with a team from one of the newly planted churches the evangelist had started.

Afterwards, we went to have a service in a makeshift church building. It was made from cardboard boxes, plastic materials to protect the cardboard from rain, and a makeshift roof. This was just where the platform was. The congregation was in an open space facing the platform. Luckily, the weather is always warm there. What impressed me most was the high church attendance and dedication to God despite the humble situation they were in.

We preached, then some team members gave testimonies and prayed for people for salvation and healing. In Africa, deliverance always pops up. People will get delivered one way or another. They have the faith of a child. We would then break into wild praise.

On our way back that night, riding on our scooter taxis, the evangelist took us to what was a private hospital. He owned it. He bought an old hotel, renovated it and turned it into a private hospital. It was still new. It consisted of one nurse, one doctor and there was only one patient at the time. He informed us of what was happening with the patient. It was a young heavily pregnant woman with unexplained fevers. She was reportedly deteriorating and they believed she may die soon as she had not responded to any medication that they tried on her. They were not sure what was wrong and had no diagnosis. The evangelist asked us to come and pray for her.

When we got there, the doctor confirmed that they didn't know what was wrong with her. She was lying in bed half-covered with a sheet as it was boiling hot that evening. She was sweating profusely and lay limp, almost lifeless. Her voice was barely audible. We asked her to try and sit up, but she couldn't. Her head was facing the other way towards the window. Her eyes were closed. When we asked her to open her eyes, she couldn't move her eyelids.

One could sense a feeling from everyone of having given up, from the patient, the doctor and the nurse. The atmosphere was saturated with disease, death and gloom.

My two London mission team mates quickly said, "Sarah, you pray for her." I nearly jumped out of that room. I had to compose myself as the other people were present and we couldn't be arguing as to who was to pray in front of them.

I just said, "We will all pray."

She had lost so much weight that the pregnancy was barely visible under the sheet.

Her breaths were very shallow. In a nutshell, she was dying. It was a very scary situation. I asked everyone to gather round and extend our hands to her. That's when the doctor and the nurse left the room. I asked the Holy Spirit to take over. I began to say some words; I don't know what I said. My teammates prayed in tongues. I went on and on praying, then they pitched in too, praying as led.

The lady moved. We pressed on, and her eyes opened. We pressed on, now with more faith, becoming louder in our prayers. She sat up and pulled the sheet to cover herself as she had nothing on due to the fevers and the hot room.

She suddenly spoke, her voice still a bit weak but audible and said she was a Christian and that the day before, God told her some people were coming to pray for her. The evangelist never said anything to any of the people there as the plan was not to go there, it was a detour; the plan was to go where we went for the outreach and back to our hotel. It just dawned on him whilst travelling back that we could go via the hospital and pray for the poor woman.

It was a miracle. She was completely healed. The doctor and the nurse came in and they couldn't believe their eyes.

The evangelist said he knew she would be healed and that's why he forced this detour. Back in the hotel, they were long expecting us back and were now getting worried. We were in an area where there was no signal or anything. Our phones were not working.

That is our God. We rode back on our scooters with our rough drivers to where we left the car.

In 2013, I seemed to be more drawn to noticing the homeless out on the streets when I walked, travelled or was evangelising in our teams. In London, street evangelism isn't easy; people are too much in a hurry all the time, and they seem pre-occupied with lots of things in their minds. To stop someone and share the Gospel takes a whole lot of effort, and on the whole, it really takes God.

The homeless seemed to be accessible and more accepting of the Gospel. This touched my heart as they would accept Jesus, get saved and then I would have to leave them there in the freezing temperatures, hungry and alone and go home to a warm house, family, hot food and a warm bed and hot bath.

Over time, my heart began to be disturbed. I started to share with the team how I felt. They were just as frustrated as I was. Some didn't understand why I was bothered, as according to them, they (the homeless) brought it on themselves.

I began to consult with God as to what could be done. God seemed to be saying, "You do something."

I didn't know where to start Or who to talk to.

I began to talk about this everywhere and to everyone who would listen.

One day, my colleague at work advised me to research and look for those who are already doing something to get some ideas.

Indeed, I began to research and consulted with God in prayer about it.

I wrote to the church about it and I was asked to provide a proposal. I did, but unfortunately, I never got a response.

I thought that lack of response meant I could go ahead thinking, if I wasn't allowed, I would have been told straight away. I had mentioned that I would not expect the church to finance the project; that this is just so they knew what I was doing.

I went on looking for venues. In April 2014, I found it. A local community hall, that offered tables, chairs, a fully equipped kitchen, bathroom and toilets, so, ideal for drop-in services. The cost was affordable and charged at an hourly rate. To start with, I signed up for 2 hours on Saturday afternoon. I paid three weeks advance to make sure the hall was secured for us, and to convince the people I meant business.

I went back so excited and joyfully informed the church about this, unfortunately this didn't go well. I wasn't allowed to do it.

Dejected and heavy-spirited, I informed the few people that were going to team up with me about this. I then went back to the people and informed them I wouldn't be hiring the hall any longer. They were shocked but couldn't do anything either. I was given my money back and that was it. By this time, invitations for the first meeting had gone out, flyers were made, and we went out distributing them and bringing awareness of what was coming to the locals and the homeless on the streets.

God never let go of my heart. In addition to the homeless, God placed in my heart the aim to reach out to the marginalised groups of people. The aim in that hall was to start with the homeless and then slowly add more services by reaching out to others like street workers, women from all walks of life and young people.

It took me some time to recover from the blow.

In 2017, I led evangelistic teams to team up and help one of the churches affiliated with ours. We held a few outreaches there. I had a discussion with the lady Pastor of that church to see if, in addition to the general outreaches, we could add specific ones, like the women's outreach, and do evangelistic events related to that. She agreed.

They had a hall, so the venue wasn't going to be an issue.

I organised flyers and everything required for the event. I got a few people to help distribute them around the area near the church.

Chapter 11. God's Faithfulness

The day before the event, I attended a prayer meeting that the church held on Friday evenings. I had begun to be part of this since we started working in partnership with them. My lady pastor friend and her people excused themselves from the next day's women's event. Another blow!

That didn't stop me, though, as the stage was already set. I had quite a few women attending. It went well. God was faithful. One lady from a Spanish church got the flyer and attended. She responded to the altar call and received deliverance from the effects of childhood abuse. I had no idea, but she came to me afterwards and informed me about it. She was in tears as she spoke. I thought, if I had cancelled this event just because people pulled out at the last minute, this lovely lady would have missed her miracle. Obedience!!!

From then onwards, I set my heart to obey God, no matter who was with me or Who was not with me.

I arranged to have the second event. I informed my lady pastor friend again. This time, they were honest enough to just not commit. I asked if I could use their hall. They didn't respond to my texts, phone calls or emails. I knew enough to question it.

I had to find a venue as it was clear I required one.

I went looking and found one in my local area.

I had a guest speaker who had written books and was involved in encouraging women to find their purposes in life. The event was better-attended than the first one. Few people from the neighbourhood attended.

Ministry time went well. I was very encouraged.

That was now the beginning of the Heart-to-Heart women's outreach ministry. This was actually created by my own experiences, in childhood and as a grown woman, relationships as well as the experience gained whilst doing street evangelism, meeting women who were being exploited and used in all sorts of evil ways by those holding them captive. The incident of the Slovakian woman I took to my house in 2009 triggered this a lot.

I am believing God for His hand upon this work. It's only the beginning.

The different disappointments and let-downs were just a means to test me. It felt like God wanted to see whether I relied on man or Him. If man lets me down and disappoints me, will I continue to trust Him and carry on even when I had no one?

Sometimes people, even leaders God places you under, will not understand your calling. They see in part. They only see people under them as serving one purpose, that of helping them with their own calling and ministry. Yes, there are such calls from God for certain people, but not everyone is called that way. Yes, people are to help others in their callings and ministry endeavours, but when God calls them for something else, they shouldn't be stopped.

Another thing is, we cannot expect people to understand what God is doing in our lives, just because they are our leaders, sometimes God tells only you. Again, your leader may certainly have been called for a different purpose unrelated to yours, and they are not obliged to go along with every member's idea or calling. Yes, it is painful when it looks like people are rejecting you, but the God that calls you knows better. He will bring it to completion in the right time, with the right team.

God's will is persistent and never lets go. If He calls you, He will keep knocking at your heart, reminding you of what He said to you from the beginning. He is no respecter of persons. No one is obliged to help you fulfil your destiny.

When God calls you, He already has a team for the work. In His own time, He will orchestrate it.

If people let you down and turn away from you, breaking their promises, don't get upset, don't get discouraged; proceed by yourself and see what God will do. He is faithful. People are fickle, unpredictable and untrustworthy, tossed to and fro by conditions; no matter who they are, even the most renowned of believers can let you down. But God is steadfast, immovable, and patient.

You may stall, you may get caught up in what is happening to and around you, getting distracted, but His call will remain upon you. His anointing for that call will remain on you. You may be tempted to react to all the deeds of men upon your life and often these reactions are fleshly and sinful as they are triggered by pain. God will always forgive you, but man may never do. Kathryn Kuhlman used to say, "You see, God will forgive you, but man will never forgive you; it's just like that."

During it all, the gift and calling upon your life are steadfast and there to stay. If you hold on to your faith in God, your destiny will come to pass. He alone will see to it. 'For the gifts and the calling of God are irrevocable.' Romans 11:29.

Sometimes God can speak and tell you He is calling you for a ministry and then you go ahead and start but nothing seems to fall into place with it. Half the time, it's because of wrong timing. When it's His timing, it will work. Not without difficulties of course, but it will work, however long it takes.

If people don't respond to your call, it simply means God has not called them with you.

The battle seemed to rage after these few events. 2018 -2019 was the worst time ever. Everything seemed to fall apart. Finances, friendships, work, losses and spiritual battles and oppositions. I lost my dear mother in August of 2019 at the peak of my hardest struggles of oppositions, denials, mistreatments, injustices, misunderstandings, false allegations, false accusations, harassment, slander, betrayals, and all. She had been my rock. I would never tell my mother about any of my struggles, because I was far away, and feared that she would be so worried about me and request that I returned home. She was very elderly, but at 91, she was still strong.

She would somehow just know and was praying for me day and night. Even when there were times when the blows were so hard and heavy that I would find it difficult to pray, she would be praying for me. Her prayer life struggled a little from when she arrived at her late 80s. She started showing signs of dementia which seemed to progress each year. By the time she reached 91, her memory had declined, her eyesight so greatly affected by diabetes that she couldn't read any longer even with glasses and relied on others to read the Bible for her. Physically, she was still stronger, given her age. She was mobile and able to feed herself and bathe herself with some assistance.

Slowly, her vital organs could not function well, and she had to be stopped, not without difficulty, from continuing with the ministry of the older women she adored so much.

Her prayer life didn't change. She would get anyone who came by or people in the house, my older sister Maria and my nephew Thabiso, to read the verses she would tell them to.

She was my rock. My children adored her. We all miss her a lot.

Words of Encouragement

To you who are currently going through tough times of any kind, know this:
God is alive and still on the Throne. He is Love. He is merciful and kind. He will never leave you nor forsake you. His promises are Yeah and Amen.

Just hang in there. He will surely come through for you.

"For I know the thoughts that I think toward you," says the Lord, "thoughts of peace and not of evil, to give you a future and a hope."   Jeremiah 29:11.

The first Heart-to-Heart women's outreach.

Chapter 11. God's Faithfulness

Above: Mali Africa mission 2009

The worship team. The night when the electricity failed, and we embarked on warfare praise till it returned. Romania mission 2014

Wimbledon missions 2013, 2014 and 2015.

Chapter 11. God's Faithfulness

Shepherds Bush Mission and weekly outreach 2014-2015.

A Journey of a Thousand Miles

Congo Missions 2015-2016

Chapter 11. God's Faithfulness

A Journey of a Thousand Miles

From Above:

First Photo: With young people and children in one of the churches.

Second photo: a dilapidated hotel used as a brothel, where we got to meet and share the Gospel with street workers in Kinshasa. 2016

Third photo: encouraging women in widow's ministry

Chapter 12.
Greater Works

God's faithfulness never left me, no matter how slow the progress, sometimes burdened with doubts, getting on and off, discouraged, and with tendencies to look to people for guidance instead of relying on God. I had to learn the hard way, as those I looked up to for guidance and help, tended to withhold it. At times, they would speak very negatively about the things I was involved in, including the writing of this book. They would rubbish my endeavours and undermine my efforts. It hurt a lot, but it actually helped me to go back to God.

At times, I would doubt even the call of God on my life. I seemed to be surrounded by three different types of people.

- Those who never say anything but surely pray for you without your knowledge. These are those who are solid. They have come to know you for who you are. Their love for you doesn't get changed by what they may hear about you.

- The second group are those who may have liked you in the past. There was something about you they liked but when you get flooded by attacks, slander, lies, spoken about badly, accused falsely, they begin to get concerned about their own reputation and begin to avoid you, stop all contacts, pretend you are not there.

- The last group are those who are only open about their friendship with you when you are doing well and liked by others. They do this for their own benefit, whatever they can get from you for themselves. As soon as you fall into some type of attack, whether it's your fault or not, they disappear or openly blame you for whatever is happening. When things get back in your favour, they are back again. It's a seesaw kind of relationship which is very selfish and unreliable.

No one is without fault. No matter how small the fault may be. This happens a lot when people are facing attacks of any kind from any source. They are prone to being wrong in how they deal with the issues they're facing, the way they react and the decisions they make.

This last group tend to be on the lookout for things like that. They fail to consider that, humanly speaking, it's hard to constantly resist the temptation to protect oneself, to reason, to explain, the list goes on. Anyone faced with unending attacks is prone to lean on this side. No one is immune from this, especially if those attacks are unfounded, false, never-ending and keep coming from the same direction or source. This group tends to get impatient with you and condone what you are experiencing; even when they know it's wrong, they publicly scorn and condemn you.

In all this, I learnt who God is; that He is not like man. He never changes. His love is not affected by what I do, what I don't do, who I am, who I am not, what I can do or what I can't do. He is reliable, honest, loyal and trustworthy.

Don't get me wrong, some people are right in seeing the wrongness in how you deal with things, but the way they go about trying to get you to see your wrongs is also wrong and not helpful. It is full of blame, accusations, harshness and unkindness. All you hear are these negative attributes, not the intentions behind them. Communication is key. How you portray and deliver your message to anyone, especially those who are hurting, is vital.

Aim at getting them to see where they are going wrong in a loving, non-judgemental manner, and see how they turn around, adjust and correct their ways. They sure will, when you operate through the Holy Spirit as He will work through you to convict them instead of condemning them. Condemnation pushes people away. Conviction brings people back to God.

People are weak. Sometimes they are more concerned about the risk of losing their friends, especially if the instruments Satan is using in your attacks are their friends. They rebuke and shame you publicly to make sure their perpetrator friends hear that they are on their side, so they don't lose that friendship by looking like they are standing with you.

On the other hand, they secretly try to make you understand that they are aware of the truth of what is being done to you and that they are supporting you, but that is only in secret. Publicly, they join the attackers against you.

If they truly cared and were sincere about it, they would have called you aside and talked to you in person about what they had seen and advise you about making changes and adjustments required. This is love. It never fails. It always achieves good results.

When you change for the better, they gain not only you but their perpetrator friends that they are so fearful to lose, as there will be peace between you and the instruments used in the attacks. God becomes happy; everything becomes good. Lives are saved and spared. They would have just allowed themselves to be an instrument of reconciliation and a peacemaker.

Choosing to have a good positive regard to both those they deem more important in their life and those they deem less important, always glorifies God and brings peace and reconciliation to people.

Public bashing never gets the attention of anyone to see what is wrong in their actions, but only serves to drive them deeper and deeper into the wrong behaviour. It stirs resentment and anger. It reinforces enmity.

When God calls for order in a person's life, He doesn't climb the highest platform, get the loudest mic, the most powerful sound system, use the strongest and most popular media source to speak to the person. He often employs His small still voice like He did with the Prophet Elijah.

'Then He said, "Go out, and stand on the mountain before the Lord." And behold, the Lord passed by, and a great and strong wind tore into the mountains and broke the rocks in pieces before the Lord, but the Lord was not in the wind; and after the wind an earthquake, but the Lord was not in the earthquake; and after the earthquake a fire, but the Lord was not in the fire; and after the fire a still small voice.' 1 Kings 19:11-13. NKJV

"Brethren, if a man be overtaken in a fault, you who are spiritual, restore such a one in the spirit of meekness; considering yourself, lest you also be tempted." Galatians 6:1. KJV (200 Bible)

Oftentimes, it's not that people don't want to change. In most cases, they just can't see things clearly due to being bombarded by what would be taking place. They need help. The problem lies with how those who see the issue and attempt to help, go about doing that. How they communicate. How they deal with them.

Now, I would like the reader to understand that I mentioned the things I talked about in this book, especially my experiences, in a good heart that has forgiven. I am not writing out of offence. It's past now. There was a time that I hurt a lot regarding all these things. Over time, with much prayer and determination to heal and move on, God helped me.

I wouldn't have managed to even write about them.

Proof that God healed me is when I was able to talk to that congregation in Yorkshire in 2010 and was able to minister and people were delivered and healed. It was after that time that I sensed God wanted me to share to help His people.

The purposes of mentioning them are:

- They are part of my life's journey

- Someone who is currently experiencing similar things will be helped.

My part in outreach and evangelism never ceased. The path was never smooth. There were many hurdles I had to jump and obstacles I had to push through, but it continued to be a forward movement.

We continued and are still doing missions and outreaches in our local areas and in the wider city and beyond. We do special outreaches at certain times in the year like Christmas, Good Friday, Easter Saturday and Sunday, Valentine's Day and Carnival time. We get involved with the other types of outreaches other members of the church are doing, such as sport, that endeavours to engage the local community and get young boys off the streets and train them to play football, as well as looking for opportunities to share the Gospel and other outreaches that hold music concerts in pubs.

Testimonies:

Here are nuggets of some of the incredible stories of evangelism and healings.

1. Maria (not her real name)

A lady in my team, one Sunday afternoon in 2015, met and witnessed to a lady who was originally from Romania.

We will call her Maria in this book.

This happened on the street outside a train station in Shepherd's Bush. Maria was devastated at the time, not knowing where she, her two young children and two sisters would be by that time the next day as she was facing eviction. New in the country, no job, no money, difficulties with the children, Maria was unable to even relate her ordeal, let alone grasp a word of encouragement.

That day, outside of that station, at the end of her tether, Maria met Jesus and accepted Him as her personal Saviour along with her children. The sister hesitated. Her face flooded with tears; Maria was inconsolable but dared to trust the only thing there was left; Jesus.

My team member testified to this and asked me to help her out with praying for Maria and her family as she needed it so badly at the time.

We made an appointment to meet with Maria again in a coffee shop near where the lady first met her.

We 'adopted' Maria from that day onwards. Practically, we helped carry some of the loads she had. We met with her almost every Sunday by the coffee shop. We provided practical help and means to some extent to ease off her ordeal, pray, counsel and do anything possible in the Name of Jesus to just hold her there. The Lord moved and they got a temporary place, shared, but at least a roof above their heads. We carried out several home visits, praying for everyone and the children who were hard-hit emotionally and spiritually by all this. Things were bad. The small boy required deliverance.

Each visit moved things a step in the right direction. The family began attending the evening service. Prayer continued even in the church prayer lines.

Maria joined my small group a couple of months later. She got baptised. The day she was baptised, the whole family, children, sisters and a brother-in-law accompanied her. We all sat at the table together with some of the team leaders. The brother-in-law was saved that day.

Later in the year, Maria was given her own beautiful place by the council, enough for her and her children. She never once stopped coming to church since we met her that day at the station, even though she now lived quite far away. You can tell what a happy woman she is now. She's following Jesus with all her heart.

Up till this day, Maria and her sisters, as well as her daughter who has grown up, are attending church every Sunday.

2. Joana

I first met Joana in church in the summer of 2015. I happened to sit next to her during the evening service.

I didn't really take much notice of her as there were many people there but I was aware that I hadn't seen her before.

It was a customary practice that, after the preaching, an altar call was made for those who would like to receive Jesus Christ as their personal Saviour.

Joana raised her hand. That was when I really began to take full notice of her.

I turned slightly to her side, smiled and congratulated her. She smiled back.

I quickly asked for a new believer's pack from the Usher and when every else was leaving, I asked Joana to spend a few minutes with me so I could pray with her.

Joana agreed and I explained to her that it is the church's practice that details of people who received salvation would be collected for the purposes of follow-up, whereby it was made sure that they didn't find themselves alone and not knowing what to do after being saved.

I also explained to her that the church practised 'small groups' ministry, whereby each group is allocated a leader and they meet once weekly for purposes of discipleship and to help one another in practical life needs.

I invited Joana to join the group I was leading. She agreed there and then.

After collecting details, I asked Joana if I could pray for her. She agreed and I asked her what she would want me to pray for specifically.

Joana began to cry and informed me that she was in a serious relationship and that they would like to get married, but the parents of her boyfriend were not agreeing with it. She went on to tearfully tell me that they loved each other very much, but due to cultural differences, her Asian fiancé's parents were not happy for him to marry outside of their traditional Indian nation. Joana informed me that she is Portuguese and said it had been a battle to the point where the boyfriend was disowned by his parents when he refused to leave her. He had not been on talking terms with them for a few years as a result.

Joana informed me that they invited him back to India saying that there was an important family event he needed to attend and that it wouldn't go on without him as all their children would be attending it. Joana expressed her fears that he may not return, that they were just about to get engaged and she thinks they tricked him so he would go there and they would stop him from returning to her.

Here was this new beautiful young lady, pouring her heart out to me, after just knowing me for a few minutes, desperate and distraught. Where do I start? I thought it was going to be "pray for my exams, or new job etc.,"- the usual stuff.

Joana was very emotional and sobbing uncontrollably. I just put my hand on her shoulder and whispered in her ear that she was now a child of God, sealed with the seal of the Holy Spirit, and nothing could take that away from her.

I went on to say the God that she just surrendered her life to, is a big God, who can turn things around in a way that can be unbelievable.

I asked her to hold my hand as we prayed for the situation, that if what she suspected was true, then we were going to ask God to work in this situation, wrought a miracle and that her boyfriend would return, they would be engaged and eventually marry. I didn't even think at the time about if this was not going to happen, what would this young new believer think of God?

On my way home, it did hit me that it may not be as we want it to be. It may not be God's will for them to marry. My thoughts went on a 'shopping spree' for all the 'if's' in the world.

Chapter 12. Greater Works

Joana started attending the group meetings on Sundays as well as church service. We prayed more as a group now into this situation. At the time, I was leading the new believer's training course on Tuesdays and I invited Joana to it. This was a course to teach about basic Bible topics such as the Holy Spirit, Salvation, Water Baptism, baptism with the Holy Spirit, church attendance and membership, prayer, fellowship etc. Each topic was discussed for a week.

She joined and completed her ten weeks.

This course was to be followed by another course for ten weeks too, which focused on getting new believers freed and delivered from life issues and unresolved life experiences that may be affecting their journey with God.

I encouraged Joana to enrol in it too. She did.

It was during this course that I encouraged Joana to think about getting baptised. She agreed and was baptised in September 2015.

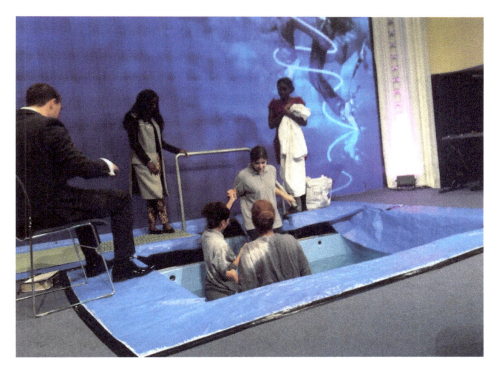

Joana being baptised.

Shortly after this baptism, Joana informed me that her boyfriend was back and they were now engaged.

A few months later, Joana informed me that her fiancé's parents had come over from India to bless their relationship and marriage.

The fiancé joined the church and I helped find him a small group to join.

Long story short, they went on to marry and were blessed with a beautiful, very healthy boy.

Joana is still in my small group as at the writing of this book and pursuing God at every level.

3. Elena and her lovely daughter

In 2016, one of the ladies in my small group called me during the week and informed me that she had met a lady in church on the Sunday before and that the lady was looking for a small group to join. My group member had taken this lady's contact numbers and gave them to me to contact her. I invited her to join us the next Sunday and she came.

After a few attendances, she settled and gained some rapport with me. She then asked me if I could help pray for a situation that she had. I met separately with her one day and she related the situation.

Elena, that is her name, was of Eastern European descent. She relocated to the UK from Russia many years ago. She was working and met and fell in love with a West African man from Sierra Leone. They never married but lived together and had a beautiful mixed-race girl. The man was a lawyer by profession.

Later on, when the girl was under 10 years of age, the father decided to relocate to the USA for work. He stopped contact with his family. One day, Elena attempted to make things work for the sake of their daughter and went to visit him in America, only to find him living full-time with another woman.

He asked the woman to give them space; she did, but things were never the same. The relationship was over. Devastated, Elena returned to the UK and got the daughter back into school. At age 13, the little girl started having some behavioural issues. She began to self-harm, experienced low mood and eventually stopped going to school. She had gained a lot of weight and was being bullied at school as a result of that.

The girl was an aspiring musician. She was in music class and played the keyboard and guitar very well.

She used to at least come out of the room once or twice a day and play her musical instruments. All this completely stopped.

Not only did she stop attending school but stayed upstairs in bed all day and night, and neglected her personal hygiene and nutrition. Things got worse; she would only talk to Elena and totally hid from everyone else.

She began to experience some paranoid delusions of some sort, perceiving danger around her bedroom and getting frightened. She reported to her mother that she could see creatures in her room that were fearful.

Elena brought her into her own bedroom and shared the bed with her. By the time we visited the house to pray, the girl's only friend was a black cat that spent hours and hours lying in bed with her.

I asked my evangelism team member who had helped me pray for Maria to come with me. We fasted for a few days prior to going, and asked Elena to fast as well.

Elena was newly saved. She had been in and out of churches.

We began with taking a detailed history from Elena just so we had a clue as to what we were dealing with.

Elena related that her mother was involved in some traditional things that were not Biblical. She said she used to carry out some rituals with a group of people that sometimes came to her house. They did strange things. She said she herself, together with her parents, was involved in an Orthodox Church and now that she was a believer, she had discovered that things that she got involved in whilst there were not of God.

Elena herself experienced emotional abuse from both parents. They were very harsh, especially the mother.

Elena went on to say that when her partner left them, she began to drink alcohol. She met a female friend who drank regularly and got her into it. She felt relieved of the hurt of desertion and rejection. She got very deep into drinking. She related that she drank daily and hopped in and out of relationships with different men and used to bring them to her house. Some stayed for some time. This affected her daughter negatively and pushed her deeper into the reclusive world.

Elena informed us that she would leave her little girl by herself in the house for days on end at times, with no food or anything. By this time, the girl was self-harming heavily. At times, she left the girl under the care of the man she would be living with at the time, who also drank alcohol. The last man was from Pakistan and was illegal in the UK. He was into some strange religious cultural practices and used to perform rituals in the house, putting things everywhere around the house. Both Elena and her girl's lives were getting worse. The man began beating her and emotionally abusing the girl.

Later, after a long time, she managed to sober up by a miracle. She stated that a woman from another church came to pray in the house. She still was not saved and didn't attend church. The situation got worse but at least she stopped drinking. Social services got involved through the GP as she took the girl to the GP for self-harming and she was referred to mental health services. They got the social services involved. The girl was removed for a short period. She stopped drinking and the girl was given back to her. She was eventually discharged from mental health.

Elena got some sense into her and asked the man to leave. It was a huge fight, but he eventually left when Elena handed him over to the police and he was deported.

Elena took a journey through her house and said she found some scary stuff all over her house; some in corners, some were strange objects, some were oils, some articles hung on certain parts of the rooms and passages.

She removed all of them and cleaned the house. Then she got someone to come and paint the house.

She herself got a little better but the girl got worse and worse.

It was for her she wanted us to come and pray.

When we got there, things were just as she said. A lovely house, very clean, but the young girl vegetating inside it.

Her keyboard and guitar were the first things we saw when we stepped into the living room. They were nicely packed away in a corner. Elena tearfully pointed at them and said, "This is what she loved to do. It was her life, but she hasn't touched any of them for over two years now."

We prayed first with Elena, got her to confess, renounce, forgive whoever she needed to, including herself and God. She took everything very seriously.

We then went upstairs to the room where her daughter was as she wouldn't come out of bed. Indeed, we found her in bed covered all over with a duvet, with the black cat lying on the side beside her, outside the duvet as if to guard and protect her. It looked at us as if it wanted to chase us away from the room.

Elena introduced us to the girl whose face and head were hidden under the duvet. She didn't respond. Elena had spoken to her about it some days before she got us to come. She had agreed for us to come. By this time, the girl was just about to turn 20 years old.

Chapter 12. Greater Works

She had been home-schooled in her early teens as she dropped out of school at age 13 due to behavioural issues.

We then informed her that we were going to pray and that it was okay for her to remain in bed. We prayed however we felt that the Lord wanted us to pray. We bound, we loosed, we cast, we broke and we did everything, everything that the Holy Spirit permitted. We then anointed the whole house with the oil I had brought from Israel.

Nothing dramatic happened.

We left but continued praying for her.

Elena continued to attend church and my cell group. After almost 6 months, Elena testified that the girl had been talking to her, not much, but she seemed a bit brighter. She also said that the girl came out of the room a few times a week now and sat in the living room on the sofa and watched TV.

We continued to pray.

We advised Elena to ask her if she could pray in her presence. It went well. She agreed.

Another three months, and the girl was now spending much more time downstairs and had begun to play the guitar for a short time a few times a week.

By the end of that year, 2016, the girl was now listening to Elena reading the Bible out loud when they were both in the living room.

In early 2017, Elena said she was asking her questions about the Bible.

Mid-2017, Elena asked her to read a few verses out loud, which she did.

Elena was led into salvation in the group as she was not saved. I informed her about the need for baptism, but she said she wasn't ready. I gave her some space to pray and seek God.

Elena changed jobs and the new job caused her to finish late afternoon on Sundays, making it difficult for her to attend. I discussed with the lady preacher of the network church we teamed up with in the mission during that time. This is the church that had to move from Clapham. I asked her to help disciple Elena and get her into her church as it was nearer where Elena lived as opposed to our one.

We paid Elena a visit with the Pastor in her house so I could introduce them to each other. Elena began attending their Friday prayer meeting and sometimes Sundays when she wasn't starting work early.

It was in April of 2018 that Elena contacted me and informed me that she and her daughter wanted to be baptised. I was not very surprised by her desire to now be baptised, but the girl!!

I really knew that our God lives, and He takes prayer seriously.

I was so shocked that I struggled to believe her. She kept asking me when they could do it. I was a bit concerned that I would fill in the forms and then they wouldn't come on the day, especially the daughter. I asked Elena to come to our church the next Sunday with her. Elena said she didn't want to come to church as yet, but wanted to be baptised. I got more concerned.

I asked her to just come by herself and fill in the form. She did and I informed her to leave out her daughter's form and that we would do it when she came for baptism. We left it that way. I still had doubts about her daughter's seriousness about this baptism.

On Sunday 27th of May 2018, the baptism Sunday, I got up so early. I prayed to God that they would come. I kept sending text messages to Elena, checking if the daughter was still coming. Elena kept reassuring me that she was coming. This was a girl that wouldn't leave her bed. The thought of taking this huge step and not only getting out of the house but travelling on public transport around crowds of people in London, was unbelievable. Only God can do this.

I took a huge step too and went to a florist shop to buy both a bunch of flowers each, still doubting whether the girl would come. I went to church, waited for them as we agreed they must be there for 1:30 pm for teaching on baptism before they were baptised. The service was to start at 2:30pm. Baptism candidates were to be there at least an hour before. It was 2 pm, and they were nowhere. I was even afraid to call any longer for fear I would hear, "We are not coming any longer".

I suddenly got a text to say, "We are just getting off the train; we are 5 minutes away." "Oh, My Lord, I thank you," I said out loud to my other group members as they stayed to support Elena.

They indeed arrived. I took them both into the teaching room, explained and apologised on their behalf to the person teaching, got the form and helped the girl to fill it in, accompanied them and left them on the front seat where all the candidates were seated. It was like a dream. They were baptised. The girl was baptised. Her beautiful face was beaming with a huge smile. She was nowhere near where she was or how she had been the day we visited their house to pray for her.

The God we serve!!

Chapter 12. Greater Works

Elena and her beautiful daughter after the baptism.

4. Odette

Odette joined my small discipleship group in 2017. She had been coming to church but didn't really know anyone, didn't get involved in anything, and wasn't committed as such.

She grew up in a loveless home environment. Father was very strict, and emotionally and physically abusive. Her mother was indifferent.

Later, Father became a Christian but never changed. He would attend church, return home and carry on the same way towards his family.

This made Odette hate church. She resented and blamed God.

She suffered from anger, self-loathing, mood swings, bad temper, irritability and avoided people.

She relocated to the UK in 1998 from Brazil.

She felt very alone and lost, and thought maybe she needed to consider attending church.

She started off by attending conferences only. This went on for 6 months.

In one of those conferences, one of the speakers preached about something that touched her heart. She felt compelled to know more about the preacher. She took their church leaflet from reception and began attending their church, even though it was very far away. It was a Pentecostal church, the New Wine Church.

Got saved and baptised her. She remained a faithful member for 7 years. Her mother passed away in 2007. Odette got angry with God, herself and everything and everyone.

She stopped going to church for 10 years.

All these 10 years were plagued with self-loathing, depression, being angry with God and everyone and negative thinking all the time.

She thought she was going crazy. It felt like she was losing her mind.

One day, she thought, enough of this, and attended the nearest church in her area which happened to be my church. That was around March 2017.

She attended till August and felt alone and lost again even though she enjoyed the services.

The next Sunday, she approached someone and asked about small groups and how she could find one to join.

She somehow was brought to me and I informed her about the times, frequency and day as well as the venue. She agreed to join and the next Sunday, I introduced her to the other members.

Over a period, she began to feel accepted and free enough to open up about her issues to us. One day, she was the only one who attended, and she went a bit

Chapter 12. Greater Works

deeper with her issues; what was still happening. She was getting very irritable and felt she still carried huge anger in her and would show it to her employers at times without realising. She worked as a housekeeper and stated that, in one of the families she worked for, she would even find herself making the children fearful of her. She would look at herself in the mirror and call herself names, punching herself and isolating a lot. Her self-loathing was increasing.

It was realised that her situation required a much deeper approach of prayer and this was communicated to the leadership who authorised the move and provided a room for it.

A fast was carried out for at least 2 days before the prayer time with one of the ladies in the evangelism team, the same lady who partnered with me before.

Prayer of deliverance and inner healing was carried out on a Sunday morning in the room provided. We led Odette in confession, forgiveness and renunciation, as well as breaking soul ties.

Things began to clear out, including her self-loathing, which was the main issue. She informed me that her mom used to say she was ugly, she was the ugliest child in the world, would spew insults and negative words to her face and called her names.

We gave her scriptures of affirmation of who God says she is, of healing and declarations of her identity in God. She got better as time went on.

She testified in every group meeting how she was noticing a great change. I gave her a list of confessions and scriptures to say to herself daily to oppose the negative thoughts when they popped into her mind.

She realised that the more she did this, the more the thoughts reduced.

One day, she surprised them by being very nice, tolerant and understanding without her realising it. It was the older child that fed back to her and told her mother about it.

Then the father, (her boss) remarked that when she came in these days, there was so much calmness and peace around the house. This surprised her, as she had worked for them for many years but they'd never said this before.

During one time of prayer, after praying for her, she felt something coming from within her right ear, and as it did, pressure and discomfort was felt along the ear canal.

She suddenly heard a 'pop' and realised something opened in her ear. She realised her hearing was more distinct and louder than usual. She had been told a few times by her bosses that she seemed to have problems with her hearing, but she was not aware of it so she used to not believe what they were saying.

When this happened, she then remembered what her boss said and believed that her right ear was indeed not hearing well.

The left ear had been compensating well.

She used to say she couldn't pray for more than 5 minutes but now she was doing her devotionals and her Bible reading, and prayer had greatly improved. She uses the Bible reading plan I recommended to her.

As at present, Odette is still doing very well.

5. Athena

From street evangelism:

Athena is an elderly Italian lady who lived in a nearby town to our church. There was a time in the mid-2000s when I had the honour to lead a team every Sunday for street evangelism in this town, when this wonderful lady was witnessed to by a member of our team back in 2014. After giving her life to Jesus, it was discovered that she had a few social and domestic issues. The team member discussed with me and we agreed to pay her a home visit to pray with her and see how else we could be of help.

Whilst talking to her in depth at her house, we discovered that she required prayer for healing and deliverance as well as befriending, as she was isolated and lonely.

We did that and kept in touch with her both by phone and through more home visits. It didn't end there; we provided practical help. We bought cleaning stuff and chose a day where we went and spring-cleaned her house. The kitchen and bathroom were very bad. We offered advice and she managed to get the council involved and her kitchen and bathroom got renovated free of charge.

We eventually managed to get her to attend church services when she felt better and she did this for the rest of that year to mid-2015 and then she disappeared.

We attempted contact by phone and home visit but to no avail.

On the first Sunday of March 2020, she came over to where we evangelise as she knew where we used to be. She came looking for us wanting to not only thank us but tell us that she was well, and things were going well. She had been away to her country visiting family all this time when we wondered what happened to her. She looked so well, so strong and clearly happy, chuckling like a child when she saw us.

6. A homeless woman from Slovakia

It was in late 2009 when, one evening, whilst out evangelising, I met this lady. I will call her Tania. As usual, I approached her to share the Gospel with her. She was sitting on a bench. Tania responded and engaged well in the conversation, accepted Jesus as Saviour into her life but I realised that something was not quite right. Her clothes were not that clean, and she was a bit inebriated. She smelled of alcohol and was slurring her speech a bit.

I then asked Tania if everything was alright. She began to cry and told me she was homeless and that she had been kicked out of a hostel and was now getting abused by men on the streets.

She begged me to help her. I took her to the evening service. She stayed throughout the service and, at the end, I presented her to our leader, the church evangelist. I informed him of Tania's ordeal and that I found it difficult to just leave her out there after she had not only given her life to Christ but informed me of her issues.

The leader found a card with numbers for homeless help and advice. They called the number and the organisation managed to find a room in one of the hostels nearby. It was around 22:00 when we finally took her to the hostel and left her there. They informed us that the hostel serves as emergency accommodation and that tomorrow they would move her to a long-term accommodation.

Luckily, Tania had a phone and we helped top it up with credit so we could get hold of her and so could she when she needed to speak to us.

The next day around 10:00, I saw several missed calls from Tania. I was in the Bible school then and had been in class when she attempted to contact me.

During the break, I returned her call and was met with floods of tears. She informed me that she had been asked to leave the hostel in the morning and that the hostel people told her they were unable to take her to long-term accommodation as she was not a UK citizen.

Tania was so distraught and so afraid at being back on the street and her sobbing just tore my heart apart. She had told me the day before that the men not only sexually exploited her but got her into prostitution to generate money which they then took to use for themselves.

I told her to go back to where I first met her and that I would be there around 4 pm to see what we could do for her. I communicated this to the leader, but they said there wasn't anything more that could be done as the only thing they would normally do is to link people with the organisation. In her case, she didn't fit the criteria for their clients due to problems with citizenship.

I was now stuck with Tania. I asked myself, am I leaving her here with all that she told me is happening to her, or what? If I do, how will I live or even sleep at night knowing what's happening to her out here? All these questions were playing in my mind.

I sought God and decided to take a huge risk and take her home with me with the aim of finding her another hostel.

My house had two double rooms, but one tiny room which my son was using. The other two were for my daughter and one for me.

I was attending Bible school by day and working night duty every other night, on top of the weekly street outreach.

I fetched Tania from where we had agreed to meet; the exact spot where I first met her.

She had very few belongings, just a medium bag with hardly anything in it. She had two mobile phones, not surprising, as they were given to her by her pimps for business.

I asked my daughter to share her room with Tania, provided a mattress and gave her our extra blankets and pillows to use. My daughter gave her a pair of new pyjamas she hadn't used yet. I had to arrange an agreement with Tania about not using either of her phones without any of us being present and that she would only use them to call her parents in Slovakia. This was to guard against her being contacted by the pimps and ending up telling them her whereabouts, which was my home address, and getting my family and I into grave danger. Tania, at first, was not happy about this but I explained my concerns and told her that if we couldn't agree on this, not only for her own safety but ours too, then she would, unfortunately, have to return to the streets.

The thought of returning to the streets was too much to bear for Tania and she agreed.

She could call home once daily. Tania wanted to stay with us but be allowed to go back to the streets during the day. I told her that would not happen as it would put us all in danger with these pimps. She was not happy with this, but it was explained to her that she couldn't have it this way. Either she stayed inside with us till we got her help, or she went back to the streets.

Tania disclosed to me that she had physical health issues, asthma and an ulcer for which she had been getting medication from her GP when she was still working as a housekeeper in the north of London. I was working in the rehab unit in the Priory at the time and had extensive experience with alcohol dependency and drug addiction. I quickly picked up that Tania was dependent on alcohol and that she was going to need some sort of detox and also she may be at risk of withdrawal seizures as well as attacks from her poorly managed asthma, as she was not taking her medication whilst out on the streets.

She also informed me that she was still registered with this GP and that she attempted to get detox from them but that they declined because of her lifestyle which made it difficult for the GP to monitor her treatment. I decided to take Tania there and discuss with the GP that she was currently safe with me and that I was a nurse and experienced in addictions, so I could do a home detox with her at my place. The GP informed me how it had been difficult treating Tania and that she had epilepsy. She also had not been attending check-ups and not collecting her prescriptions.

I managed to assure the GP that I would take personal responsibility to make sure she took her medication and would report to them when there were problems.

Her GP eventually agreed and issued us with a week's worth of detox as well as inhalers and anti-epileptic medication.

Tania also told me that the last hostel she lived in had all the information about her parents as she wouldn't tell me much when I asked her. I took her to the hostel and they indeed knew her and told me they had to kick her out as she was prostituting herself inside and causing fights between the men as it was a mixed hostel.

Tania had been kicked out of several hostels for drinking alcohol and prostitution.

The hostel staff did not want to give Tania another chance to stay there, saying that one man nearly killed another man as a result of Tania playing them.

I then asked them to help contact her parents in Slovakia and tell them what was happening here and that they needed to rescue her from the streets. The staff made contact whilst we were there, and Tania got to speak to her parents. They arranged to purchase an electronic flight ticket and send it to the staff for Tania to return home. All this was not done in one day but took a whole two weeks to come through. Meanwhile, Tania remained at my place. It was scary and very risky, but God was faithful. When I informed the evangelists about this, they warned me that this was too risky; they wouldn't advise me to take it on. However, if I felt I had to do it, I could go ahead but they would not be involved.

Long story short, Tania managed to fully detox with no complications and had a whole two weeks of sobriety before leaving the UK. The arrangement of her departure was that as I was attending college and working, the hostel staff agreed to help take her to the airport. Tania eventually went home and escaped death on the streets of London.

God is amazing.

There are many more stories and testimonies, but I won't be able to put them all here. I would leave you with this one though.

If you are discipling someone, don't get discouraged when they seem to take one step forward and three back. Hang on to them. God knows.

If you are involved in reaching out to the lost, don't get discouraged; when some days are darker, there is no catch, or you caught fish but it seems they all slip through your fingers, hang on to it. God knows.

It is never in vain. Isaiah 55:11

Chapter 13.
Total healing

Healing comes after total forgiveness.
In this chapter I am going to look at:

- what forgiveness is
- what forgiveness is not.
- what unforgiveness can do to you.
- how to forgive
- how you know you have forgiven

What forgiveness is:

Forgiveness is the intentional and voluntary process by which a victim (person wronged) undergoes a change in feelings and attitude regarding an offense, let go of negative emotions such as vengefulness, or expectations and wishes for punishment of the offender, however legally or morally justified it might be, and with an increased ability to wish the offender well.

What Forgiveness is NOT:

Forgiveness is different from:
- condoning - failing or refusing to see the action as wrong and being in need of forgiveness.
- excusing - not holding the offender as responsible for the action.
- forgetting - removing awareness of the offense from one's consciousness.
- pardoning - whereby a representative of society such as a judge, steps in and grants an acknowledgement of the offence.
- reconciliation - restoration of a relationship. I know this may sound tough to some readers, but yes, it is not a must and sometimes, not advisable to return to the same situation, person(s) that brought about the offence in the first place, especially if they have not stopped their actions towards the wronged person.

Reconciliation can be done but wisdom and care should be applied and clear judgement of the situation to see if it is ideally wise and safe for someone to get back with those causing them harm and refusing to stop doing so to them or to a situation or place where their harm is coming from.

One can forgive and move on. It is OK. This means the person puts everything out of their lives and stops talking about the issues and the perpetrator(s).

In most contexts, forgiveness is granted without any expectation of restorative justice, and without any response on the part of the offender. For example, one may forgive a person who is dead, or still alive, but who is not willing to acknowledge their actions to the person wronged.

In real practical terms, it may be necessary for the offender to offer some form of acknowledgment, an apology, or even just ask for forgiveness, in order for the wronged person to believe themselves able to forgive as well, but this is rare. It takes humility on the part of the offender to do this.

No one, not even God, I believe, expects anyone to continue to stay with or get back with someone who, for instance, subjects them to unending continuous emotional, psychological or physical abuse.

The emotional and psychological abuse will eventually turn them into a mental invalid. It doesn't only affect all aspects of the person, their family and friends, but society at large. They end up needing care as they wouldn't be able to do that for themselves any longer, accessing public funds as they wouldn't be able to function in a job, they wouldn't be able to carry their duty and responsibilities as a spouse and parent resulting in a dysfunctional family unit with children ultimately becoming the same. Then they do the same things done to them or not done for them by their parents to their own spouses and children. Those children carry on the legacy of a dysfunctional family unit. Society is affected, the economy is affected, through the loss of manpower and the burden upon the government to step in to help.

The physical abuse, in most cases, ends up in the death of the victim if they continued to stay with or got back to the perpetrator.

You can forgive and move on. You are not obliged to remain with the perpetrator in an abusive relationship, whichever type of relationship it may be, intimate, friendship, professional or spiritual. Emotional and psychological abuse is the worst and most hidden from everyone else outside of the victim. It may be observed at times by immediate family members and some close relatives or friends, but oftentimes it gets missed and is quite hidden from everyone purposely by the perpetrator. They are skilled in doing this. They isolate the victim, remove all possible help from them by lying to their friends, family members, relatives, acquaintances and bosses as well as colleagues about the victim, portraying them as mentally unbalanced and not to be listened to or believed. The coin flips to them being abused by the victim to gain sympathy and support from all these people, with the victim becoming ostracised by all of them, viewed as a very bad person from what they are told by the perpetrator and ultimately they shun the victim and isolate them, doing exactly what the perpetrator wanted.

God understands and sees this. He understands the reasons why reconciliation is not always the solution and is not proof of forgiveness. Forgiveness happens in the heart first. The offended takes a heart decision to forgive and release the offender and move on with their life.

True genuine forgiveness is not easy. It takes the help of the Holy Spirit.

Consequences of staying with unforgiveness

- it affects relationships
- It breeds negative emotions
- It promotes distrust, which leads to isolation and separation
- It causes division

It affects health, physically and mentally.

People who live with unforgiveness are prone to heart disease, ulcers, gastritis, cancer, asthma, and colitis. Research has shown that chronically angry people die at a younger age than non-hostile people.

Mentally, it makes the person harbour grudges which survive on anger; when things don't change, the anger is turned inward, leading to depression and anxiety. If depression is not properly addressed, part of which can be by forgiving, then it can trigger underlying severe depressive conditions like Bipolar mood disorders or, in some cases, schizophrenic symptoms and suicide.

Don't get me wrong. These conditions can be caused by chemical imbalances but will be aggravated by unforgiveness.

Bitterness causes one to stay in fight and flight mode.

It creates feelings of doom and gloom, irrational fears, unwarranted guilt and these will come out in speeches and non-verbal behaviours. Words become sharp and biting, harsh and hurtful. Communication is conveyed with bluntness and requests are barked at people.

Psychologically, it affects your perspective on things. You expect doom and gloom. You expect to be treated badly. You write people off. If the perpetrator is a teacher, all teachers are bad; if it is a priest, all priests are bad; if it's a man, all men are bad; if it's a woman, all women are bad. The list goes on. Satan will always find instruments to use in all situations to reinforce this.

Spiritually, it can affect how you see God. It reverses what God says about His love for His people, including you. You tend to think that God has favourites like people do. You tend to think that God, like people, will only like you when you do things for Him, when you are being good and when things are going well.

He becomes unpredictable just as people are. His love depends on your 'goodness'. This affects your trust in Him.

You believe Him to be causing bad things to happen to you, as if He is punishing you. Like people do. Scripture can become blurry.

Satan thrives on this. He will work overtime to make sure you never get to grasp the unconditional, unending love of God that is there always, despite what you do and what you don't do.

The only unfortunate thing is that oftentimes, there is no help in the church for this kind of people. They are often labelled, and in most cases publicly, as problematic, hindrances to the work of God, burdens, high maintenance, unbelieving, immature, critical, hateful, bitter, angry and weak. In as much as all these characteristics may be true at that time, they don't remain like that forever and they don't deserve all the name-calling and labels as well as being blamed for what is not going well in the church or whatever organisation. That's the last thing they need. They need help. They need love. Some people have left the church as a result. As the scripture says, "We, then, that are strong, ought to bear the weaknesses of the weak, and not to please ourselves.

Let every one of us please his neighbour for his good to edification". Romans 15:1-2.

The ultimate effect on relationships:

Marriages break. Families separate. Friendships end. Work is affected. Trust is lost.

When to forgive

Biblically, it's as soon as possible.

Humanly speaking, do it as soon as your conscience reminds you.

"Be ye angry, and sin not: let not the sun go down upon your wrath". Ephesians 4:26 King James Bible

How to forgive

There are many ways to exercise forgiveness

- If you are lucky, the offender may initiate a move through their conscience and ask for forgiveness. This is the easiest way to settle things but unfortunately, many offenders never do. That's the reason Jesus wrote this verse. "Then said he unto the disciples, It is impossible but that offences will come: but woe unto him, through whom they come" Luke 17:1. You will notice here that Jesus emphasised His message, not only on the fact that offence will come, but more on the fact that those through whom they come are in a far worse state.

- Writing a letter to the offender especially if they are deceased. You can write all that you wanted to say to them, if you had the opportunity to say it when they were still alive. Read it out loud, either by yourself, or in the presence of someone, and then destroy the letter. Note that the dead person will never get to know about it, but this tends to promote a feeling of a clear conscience on your part and brings the much-needed healing.

- You can do it verbally or telephonically only if you know the person knows about the wrong they have done. Otherwise, it can create a mess. There are psychopathic, narcissistic and antisocial people out there, who thrive on hurting others. It has become so much a part of them that they don't feel anything any longer after they've done or said something bad to another human being. Their consciences are dead. These are those you will need to just forgive without bothering to approach them and don't consider reconciling with them as they are toxic. God will see your good heart and you will be rewarded for it.

- You can do it through a third person, a mediator. This could be a counsellor, a friend, church leader, neighbour, relative or anyone willing to take part in this.

Why Forgive

- From a Christian Perspective

- A MUST and NOT AN OPTION

- Forgiveness is not an option to a Christian; rather one must forgive to be a Christian. Forgiveness in Christianity is a manifestation of submission to Christ and fellow believers.

- God demonstrated a whole lot of examples of forgiveness throughout the Bible.

- I will mention some here.

- In Mark 11:25: "And whenever you stand praying, if you have anything against anyone, forgive him, that your Father in heaven may also forgive you your trespasses."

- In Matthew 6:14–15: "For if you forgive men their trespasses, your heavenly Father will also forgive you. But if you do not forgive men their trespasses, neither will your Father forgive your trespasses."

- Jesus speaks of the importance of Christians forgiving or showing mercy towards others. Jesus used the parable of the unmerciful servant -Matthew 18:21–35, to say that we should forgive without limits.

- Parable of the Prodigal Son in Luke 15:11-32 is the best-known parable about forgiveness and refers to God's forgiveness for His people.

- In the Sermon on the Mount, Jesus repeatedly spoke of forgiveness; "Blessed are the merciful, for they shall obtain mercy". Matthew 5:7

- "But I say to you who hear: Love your enemies, do good to those who hate you, bless those who curse you, and pray for those who spitefully use you. To him who strikes you on the one cheek, offer the other also. And from him who takes away your cloak, do not withhold your tunic either." Luke 6:27–29.

- Be merciful, just as your Father also is merciful." Luke 6:36

- Forgive, and you will be forgiven." Luke 6:37(b)

- Last but not least, it is said, "Then Peter came to Him and said, "Lord, how often shall my brother sin against me, and I forgive him? Up to seven times?" Jesus said to him, "I do not say to you, up to seven times, but up to seventy times seven." Matthew 18:21–22

- Lastly, Jesus asked for God's forgiveness of those who crucified him. Then Jesus said, "Father, forgive them, for they do not know what they do."

- And they divided His garments and cast lots. Luke 23:34

- The greatest forgiveness was when God forgave all humanity by providing a sacrifice for their sins to obtain salvation.

- "For God so loved the world that He gave His only begotten Son, that whoever believes in Him should not perish but have everlasting life." John 3:16

- How do you know you have forgiven?
  - When you can speak of the offence from a point of reference as opposed to a point of pain.
  - When you talk about the issue, you don't hurt any more.
  - The reason you mention the deeds is to help others without mentioning the perpetrator or offender's name.
  - When you sincerely love the perpetrator and want the best for them. You pray for them just as God commanded.

"You have heard that it was said, 'You shall love your neighbour and hate your enemy.' But I say to you, love your enemies, bless those who curse you, do good to those who hate you, and pray for those who spitefully use you and persecute you, that you may be sons of your Father in heaven; for He makes His sun rise on the evil and on the good, and sends rain on the just and on the unjust." Matthew 5:43-45

God will always send someone to you when you least expect it.

  - Another way to know you have forgiven is to serve and bless the perpetrator. Help them where they need help. Do things for them.
  - NB: Only if the perpetrator is a normal person and doesn't fit the criteria for narcissism, antisocial personality and psychopathic personality. These ones, you forgive and remove yourselves from them. They will

cause you great harm, and if you stay too long, permanent emotional and psychological, even physical damage.

- When you see them or hear their voice or think about them and what they did and perhaps are still doing to you, you feel sorry for them, feel empathetic towards them, as truly speaking, they are the one suffering, not you. The hatred of you that causes them to do things to you is causing them unhappiness, hurt and loss of peace. It's something great about you that makes them jealous and envious of you. They constantly secretly compare themselves with you, only to realise they are way short of your good natural traits and virtues. That's when you begin to sincerely pray for them. It's hard to do this when you are still hurting and offended.

- The other way is not talking about and not finding yourself itching to tell everyone about the offence.

- When revenge, paying back and retaliation become not an issue any longer to you.

It's natural for all humanity, at first instance, to have hard feelings towards those who offend us. You don't think twice about it. It takes prayer, meditation on the Word of God and truly wanting the best of God for you and them to get to a point where you are free of thoughts and acts of retaliation and revenge.

- When you have come out of the denial phase. That is, you have stopped using the defence of "I moved on, I let it all go", when you truly know that what you did was just to put it under the carpet, and deny you are hurting.

The virtue of honesty helps you to face up to the fact that you are still hurting, and you need God to help heal. Accept that the pain is there and if the pain is still there, you have not let go but are in denial. Denial is very similar to avoidance; avoiding the truth of the situation. It's normal to hurt when offended or attacked, and God understands this. But you need to pray for healing and come out of the hurt as quickly as possible.

- When you fully accept that God loves the offender just as much as He loves you.

As human beings, we tend to think that God hates bad people. He hates their actions and deeds but not the person. The moment you can separate the deed from the person, you will be able to love them just as God loves them. Remember that God doesn't see them as different from you. Both of you need His mercy in different areas. Just as much as He loves you, despite your own shortcomings, He loves the perpetrator the same way despite their shortcomings.

I am not the expert in this topic; however, my personal experiences have led me through the road of forgiveness.

Chapter 14.
Abuse

BONUS Chapter dedicated to all you survivors of this demonic act and the organisations geared at helping those affected.

In this chapter, we will look at types of abuses and rape, types of people who tend to be perpetrators and why they do these things.

We will also look at tell-tale signs that you may be involved with one of them.

We will look at what to do when you find yourself trapped in that kind of situation.

Types of abuse

There are different types of abuse that perpetrators use against their victims; most abuse will overlap.

Types of abuse are:

a. physical
b. spiritual
c. sexual
d. psychological/emotional/verbal
e. financial

1. Physical

Physical abuse is the use of physical force against someone, in a way that inflicts injuries and/or endangers that person. It mostly, but not solely, happens in Domestic abuse. Domestic abuse rarely starts at physical assault. Perpetrators will resort to physical abuse when they feel their victim is challenging them.

Examples of physical abuse include:
– Punching
– Hitting
– Spitting
– Kicking

Chapter 14. Abuse

- Strangling
- Restraining
- Burning
- Scalding
- Stabbing
- Head-butting
- Forced traumatic sexual acts
- Biting
- Squeezing
- Shoving
- Suffocating
- Pushing
- Grabbing
- Choking
- Throwing
- Breaking bones and causing fractures
- Using weapons
- Poisoning
- Throwing things
- Forced feeding
- Attempts to kill
- Reckless driving
- Pulling hair
- Murder

2. Sexual

Any situation in which someone is forced to participate in unwanted, unsafe or degrading sexual activity, even when it's with a partner, is sexual abuse.

- Rape (forced penetration)
- Sexual assault (vaginal, anal or oral)
- Sexual assault using objects - sex toys, broken glass, bottles
- Forcing a partner to have sex with others and/or the partner, boyfriend or husband giving their female or male mate to others to have sex with them. It

can be a group of people or one person. It can be done in exchange for money or just as punishment.
– Forcing sex in front of others. Making the partner watch or mimic pornography
– Unwanted fondling/inappropriate touching
– Forcing sex in ways that hurt, degrade or following a physical beating
– Videoing / photographing them doing sexual acts
– Pinching or biting breasts and buttocks
– Name-calling e.g. frigid, whore
– Criticising them sexually
– Forcing them to strip or forcefully stripping them
– Sadistic sexual acts
– Forcing them into prostitution

The following forms of sexual abuse affect mainly the psychological/emotional being of a person.
– Withholding sex and/or affection
– Having sex conditional on the partner's behaviour
– Minimising or denying their feelings about sex or sexual preferences
– Forcing or coercing them to act out fantasies they are not comfortable with

3. Psychological/ Emotional/ Verbal

Emotional and mental abuse is often subtle, and, in some cases, victims don't recognise they are being abused. This kind of abuse will wear victims down, often over a long period of time, until they take responsibility for their abuser's actions and behaviour towards them, or simply accept it.

The abuse can use both verbal and non-verbal communication. The impact of psychological abuse is often deeper and longer lasting than physical abuse.

Methods are:
– Name-calling
– Constant insults
– Shaming and humiliating the person in public, with put-downs disguised as jokes
– Nasty and hurtful sarcasm

- Only engaging in conversation with the person when the perpetrator decides the time is right
- Criticism or constantly correcting everything the person says or does
- Refusing to listen to anything the person has to say
- Not allowing the person to voice their opinion or have an opinion of their own
- Denial – perpetrator pretending they haven't said or done something
- Silences and sulking for days
- Blocking and diverting them if they want to say something
- Perpetrator decides what subjects can and cannot be discussed
- Trivialising and minimising anything the person say, and making it seem insignificant
- Twisting and turning every situation around so it's always the person's fault
- Screaming and shouting at them in private or public
- Laughing or making fun of them in an inappropriate way
- Leaving nasty messages by texts, voicemail, and other social networking platforms.
- Accusing them of unfaithfulness falsely and not trying hard enough to help the situation at hand or purposely doing something to annoy them
- Perpetrator blaming them for their own failures or mistakes
- Perpetrator cheating in the relationship and talking purposely about the other person to the partner
- Perpetrator making passes at, or flirting with, other people in front of the partner
- Stalking and spying on the partner physically or by social networks, phones, even hacking into their emails, phones and getting other people to follow them everywhere they go and report to them.
- Badmouthing them to their bosses or business partners or friends, sabotaging their success in what they are involved in. (i.e. work, career, business and friendships)
- Isolating them from everyone including friends and family, choosing friends for them.
- Controlling their movements
- Instigating people to treat them badly

4. Financial

In addition to hurting their partners in ways mentioned above, perpetrators may also hurt them financially.

Examples:
- Controlling all the finances
- Not allowing the partner to see any bank statements, bills, or any financial transactions
- Putting all the bills in the person's name then not paying them – destroying their credit or chance to set up their own bank account were they to leave them
- Setting them up to stay dependent on them.
- Withholding money or credit cards
- Not allowing them to have their own bank account
- Perpetrator not paying bills and spending the money on themselves (alcohol, gambling, trips, treats)
- Giving them an allowance, which is not enough to buy what they need
- Making them account for every penny they spend and inspecting all receipts
- Stealing or selling the person's possessions or demanding money from them
- Exploiting the person's assets for the perpetrator's personal gain
- Preventing them from working or choosing their own career
- Making them work from home so the perpetrator can "keep an eye on them" —sabotaging their job (making them miss work or calling them constantly whilst at work)
- Making them beg for money
- Setting up financial loans, credit cards, hire purchase agreements by forging the person's signature or making them sign the paperwork
- The perpetrator refusing to work or contribute to the financial running of the family and house

5. Spiritual

Spiritual abuse can be hard to detect, especially if you are not knowledgeable in that religion, culture, beliefs or traditions. Spiritual Abuse is real and you are not going crazy.

Examples:
- Using the person's faith or spiritual beliefs to manipulate them
- Preventing them from practising their faith or spiritual beliefs
- Ridiculing their religious or spiritual beliefs
- Forcing the children to be brought up in a faith that their mother has not agreed to
- Threats to harm or kill in the name of 'honour'
- Using religious teachings or cultural tradition as an excuse for violence
- Denying access to ceremonies, places of worship, land or family
- Forcing the person to do things against their beliefs
- Forced marriage
- Dictatorship and Authoritarian type of leadership styles that Lord over their flock
- Demanding honour and loyalty from members and ridiculing or shaming those who question certain acts from leaders.
- Twisting scriptures to back their opinions or actions
- Electing an Elite group of 'yes men' that agrees with anything the leader says or does.
- Employs favouritism in their dealings with their members

Other examples:

- Leaders who tell you that even though you are burnt out and losing your health, you have to stay in whatever it is you are involved in because if you stopped, or took time off, you would lose all your gifting to do any future ministry.

- Leaders who found ministry to be a vehicle for their great gain, twisting Scriptures to manipulate donors for their personal gain.

- They typically chase after wealth at any cost, and often at the expense of the very people they shepherd.

- Leaders who place themselves above God, refuse to admit their wrong-doings and employ threats, isolation, ostracism, subtle or straight forward verbal attacks from the pulpit upon the person who brought up a concern about them that others saw.

- Leaders who have a distorted view of respect. They forget the simple principle that respect is earned, not granted. Abusive leaders demand respect without having earned it by good and honest living.

- Leaders who demand loyalty as proof of the follower's loyalty to Christ. It's either their way or no way. And if a follower deviates, they will be guilty of deviating from Jesus or God.

- They often see themselves (their church) as the only one that is really following Jesus and having the right theology. They, therefore, use this to coerce followers to do things, think or handle things their way and never have their own revelation straight from God or Scripture. They preach about the gift of the Holy Spirit given to every believer but deny believers to commune with, get revelation from and function in the anointing of the same gift of the Holy Spirit. Unless the leader is alright with it, it is always deemed wrong and a believer gets shut out. Everyone else is wrong, misguided, or stupidly naive.

- Leaders who create a culture of fear and shame. Practising a culture of fault-finding and naming and shaming to their followers for correction of what is perceived as sin or wrongdoing. Often there is no grace for someone who fails to live up to the church's or ministry's expectation. And if someone steps outside of the often-unspoken rules, leaders shame them into compliance. Leaders can't admit failure, but often search out failure in others and use that knowledge to hold them in fear and captivity. They often quote scriptures about not touching God's anointed or bringing accusations against an elder. Yet, they often confront sin in others, particularly the ones who bring up legitimate Biblical issues. Or they have their circle of influence take on this task of silencing critics.

- Leaders who immune themselves from criticism by placing people around them whose only loyalty is to the leader. These leaders and churches view those who bring up legitimate issues as enemies. Those who were once friends, immediately become enemies once they raise a concern about them or the church. Sometimes, these folks are banished, told to be silent, or shamed into submission.

- Leaders who use exclusivity for loyalty. Followers close to the leader or leaders feel like lucky insiders. Everyone else is on the outside.

- If someone on the inner circle speaks up about abuse, lapses in character, illegal acts, or the leader's dictatorship, that insider immediately moves to be an outsider. Fear of losing their special status often impedes insiders from speaking up.

- There is often a charismatic leader at the 'wheel' who started off well, but slipped into arrogance, protectionism and pride. Where a leader might start off being approachable and interested in others, they eventually withdraw to a small group of "yes men and women" and isolate from the needs of others. This small group comprises of people who 'worship' the leader. Their payback is the recognition and favours they receive from their 'hero'. They are often highly educated people whose positions in society make the leader feel good about themselves. They are, in most cases, very non-spiritual. Their prayer life is non-existent, their worship is weak, they carry no anointing. They are sitting in positions that require certain anointing that they don't have, and the outcasts are those who God has specifically anointed for the God-given purposes of the ministry in question. Things don't change. God is blocked from working as His vehicles are pushed away.

- Leaders who are fearful of the anointed followers under them and perceive them as a threat to their position.

- Such churches harbour a cult of personality, thinking that if their hero left, the ministry or church would collapse, as, in their view, it is entirely dependent on this leader to hold the place together. They become indwelled by the demon of idolatry.

- Leaders who demand blind servitude of their followers, but live prestigious, privileged lives. They live aloof from their followers and justify their material extravagance as God's favour and approval of their ministry. Unlike Jesus' instructions to take the last seat, they often take the first seat at events and court others to grant them privileges.

- Leaders who hold to outward performances but reject authentic Spirituality. Leaders who place burdens on followers to act a certain way, maybe even dress a certain way, and have an acceptable lifestyle, but they often demonstrate greed, and uncontrolled addictions behind closed doors.

Types of people who are likely to be abusive:

Why and How they became that way:
There are many types, but in this book, I will talk about three of them.

A. The first most abusive personality type: The Narcissist

It can be hard to spot a Narcissist, especially at first instance, because they seem powerful, intriguing and captivating, but also wounded, helpless and vulnerable at the same time.

Narcissism develops from an early childhood trauma when a child learns that they cannot show their "authentic self" due to an unavailable, selfish or neglectful caregiver. In order to survive, the child develops a "false self" as a defence to protect against the emotional pain and rejection of the primary attachment figure.

This false self becomes the way the person learns to exist in the world. Essentially, these people are unable to acknowledge their internal pain and vulnerability and go through life pretending to be someone they are not. Because of this, they use external validation to feed their ego, numb their childhood trauma and feel better about themselves.

Narcissists lack a coherent sense of self, so they use external things to feel worthy and powerful. Things such as:

- Seeking out travel, expensive clothing, powerful jobs or beautiful partners to project to the world that they are "good enough."
- Using life experiences, things and interesting stories about their lives to feel worthy and lovable. They are storytellers. They love to hear their own voices.

The moment that they feel they are safe in a relationship and know that they have been unconditionally accepted, their true character begins to show. They suddenly become critical, selfish and demanding, twisting things to make the other person feel crazy and demanding that everything is on their terms.

A narcissist is a wolf dressed in sheep's clothing and sheep dressed in wolf's clothing. Dr Jekyll & Mr Hyde. They are wounded children deep in their soul. They suffer from a lack of emotional intelligence. Their mental and emotional growth got stunted around age 5, hence the childish behaviour. They go through life longing for acceptance and love, while at the same time, destroying everything and everyone around them, causing havoc and breaking heart after heart.

Tell-tale signs you may be involved with one:

1. Storytelling

Narcissists LOVE to tell stories, especially stories about themselves, their lives and their victories. They like to be viewed as conquerors. They will never once talk about the trauma that happened in their childhood. They don't want anyone to know this. They tend to have one narcissist parent with whom they are stuck for life who contributed greatly to their personality and will make sure the bad family stuff never gets out. This parent will never want to leave the narcissistic child, even when they are a fully grown-up person.

To the narcissist, there is nothing more externally validating than having a great story to tell that makes them feel "special" or "better" than everyone else. That is why narcissists often seek out adventure, travel, care about their external appearance and want to have "the best" of everything.

Everything about them 'is the best'.

2. They have a poor tolerance of those they view as weak.

This is because they see themselves in these people as their true self is weak. They love befriending the strong, the successful, the rich, the gifted and the famous. This feeds on their sense of false self.

Often, they will dominate conversations and exaggerate their accomplishments.

3. They become the "life and soul" of the party.

However, at the same time, they feel inadequate and lonely if their story gets old or someone has a better one. Because of this, the narcissist will resort to putting down others to defend against feeling less superior.

If they perceive that someone is coming up greater than them, they attack the person, often verbally through sarcasm, gossip, slander and anything that will take away credit from the person.

4. Inability to form lasting relationships.

When relationships start, the narcissist can come across as being extremely charismatic, flattering and seductive. They can make a person feel extremely special in their quest to win them over. However, they are not able to love others in a normal way.

For them, people and relationships serve a purpose: to feed their ego and validate their "false self." Narcissists use love to fill their internal void and temporarily fulfil their need for intimacy. As soon as they get what they need, they will begin to devalue the person and eventually drop them without looking back.

5. Playing mind games.

They are unable to give and receive love due to the deep void inside of them stemming from unloving primary caregiver in childhood. They learnt to earn their love and they were made to feel never able to reach the bar set by their childhood caregiver in fulfilling that which was required of them to earn their love. They do exactly the same in their adult lives in relationships, making their significant other always feel like they have to keep earning their love by complying with the narcissist's abuse.

This leaves many people feeling confused, traumatized and guilty. "How can someone pursue you so much and then be so hurtful?!"

This is only because to them, people and relationships do not matter. They only serve a purpose to get validation. You are essentially just a character in the play that they have created to uphold their "false self" and validate their image, just like an actress who, after playing their role in the story, gets replaced by the next best thing. This stage comes only after they have criticised, ridiculed and devalued the person to the point that the person feels like they are the problem (it's never the narcissist).

This is extremely painful, especially if the narcissist moves on quickly to another relationship and is "charming" the new person.

NB: the new person will soon be treated the same as you. Everyone gets that in the life of the narcissist. They hop from relationship to relationship and are master cheaters.

The narcissist cannot change how they relate to people.

The new actress is only a temporary stand-in and their faith within the relationship is no different than the previous person's.

In the beginning of the relationship, the narcissist behaves like a normal person. They seem to be loving, give the other person attention, maybe even gifts, but this is never lasting.

Psychology says that the narcissist sees people in black and white and does not allow any grey areas. That is, the partner at first comes across as perfect, like how the narcissist's psyche makes them see themselves, hence so much denial of their true flawed self.

After a while, they realise that this person has flaws just like everyone else.

The poor judgement of the person, false belief about them and how they viewed them comes tumbling down.

Now, this perfect soulmate is flawed. They don't fit their criteria of a soulmate any longer. Remember that their mind was programmed by their narcissistic caregiver in childhood, for perfection and denial and shunning of anything flawed or wrong, hence the twisted psyche of grandiosity.

They have trouble seeing the fact that everyone makes mistakes. Everyone falls short at some point; it's human. They now develop a compulsion to discard this flawed person and go on another hunting spree for a perfect soulmate who, like them, has no flaws. (Remember that they are the worst flawed person of them all but they have programmed their mind to deny this, to save sinking into insanity with the load of guilt.)

Due to an insatiable need to be admired, praised, validated and recognised, they find one partner not satisfying of all these requirements at the same time. They deem them flawed as a result. The person with the disorder may lash out in different ways due to disappointment that the partner is not the person they imagined them to be.

It is a huge demand upon the partner to constantly have to notice what the narcissist is doing and never fail to praise, validate, comment, admire and lift them high. After some time, as a human being, the partner gets tired of this and this makes the narcissist angry and they begin to devalue the partner as punishment for failing to do their job by ways spoken of in the above paragraph such as ridiculing, publicly insulting you, cheating on you or flirting with other women/ men publicly or in hiding, belittling you and everything you do or say publicly, harshly criticising you often publicly, putting you down all the time, both publicly or in private, badmouthing you to everyone including your friends, family, relatives, the religious organisation you belong to and your workplace.

They steal your friends.

Lastly, they fear commitment which stems from inner turmoil due to low self-worth and feelings of inadequacy, especially around their manhood. They are constantly comparing themselves to other men and thinking they can't measure up, hence the extreme control and jealousy over their partner.

6. Avoidance of Responsibility:

Narcissists are unable to face their own flaws or acknowledge any mistakes they have made or short comings. What can be more threatening to the "false self" than admitting that you may not be perfect?!

They blame everyone other than themselves.

If the other person gets out of the relationship, they must be prepared:

Family and friends who are close with the narcissist will hear stories that point to them as the one who ruined the relationship and makes them look like the victim. When things don't go the way the narcissist wants, they can become easily angered, throw a tantrum, use negative comments, ridicule, withdraw love and play an unavoidable "blame game". Remember these people's emotional development is around age 5.

7. Poor or lack of Follow-Through: Another way to spot a narcissist is to measure their actions against their words. Many narcissists lack reliability. They lie easily and find it difficult to keep their word.

They exhibit such behaviours that range from regularly breaking appointments, to habitually failing to fulfil promises and agreements.

Their lack of dependability can be emotional as well - being there for the person one minute and gone the next. Inconsistency is one of the signs a person may be dealing with a narcissist who is on their own timeline.

8. Sense of Entitlement

The Narcissist expects special treatment from others. In their world, they deserve to have the "best" even if they didn't put in the work or effort to get it. Whether that's a job, partner, food or accommodation, they want the preferential treatment. They are master manipulators and are very good at getting what they want out of others, without much effort on their part. See how they treat people who can get them what they want, then notice if they say something negative about that same person later. Only because according to the narcissist, why would that person deserve something that they think they deserve?!

In relationships, they are the most important party in it. The other person's job is to lavish them with gifts, but they never once think of giving them any because they view themselves as the superior, most important person in the relationship. The partner is regarded as their servant; in fact their slave, their possession.

9. They lack empathy

They are unable to love as normal people do. They suffer from self-loathing from the childhood abuse they received mainly from their caregivers. They were taught by how they were treated to always please the main caregiver, be good and perfect and were never allowed to be children who make mistakes and are still loved by their parents. This is primarily due to their caregiver being narcissistic themselves, needing constant praise, validation, recognition and admiration. The caregiver used their children as those to provide them with these things. In the middle of this, they focused on themselves and their own need, became the most important person, disregarded the needs of their children, and used them as tools to provide for them. Children were not allowed to be weak, show negative emotions or admit to failure. This would bruise the narcissistic caregiver's ego. They will punish the child for this so severely and harshly to teach them to never ever do that again. As a result, children learn to only exist to please the caregiver (mother or father mainly).

They learn to put themselves last. They learn not to matter. Eventually, they don't feel they exist. They become invisible and only the narcissistic caregiver exists. They lose self in the process and their self-worth and value go out of the window for life. They then experience a constant feeling of unworthiness, failure, self-loathing, unlikability, unable to be loved, deep depression and anxiety. Their small psyche becomes unable to contain this pain. It develops a false self opposite to the true self, that of power, superiority, beauty, success, charm, importance and happiness. This is so their psyche can survive, otherwise the pain is so severe, they will end up becoming a mental wreck unable to function, or even compelled to commit suicide.

The false self formed in early childhood to cope will carry on till adulthood, and all their life, unless treated with years of psychological interventions. To maintain this false facade and double persona, they then need constant reassurance and reminders of how successful, powerful, important, superior and above everybody else they are by others mostly with high empathy qualities. This silences their inner truth about who they really are and how they really feel inside. The feelings of unworthiness, failure, self-loathing, unlikability, inability to be loved, deep depression and anxiety are constantly popping into their head, pushing to surface to the fore. They constantly battle to push them down and they can't without the help from outside, hence needing so much constant reassurance by way of praise, validation, affirmation, applause, acceptance, adoration, attention and love.

The constant need for this, and the never-ending void inside, compel them to constantly seek people with empathy to fulfil this need. If the person with empathy fails to keep up the high demand, as they sure will get tired as a human being, the narcissist sulks, rages and punishes them for failing them. This is all psychological. In most cases, the narcissist may not ask you in person to do this, but they somehow effectively communicate it to you. At times, they use third parties to ask you to do this on their behalf.

The person with high empathy qualities is viewed and regarded by the narcissist as an extension of themselves. It's bizarre but true. In their twisted mind, you are part of them, to help erase their true self. The good qualities of being able to get in touch with your feelings, to feel happy, to accept yourself as you are, to love, to receive love, to feel concern when others hurt, to feel remorseful when you wrong others, kindness, authenticity, a caring nature, carefree disposition, outgoing and adventurous; the narcissistic person will try and pass them onto themselves by mimicking and mirroring you, to make them feel human, feel alive and feel they exist. It helps them feel they are like others. This helps boost their image and portrays themselves as a good, successful, loving, kind person to the world at your expense.

The bizarre thing is, the very qualities in you that they admired and were attracted by, are the very things they target and destroy to leave you completely sucked out and empty. This is the typical product of any abuse, but more so, the emotional and psychological type.

As you keep on giving these qualities to them, they, in turn, portray you to the outside world as being the person they truly are, the damaged child, who is unable to love and receive love, unable to form any lasting relationships, who sabotages every chance they get to form those relationships by hurting the other person. They can only take from the other person, they can never give as they don't have any love to give anyone. Their romantic relationships are always one-sided, with the other person taking all the responsibility to make it work, love them and be there for them. They never do the same as they believe the other person is inferior to them and that it's their job to take responsibility to make it work. This stems from their acquired sense of grandiosity.

It is the direct opposite of who their partner really is. In a nutshell, the partner swaps personalities and qualities with the narcissist. They need the empathic partner there, always, because it's a constant phenomenon, it's short-lived, and it needs reinforcement all the time.

If you let it persist, that is, stay with them longer, they will suck your core being out of you totally and replace you with them, psychologically and emotionally till you are but just a shell of a person, no use for anything any longer. Then, they dump you and go looking for a new person with high empathy to continue. It's a life-long thing. Psychology professionals say there is a consciousness and awareness on the narcissist's part about the abuse, but their poor impulse control, sense of entitlement, superiority and grandiosity characteristics block them from stopping this as they have an inflated false persona; only they come first, their needs are to be met and by you, no matter how.

They were attracted to you in the first place by your good character traits.

10. Poor impulse control

They are unable to control how they feel, which in most cases, if not all cases, is negative. They are fuelled with negativity and go around spewing it everywhere, hence the critical spirit, the tendency to put others down, look down on others, or rubbish what others say or do.

They are quick to perceive attack even if it's not there. They harbour feelings of paranoia, always sensing that other people are against them. They lash out either verbally or physically (physical actions are rare, they are employed as a last resort), at the slightest thought of being opposed, criticised or disagreed with. They may write about it on social media platforms, make a video, go tell others about it or use any platform they can get to lash back at the person they now perceive as their enemy. They are usually harsh, blunt and bark when they are angry. Their relationships are always conflicted, short-lived and very shallow.

They act on their negative feelings too quickly without giving it a second thought to verify if what they think is true or not.

They get involved in things that may be binding without thinking and can find themselves entangled in difficult situations as a result.

11. Projection

In Narcissistic people, as mentioned earlier, their psyche buried their true self, the one with all the negative traits that developed during their abusive treatment by their caregivers, usually around age 5. Therefore, narcissistic people deal with life in a childish way, especially relationships. They need to be cared for as a child would. They never care about anyone as a child wouldn't know how.

Their brain then developed coping mechanisms to escape the never-ending painful memories of the bad treatment they endured. These coping mechanisms serve to uphold the false self developed by their psyche to replace their true self, which is unbearable to them and everyone else.

The most used defence is projection. Remember that the narcissist now views themselves as without flaws, a perfect being that is so powerful and above everyone else.

In their new created mind, they can't be wrong, they can't be defective. They can't fall short of anything. In reality, and especially to those closest to them, they are as defective, get things wrong most of the time, lie to cover up their shortcomings, suffer from envy and are jealous of those they perceive as 'competing' with them.

NB: Anyone that seems to be more successful than the narcissist will be envied by them and they will begin to compete with this person but go around saying the person is competing with them.

One of their weaknesses in relationships is cheating. It is called Triangulation. They always have more than one partner or lovers. Their relationships always have a 'shelf life'. This is for security reasons to avoid running out of someone to provide them with their basic needs to sustain their false persona, should their partner leave. They always know from the beginning of a relationship that the partner, at some point, is going to leave them just like all others.

The other reason is they keep hunting for more admiration, love, acceptance, praise, validation and affirmation as one person (partner) is always never enough to provide all these benefits. It also provides them with a sense of importance (arrogance, grandiosity) which is one of the main character traits of these people. They like being sought-after, being chased.

Fear of abandonment also plays a major part in causing them to cheat.

Because cheating is negative and bad, and they have now falsely acquired this super-human, unflawed personality, it becomes difficult to accept they can do such a thing. Their psyche now resorts to the familiar thing of denial of their true self and acknowledges the cheating but projects it to their partner. The partner is the one cheating; they have swapped roles; they have taken the partner's good self and clothed themselves with it and threw their bad self onto to them. Only bad people cheat and that cannot be them. The reason why their psyche is like this is, their narcissistic caregiver, during childhood, 'programmed' them to be perfect and denied them allowance of any wrongdoing. If the caregiver did something wrong or fell short of something, they denied it and projected it onto them as a child. They were made to carry the blame for what their caregiver did. They ended up with guilt, self-blame, self-loathing, feelings of inadequacy, worthlessness and everything wrong about them. Their psyche, as protection to the system from collapsing, developed this super-human, unflawed person, which is false anyway, to the extreme end of perfection. If you are not the real you, then you are the direct opposite of you. Hence, they target and get drawn to good people full of empathy and genuine love, concern and consideration for others. That's what they lack and MUST find it somewhere, somehow to replace their lack. Unfortunately, this is done in ways that harm others, those they derive these attributes from. That's where the abuse comes from, always blaming them for what they themselves did, always fault finding with them, always putting them down because they want them to take their true self of defective nature. They project the way they feel inside onto their target. They MUST be blameless. They are perfect.

I only gave two examples of what they can project to you, but they will project anything and everything they feel doesn't fit the false self they have acquired.

12. Control and Manipulation

Narcissists employ various ways to exert control over you and manipulate you to do and be what they want.

One of the most common ways is what in psychology and psychiatry is called 'gaslighting'. This is a phenomenon whereby the partner/ target starts to self-doubt. They begin to think that something is not quite right with their mind.

This occurs because the partner began to perceive that the narcissist was not who they really seemed to be, not as nice and loving as they portrayed themselves, that their behaviour is not right, especially towards them. They see that they tend to say things to them that are not nice like subtle insults, put-downs, publicly flirting with other people of the opposite sex and deliberately making them see it, betraying them, lying, cheating, etc. Then the partner starts to feedback to the narcissist about how these behaviours are affecting them. The narcissist will deny all of them point-blank, saying the partner is imagining things, the partner is oversensitive, the partner is overreacting and suggests the partner needs to have their mind checked because it seems they are beginning to see and hear things that aren't there, while perfectly knowing that the partner is 100% right.

If the partner lives with them, the narcissist will hide and move things around in the house from where the partner put them so the partner can't find them when they look for them and then put them back when the partner asks them about the whereabouts of those things. The narcissist will then tell the partner to go check again. On this occasion, the things are there, exactly where the partner put them in the first place, but they were not there earlier. The narcissist will then emphasise the fact that the partner is not right in their mind and needs to seek help.

Over time, with repetitions of these mind games, the partner begins to believe what the narcissist is saying about them and in so doing, they doubt their own sanity and give the narcissist full control over them.

The other most common way is to criticise everything the partner does, their accomplishments, their endeavours, their plans, their friends, the way they dress etc., to a point where if the victim doesn't seek help, they will become very isolated with no friends, but only the narcissist, who now has full control over them.

They stalk the partner in many subtle ways, by cyber-stalking, on social media platforms, they get other people to place tabs on them, constantly checking, stalking the partner and reporting back to them (flying monkeys).

The narcissist will mistreat and abuse the partner but tell them it's not abuse but teaching and training them to be a better person because there's something wrong with them.

Remember that the person targeted is always a romantic partner, or in the case of children, it will be the primary caregiver. Ask yourself this; if the partner is that mentally defective as the narcissist makes them and everyone think, how did they live successfully and survive all these years before meeting the narcissist?

This thought is what liberates the partner in the end. Looking at how far they've come and things they accomplished, friendships and relationships they managed to have and keep, jobs they kept so well, their joys and happiness all these years before meeting this person, and now, all of a sudden, they are supposed to be an invalid needing the narcissist to survive?

Unfortunately, most people are naive; they are gullible enough to just believe what the narcissist says about the partner.

What this aims at doing is removing the partner's good qualities and replacing them with what the narcissist knows is their true hidden self, whilst the narcissist uses this to make themselves look good, powerful, intelligent, successful and totally with it, to the outside world. You swap personalities. They take yours and give you theirs. They learnt this technique at an early age under the 'training' (abusive treatment) of their narcissistic caregiver. They have done this to every empath they had in their lives and they always have one, always, because they can't survive without swapping personalities to avoid and bury the deep emotional pain acquired in childhood.

Their primary caregivers would have been narcissistic and displayed a very distant, indifferent, uncaring, harsh, critical, punitive interaction with them as a child and demanded attention, praise, adoration, affirmation from them instead. This is how they were made to earn the love from the caregiver, to always seek to please them, but they found that they were never able to satisfy them, no matter how hard they tried, resulting in ill-treatments, mainly emotional abuse but it can become physical.

They learnt to demand attention and punish those who are perceived to be withholding it.

They aim at changing the personality of the other person to fit their model, that of stopping loving yourself and only existing to please, validate, praise, affirm and honour them.

If you still love yourself, give yourself or others attention, they feel you are neglecting them, you are not doing your duty.

They accuse you of being unteachable and refusing to change.

They want you to abandon your values in favour of theirs. This is totally removing your core being. You cannot have an opinion. You've got to agree with them in everything, believe in what they believe, see things how they see them, love those they love and hate those they hate. You cease to exist. You are now ONE with them. They adopted you into their being. It's their way or no way. They've gained total control over and manipulated you to the core. That's when they have conquered you. This results in you stopping to live. You exist to make them live.

If they can't control you, they control how others see, think of and view you. Hence, they engage in smearing your name and portray you as a bad person when they are seen as a good person (in their false facade). They influence others to place tabs on you, stalk you, and lie about you.

Facts and information gathered are twisted and made to have you look bad to everyone.

13. Multiple personality/ alter ego

Dr Jekyll & Mr Hyde

There are different opinions as to whether Narcissists know what they are doing when they hurt others. The most common belief is that they know. They are unable to stop themselves due to poor impulse control and they are unable to feel the pain they cause another, like empaths do, because they lack empathy.

The reason why most people believe they know what they are doing is because they will always reserve the cruellest destructive behaviour and hurt for those closest to them, especially in relationships. They display visible pleasure when they see their target crying.

They know they are not normal. They are not like most good people. They discovered this about themselves over the years when they lost good people in relationships and were unable to keep any relationship. They also learnt this from feedback given by all their partners over the years as to how they treated them. They know now that they are sabotaging their relationships. They just can't stop doing what they are doing to their partners because that will cause them to admit they are defective, weak and accept and face their hidden childhood issues.

There is, however, a need in them to appear normal and decent to the rest of the public. They behave better outside their homes and away from their significant others. They are aware that their real self is bad and makes them unlikeable, so they try hard to mimic and mirror people with good qualities when out in public and the world at large. They may or may not be abusive with their family of origin, parents and siblings.

This is the reason people do not believe that narcissists are abusive with their own family because they treat other people differently. They perform distinctively for different audiences.

They will manipulate or use the other people but in a different way than they use and abuse the closest person(s) to them. This is when they are referred to as wearing many masks.

It is because of these differences in behaviour that they are able to convince others to serve them as their "flying monkeys", people they 'befriend' for the purposes of using them to help stalk, punish, collect information by placing tabs on their partners, help spread false rumours and slander them.

They often appear nice to these people and hide the nastiness they display to their significant others.

Different behaviours to different people and audiences as well as different masks. Narcissists are great actors and manipulate everyone and everything. That's where the label Dr Jekyll and Mr Hyde comes from.

Unfortunately, to the detriment of their partners, people tend to be fooled by the narcissist and believe what they say about them, hence their willingness to feel sorry for them and help them punish who they now view as the 'bad' person.

There is more on this type of personality, but for now, we will stop here and look at the other two most common abusive personality types.

B. The second most common abusive personality is: The Antisocial

This type of people has a long-term, pervasive behavioural pattern that majors in exploiting, manipulating, and violating the rights of others. This behaviour has a very short bridge between disturbing and criminal. They are usually hostile and deceitful. These behaviours would first appear in childhood. When they were young children, they engaged in tormenting and torturing animals as well as in bullying and intimidating others. They engaged in theft and often vandalism and set fires to destroy property.

Individuals with antisocial personality disorder have a complete lack of remorse for their behaviours. They may fake it when it benefits them.

Just like the narcissist, prognosis for the disorder is poor.

C. The third most abusive personality type is: Borderline Personality Disorder (USA) /Emotionally Unstable (UK)

This personality involves intense and unstable relationships, self-perception and moods. People with BPD/EUPD tend to have poor impulse control. They frantically avoid abandonment, they are impulsive, they exhibit and engage in suicidal acts or self-harming behaviours, they feel empty, they have difficulties managing their anger and may be paranoid.

These people's relationships of any kind are intense, chaotic, and full of conflict, and largely around intimate ones.

They also have severe issues with interpersonal relationships, whether they are romantic, casual, or professional. These issues result in the chaos and rollercoasters that affirm the inner and outer experience of the person.

Studies have shown that women are more affected by this disorder, but it largely affects men too, especially those who tend to have gender issues.

How do relationships start with these types of people?

Excitement is the first part and experience in the relationship. They are full of fun in the beginning but later in the relationship, turmoil and pain come in, leaving the other party deeply hurt and confused.

Reason why people go on to have relationship with such a person:

These people are often naturally kind, caring individuals with a lot of positives to offer in a relationship, hence people are most frequently drawn to them. The attraction is the initial excitement and passion they bring to a relationship. The relationship goes through an intense "honeymoon" period. The person with the disorder puts the other party on a pedestal, feeling like they have found the perfect match. They are unaware of the fact that they are, often unconsciously, really looking for a rescue from their emotional pain and chaos troubling them inside.

The other person, at first, is captivated and flattered by the attention, the intense 'love' the other person is showing them, and it makes them feel so needed and purposeful. Everything in the relationship is intense at this stage, including intimacy. (NB: for Christians, sex before marriage is forbidden by God) Unfortunately this is short-lived and once the 'honeymoon' phase fades away, problems start to emerge.

It's during this phase that the person with the personality begins to see that the other party is indeed not flawless. The poor judgement of the person, false belief about them and how they viewed them comes tumbling down. This is because people with BPD/EUPD see things in black and white. There are no grey areas.

They have trouble seeing the fact that everyone makes mistakes and then forgiving them.

The person with the disorder may begin to be abusive towards their partner, lashing out, out of disappointment that the party is not the person they thought they were. Very similar to narcissism.

That's when it may switch to an abusive relationship. Some of the tell-tale signs I spoke about earlier may begin to surface. Some will be inflicted to the person themselves, but the aim is to punish the other party. Things like self-harming, attempting suicide, threats, physical abuse, mostly verbal and emotional abuse, withholding love and sex, harshness of words, name-calling, hatred, destruction of property and things, the list goes on.

Some of the symptoms including the ones mentioned above are:
- Powerful emotions that change quickly and often
- Periodic bouts of anxiety and low mood
- Inappropriate hostility and antagonistic behaviour
- Poor impulse control
- Emotional eating habits that may or may not fit the diagnoses of bulimia or anorexia.
- Intense fear of abandonment and being alone
- Unstable sense of self
- Feelings of emptiness and worthlessness
- Dissociation. Tendencies to mentally separate oneself from an event, incident or actual situation.
- Tendencies to experience stress-related paranoid ideation

It has been said that symptoms vary slightly in men affected by the illness. Men tend to display all or some of these symptoms:
- Aggression and being easily provoked; anything someone else say which could be perceived as criticism can send the male into a rage.
- Controls others through criticism and tends to be overly controlling in intimate relationships by using criticism.
- Extremely jealous – when another man appropriately compliments their significant other, they will take it as an attempt to seduce their lover and trying to take the person away from them.
- Emotionally detached – they never share their inner emotional experience with their significant other.
- Inability to form lasting friendships – rejects every friendship or potential friendship after only a short period of time.
- Holds grudges – may hold a grudge for months, even years
- Substance use

- Fear of commitment which stems from inner turmoil due to low self-worth and feelings of inadequacy, especially around their manhood. They are constantly comparing themselves to other men and thinking they can't measure up; hence, they feel threatened whenever other men innocently say something nice to, or about, their significant other.
- Extreme fear of rejection and abandonment.
- Poor communication skills especially in relationships; inability to sit down with significant others and discuss issues.

If the other party has within them the strength to persevere and they really love the person, despite the recurrence of negative cycles, it is possible to make these relationships work. It takes a generous amount of commitment, patience, and understanding to pull it off.

This is the time you need to step back a little and decide whether you're willing to go all in and do whatever it takes.

Once you've decided to move forward with the relationship, the next step involves learning how to deal with someone with borderline personality disorder.

It's hard work but professionals believe it's doable.

The following are some of the ways:

a. Learn all you can about the disorder by reading about it.

b. Assist and help the person to be willing to admit there is a problem and seek help. There is no medication to treat this disorder unless it is accompanied by other disorders, then treatment will be geared at those disorders.

Main treatments are through psychological approaches where the person gains self-awareness and learns skills to deal with their unstable emotions.

c. Do what you say you'll do.

Be consistent. Don't muck about. Whatever you promised to do, do it. Whatever you told them you won't do, don't do it.

It's that simple. Staying consistent and predictable will help alleviate the person's intense and excessive fear of abandonment. Just simply keep your word.

d. They tend to be labile in mood.

They are able to cry and laugh at the same moment. This is how their internal emotions are.

Sometimes, despite your best efforts, you still end up the target of a tearful meltdown; don't get sucked into the drama.

e. Give honest, gentle feedback.

Often, their perception of things is incorrect. Whenever they seek your support when there has been a conflict and you were not at the scene, avoid affirming their innocence in it as it may turn out to be them who was wrong.

You may need to gently keep on making them see how their behaviour impacts others. So honest feedback is vital.

f. Avoid rescuing.

Encourage the person to take responsibility for their choices and actions. For example, if they overspent and now can't afford a new hairdo, don't jump in.

g. Avoid getting into arguments.

Since people with BPD/ EUPD have trouble with (self) identity and awareness, they frequently think comments are directed at them, when sometimes in fact, they are not.

They perceive things differently.

Example:

- When the other party brings them flowers, they may start to suspect you're cheating.
- When they are complimented about something they did, they may say you're secretly making fun of them.
- When this happens, that they misinterpret something you've said, you may have to bear a moment or a period of a raging fit and be told how disgusting and judgmental you are. Stay away. Avoid getting involved.
- Explain your true intentions and stay calm.
- It can be exhausting and the struggle will sometimes leave you feeling powerless and defeated.
- Just focus on the positive aspects and good days.
- Whether you're just dating or are married to someone with borderline personality disorder, making the relationship work won't be easy, but it can be done.
- It Is still a little better than a relationship with a narcissist.
- Remember, it takes two to tango. You have your 50% worth of responsibility to play in any relationship which accounts to its success or failure.

There are similarities and differences between borderline and narcissistic personality disorders. We will first look at similarities. The major issue that underlies both disorders are:

- Insecurity.

There are fears beneath the surface that are very overwhelming and distort the person's perceptions of themselves and others. As a result, people with these personality disorders both tend to experience patterns of unstable or destructive relationships.

- Abandonment is a common theme in both cases.

Someone with borderline personality disorder may act out their intense fears of abandonment to such an extent that they drive their significant other away.

Someone with narcissistic personality disorder, on the other hand, is more likely to be the one abandoning their significant other. This is because of their arrogance and inflated ego. They would rather be the first one to leave before someone has the chance to leave them to otherwise reinforce their superiority.

- Both disorders are characterised by isolation. People affected by these disorders may spend much of their lives in isolation.

- They tend to struggle to hold a job, due to interpersonal difficulties, impulsivity and arrogance.

- There are mood-regulating issues with both disorders. They face high risks of co-occurring disorders, like depression, anxiety Bipolar, substance-use disorders, eating disorders, and PTSD.

- People with these personality disorders are highly unlikely to seek help for treatment of their distress. Those with narcissism tend to believe in their disordered perspective and are unlikely to see that their beliefs are off-base.

- Both disorders require enough time and patience to begin to untangle the deeper insecurities and fears.

Then, let's look at differences.

A. Borderline Personality Disorder

Cindy is diagnosed with borderline personality disorder at age 18. She has always been subjected to feelings of inadequacy and is terribly concerned that she is unlovable. She finds herself always seeking attention because of a hidden fear of the void inside. She tends to feel like intimacy and validation from others are lacking. This causes her a great fear of being without her close personal connections. Cindy desperately fears abandonment, and many of her thoughts and reactions are aggravated by that fear. Cindy also finds that her very sense of self depends on this volatile attachment to others.

When Cindy was diagnosed, her history consisted of the following:
- Desperately trying to avoid abandonment
- Highly depended and clingy behaviour
- In relationships, Cindy tends to idealise and then later devalue her boyfriends, finding the same qualities in them that attracted her in the first place now repulsive.
- Struggles with an unstable sense of identity and self-image
- Displays poor impulse control and engages in activities or actions that make her regret afterwards
- Experiences lots of emotional rollercoasters; finds it difficult to control her negative feelings, getting quite irritable and frighteningly angry
- instability, including anxiety or irritability
- Feeling low, empty, unmotivated
- Episodes of intense anger and outbursts
- A disconnection from reality and other dissociative symptoms, including suspicion and paranoia
- Self-harming behaviours and suicidal ideation and attempts

B. Narcissistic Personality Disorder

John is diagnosed with narcissistic personality disorder and is convinced that he is special to the point of superiority. However, this belief is built on an unstable foundation, a foundation designed to distract his psyche from the underlying fear that he is actually worthless. He constantly feels threatened by anything that compromises his self-esteem. John's efforts are dedicated to preserving the illusion of superiority rather than addressing the fears and vulnerabilities below the surface.

To the outside world, John seems confident and well put together, but it is because he truly believes in the exaggerated positive qualities ascribed to himself and feels the strong need for others to also believe in how special he is.

When John was diagnosed, his history consisted of the following, some of which other people observed and remarked about:
– Lack of empathy for others
– Bragging about his superior traits and accomplishments

- Insulting others or otherwise making himself look better at the expense of others
- Flattering or criticising depending on whether others flatter or criticise in return
- Sensitivity in the face of criticism or even potential criticism
- Dominating interactions and relationships
- Aloof and distant
- Needing attention and flattery
- Fantasising about power, fame, and wealth
- Moodiness
- Impatience
- Envy, resentment, and revenge
- Difficulty adapting to change

I elaborated a lot more on the Narcissists and a bit on the Borderline Personality Disorder because they are the two most common and often left untreated. Most people suffer abuse at the hands of these people due to lack of awareness.

To conclude this chapter, I would like to touch a little on marriage.

I believe that God designed marriage. Therefore, I believe that it is His desire to have each and every one of His people married, with families to multiply and replenish the earth as He said. Genesis 1:28.

As I mentioned earlier, it takes two to build a relationship and it takes two to ruin it.

Each partner has their 50% share of responsibility. When a relationship succeeds, it's because both partners played their individual part well.

Likewise, when it crumbles, both parties are responsible, no matter what.

Let's take a look at some advice for those in marriage. They can also help those who are in serious relationships looking at taking them to a higher level.

1. There is nothing that threatens the security of a wife than the thought of another woman competing for the attention and affection of her husband or husband-to-be.

Nothing is more painful. Nothing is more disrespecting. Nothing is more insulting. Nothing is more belittling and degrading.

2. Marriage flourishes when the couple work together as a team; when both husband and wife decide that winning together is more important than keeping score.

Good marriages don't just happen. They are a product of hard work.

3. Your children are watching you and forming lasting opinions on love, commitment, and marriage based on what they see in you. Give them hope. Make them look forward to marriage.

4. Husbands: The reason why other women look attractive is because someone is taking good care of them. Grass is always green where it is watered. Instead of drooling over the green grass on the other side of the fence, work on yours and water it regularly. Any man can admire a beautiful woman, but it takes a true gentleman to make a woman admirable and beautiful.

5. When a husband puts his wife first above everyone and everything except God, it gives his wife the sense of security and honour that every wife hunger for.

6. A successful marriage doesn't require a big house, a perfect spouse, a million dollars or an expensive car. You can have all the above and still have a miserable marriage. A successful marriage requires honesty, undying commitment and selfless love and Jesus at the centre of it all.

7. Pray for your spouse every day; in the morning, in the afternoon and in the evening. Don't wait until there is a problem. Don't wait until there is an affair. Don't wait until something bad happens. Don't wait until your spouse is tempted. Shield your spouse with prayer and cover your marriage with the fence of prayer.

8. The people you surround yourself with have a lot of influence on your marriage. Friends can build or break your marriage; choose them wisely.

9. One spouse cannot build a marriage alone when the other spouse is committed to destroying it. Marriage works when both husband and wife work together as a team to build their marriage.

10. Don't take your spouse for granted. Don't take advantage of your spouse's meekness and goodness. Don't mistake your spouse's loyalty for desperation. Don't misuse or abuse your spouse's trust. You may end up regretting it after losing someone that meant so much to you.

11. Beware of marital advice from people who are not committed to their own family. If you really need Godly advice, seek it from God-fearing, impartial and prayerful mature couples whose resolve has been tested by time and shaped by trials.

12. Dear wife, don't underestimate the power of the tongue on your marriage. The tongue has the power to crush your marriage or build it up. Don't let the Devil use your tongue to kill your spouse's image, self-confidence and aspirations. Let God use your tongue to build up your marriage and bless and praise your spouse.

Courtesy of Bishop David Oyedepo.

Another set of advice this time pointing to men. What does the Bible say?

HOW TO TREAT YOUR WIFE:

Your woman reflects you. If you are happy about yourself, you have inner peace and you love yourself, you will treat her well. Likewise, if you hate yourself, you will treat her bad.

- Don't shout at your wife when you are talking. It really hurts her. Proverbs 15:1
- Do not speak evil of her to anyone. Your wife will become who you call her. Genesis 2:19
- Do not share her love or affection with another woman. It is called adultery. Matthew 5:28
- Never compare your wife to another woman. If the other woman was good for you, God would have given her to you. 2 Corinthians 10:12
- Don't ever allow her to beg you for sex. She owns your body just as you own hers.
- 1 Corinthians 7:5
- -Be gentle and accommodating. She has sacrificed so much to be with you. It hurts her deeply when you are harsh and irritating. Be tender. Ephesians 4:2
- Hide nothing from her. You are now one and she's your helpmate. Let there be no secret you are keeping from her. Genesis 2:25
- Do not make negative comments about her body. She risked her life and beauty to carry your babies. She is a living soul, not just flesh and blood.

- Do not let her body determine her worth. Cherish and appreciate her even till old age. Ephesians 5:29
- Never shout at her in the public and in private. If you have an issue to sort with her, do it in the privacy of your room without raising your voice. Matthew 1:19
- Thank and appreciate her for taking good care of you, the kids and the house. It is a great sacrifice she is making. 1 Thessalonians 5:18
- All women cannot cook the same way; appreciate your wife's food. It is not easy to cook three meals a day, 365 days a year for several years. Proverbs 31:14
- Never place your parents and siblings before her. She is your wife. She is one with you. She must come before your family. Genesis 2:24
- Invest seriously in her spiritual growth. Buy books, tapes and any material that will edify her and strengthen her walk with God. That's the best thing you can do for her. Ephesians 5:26
- Spend time with her to do Bible study and pray. James 5:16
- Make time to play with her and enjoy her company. Remember when you are dead, she's going to be by your grave but your friends may be too busy to attend your funeral. Ecclesiastes 9:9
- Never use money to manipulate or control her. All your money belongs to her. She is a joint heir with you of the grace of God. 1 Peter 3:7
- Do not expose her weakness. You will be exposing yourself too. Be a shield around her. Ephesians 5:30
- Honour her parents and be kind to her siblings. Song of Songs 8:2
- Never cease to tell her how much you love her all the days of her life. Women are never tired of hearing that. Ephesians 5:25
- Grow to be like Christ. That's the only way you can be a good and godly husband. Romans 8:29.

Additional points to both men and women

1. Everyone you marry has strengths and weaknesses

Only God has no weakness. Every rose flower has its own thorn. If you focus too much on your spouse's weakness, you can't get the best out of their strength.

2. Everyone you marry has a past, some darker than others.

No one is an angel, therefore, avoid digging one's past. What matters is the present life of your partner. Old things are passed away. Try to forgive and forget. The past can't be changed. So, focus on the present and the future!

Remember, there is no saint without a past.

3. Every marriage has its own challenges

Marriage is not a bed of roses. Every shining marriage has gone through its own test of hot and excruciating fire. True love is proven in times of challenges. Fight for your marriage! Make up your mind to stay with your spouse in time of needs. Remember this is the vow you made on your wedding day!

4. Every marriage has different levels of success

Don't compare your marriage with anyone! We can never be equal; some will be far in front and others far behind. To avoid marriage stresses, be patient, work hard, and with time, your marriage dreams shall come true.

5. Marrying is like declaring war

When you marry, you must declare war against enemies of marriage. Some of the enemies of marriage are: ignorance, rumours, prayerlessness, unforgiveness, adultery, third party influence, stinginess, stubbornness, lack of love, rudeness, wife battery, laziness, complaining, nagging, pride, divorce etc. Be ready to fight to maintain your marriage zone.

6. There is no perfect marriage

There is no ready-made marriage anywhere. Marriage is hard work; volunteer yourself and perfect it daily. Marriage is like a MOTOR CAR with a transmission, gear box, etc. If these parts are not properly maintained, the car will break down somewhere along the road and expose the occupant to unhealthy circumstances.

Many are careless about their marriage… Are you?

If you are, please pay attention to your marriage.

7. God may not give you the perfect person you desire but He will give you the right person.

God gives you she or he, in the form of raw materials for you to mould what you desire. You may desire a woman who can pray for one hour, but your wife can only pray for half an hour. And with your love, prayer and encouragement, she can improve.

8. Marriage involves risk-taking

You cannot predict what will happen after marriage, as situations may change, so, leave room for adjustment. Pregnancy may not come in the next few years. You may get married to her because she's slim, but she becomes a little fat after a child. He may lose his beautiful job for years so that you must bear the financial responsibility of the family until he gets a new job. But with God by your side, you will smile at long last.

9. Marriage is not a contracted job but permanent

Marriage needs total commitment; love is the glue that makes a couple stick together. Divorce starts in the mind. Never think of divorce! Never threaten your spouse with divorce. Choose to remain married! God hates divorce. Malachi 2:16

10. Every marriage costs a price

Marriage is like a bank account. It is the money you deposit into your bank account that you can withdraw. If you don't deposit love, peace and care into your marriage, you are not a candidate of a blissful home. There is no free love in marriage. You cannot love without giving and sacrificing. You cannot receive love either from your spouse without giving them your love first.

Perfect love is a decision. Love is a deliberate decision and commitment towards a partner.

May God grant you the grace and wisdom to succeed.

Ephesians 5:25: "For husbands, this means love your wives, just as Christ loved the church. He gave up his life for her."

Genesis 2:24: "Therefore a man shall leave his father and his mother and hold fast to his wife, and they shall become one flesh."

"The soothing tongue is a tree of life, but a perverse tongue crushes the spirit." Prov. 15:4

Be an encourager, a joy-giver, a fun-filled, high-spirited person, positive, full of faith, an exhorter, with the ability to look and find goodness in someone, and when you do, tell them.

Give everyone the benefit of the doubt; believe in them.

Be a lifter not a put-down.

Choose your words wisely. If you need to give "tough love" to someone, make sure you have built a trusting relationship and have a good rapport with them, otherwise, the intended good, can end up messy.

Do unto others what you would like them to do unto you.

Conclusion

Get Out of the JUDGEMENT Seat
It belongs to God and ONLY HIM.
"You will be judged in the same way that you judge others." Matthew 7:2.
The reason I am saying this is oftentimes, as humans, without thinking sometimes or just out of habit, we tend to be quick to judge people when we really don't have a clue as to their life history and factors that shaped them throughout life from conception.

We condemn someone for stumbling this morning, but we didn't see the blows they took yesterday.
We judge someone for a limp in her walk, but we can't see the tack in her shoe.
We mock the fear in their eyes, but we have no idea just how many stones they have ducked or how many darts they have dodged.
Are they too loud? Perhaps they had to be or get neglected again.
Are they too timid? Perhaps they had to be, or maybe they just feel that way for fear of failing again.
Are they too slow? Maybe they fell the last time they hurried.
YOU. JUST. DON'T. KNOW.

Only one who has followed yesterday's steps can be their judge!
Not only are some of us ignorant and perhaps stupid about yesterday, perhaps some of us are ignorant and may be stupid about tomorrow.
Dare we judge a book while chapters are not even yet written?
Should we pass our verdict on a painting while the artist still holds the brush?
How can you just simply dismiss a soul until God's work is complete?
"God began doing a good work in you, and I am sure he will continue it until it is finished when Jesus Christ comes again" (Philippians 1:6).
Remember that: This verse applies to them too.

I know you are reading this right now
I know some of you may be hurting
Some of you may be in the middle of an abusive relationship
I want you to know
You are NOT ALONE

God is right there with you, during that pain. "The Lord is close to the broken-hearted and saves those who are crushed in spirit." Psalm 34:18

It is in your pain that God is closest to you, whether you are aware of it or not.

Lightning Source UK Ltd.
Milton Keynes UK
UKHW020934120920
369709UK00005B/29